IMAGES
of America

THE COLE CAMP AREA

I0806455

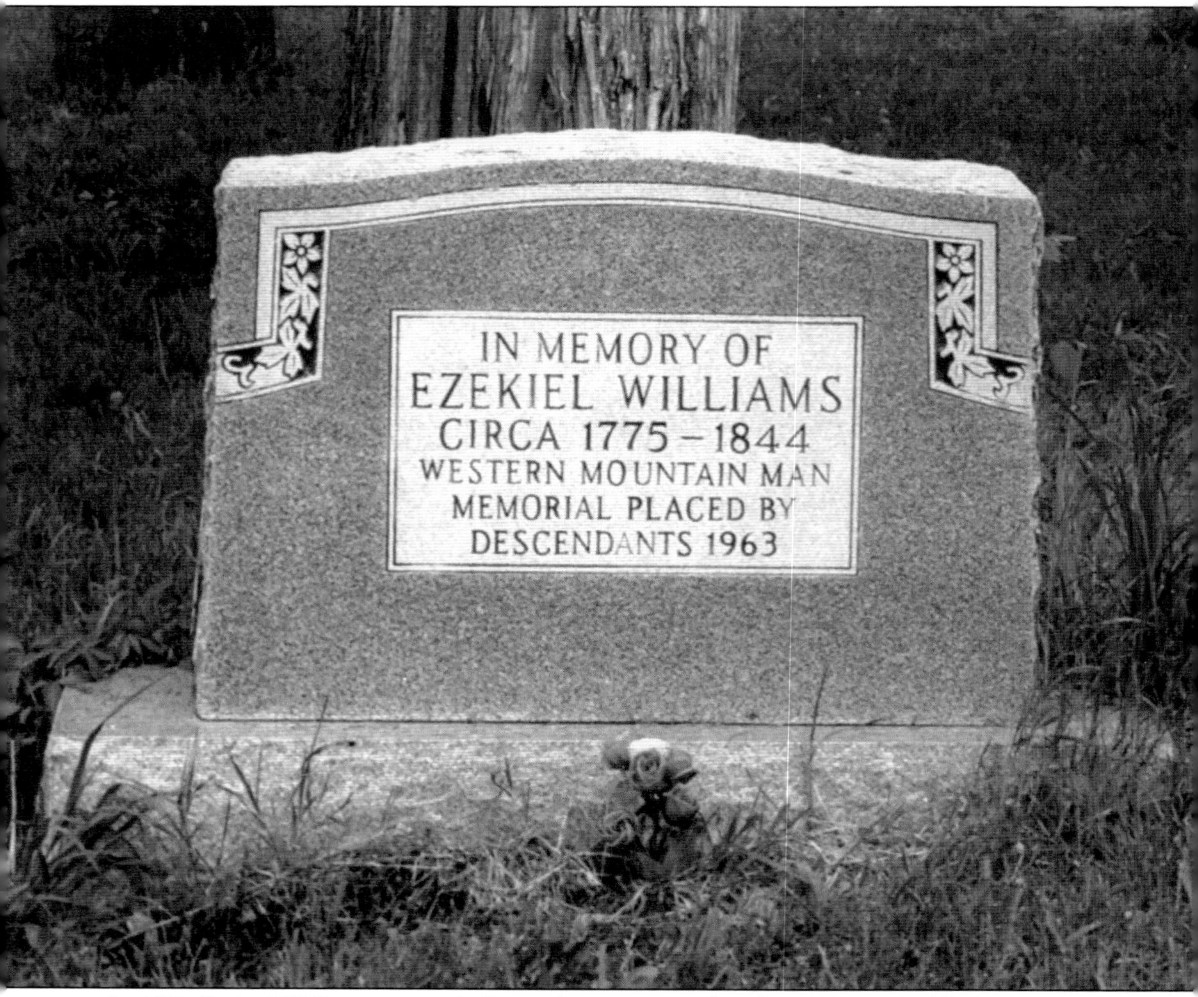

In 1818, Ezekiel Williams, an early Kentucky trapper and explorer, was named by William Clark to lay out a military road between Palmyra, Missouri, and Fort Smith, Arkansas. Williams liked what he saw of the area through west central Missouri and returned in 1830 to retire. He gave the name Cole Camp, based on the magisterial district of his native Kentucky, to a post office he opened south of the present site of the city of Cole Camp. Williams died at age 69 on December 24, 1844. His grave is located at the Union Williams Church Cemetery, three miles south of Cole Camp on Highway F, which is the old Military Road route he once surveyed. (Courtesy of the Cole Camp Historical Society.)

ON THE COVER: In this 1916 photograph, J.F. Howe, the cashier of the Bank of Ionia, watches as bank president Clarence Schnabel operates a modern adding machine. Customers evidently had a choice of many calendars and clocks to consult. (Courtesy of the Cole Camp Historical Society.)

IMAGES
of America

THE COLE CAMP AREA

Kenneth L. Bird and the
Cole Camp Historical Society

ARCADIA
PUBLISHING

ISBN 978-0-7385-8300-6

Published by Arcadia Publishing
Charleston, South Carolina

Printed in the United States of America

Library of Congress Control Number: 2010934828

For all general information, please contact Arcadia Publishing:
Telephone 843-853-2070
Fax 843-853-0044
E-mail sales@arcadiapublishing.com
For customer service and orders:
Toll-Free 1-888-313-2665

Visit us on the Internet at www.arcadiapublishing.com

This book is dedicated to Mr. and Mrs. E.L. Eickhoff Jr.

Contents

ACKNOWLEDGMENTS

The author is indebted to the following people and organizations who have contributed to this book: the Cole Camp Area Historical Society, the Cole Camp Museum, the Benton County Historical Society, Mrs. Sandra S. Bird, Mrs. Shirley Cash, Mr. and Mrs. E.L. Eickhoff, Mrs. Stella Frisch, Mr. Robert Hare, Mr. Richard Harms, Mr. Neil Heimsoth, Mrs. Ruth Kersey, Mrs. Donna Lambert, Mr. Jeffery Lutjen, Col. Robert Owens, Mr. Harold Steffens, Mr. J.D. Williams, and Chief Storm Walker.

Unless otherwise noted, photographs appear courtesy of the Cole Camp Historical Society.

INTRODUCTION

The Cole Camp, Missouri, area includes the northern portions of Benton County and the southern portions of Pettis County in west central Missouri. Existing communities include Ionia, Lincoln, and Mora, with former sites known as Crest, Melton, Raymond, and Tahoma. The area was first explored by early Spanish and French scouts and trappers in the 1700s. In 1829, a trapper named Ezekiel Williams settled in the area, giving his name to Williams Creek. He established a trading post and a post office named after his native Cole Camp Township in Cumberland, Kentucky.

The site of the town of Cole Camp was laid out in 1839, and its first home was built by Dr. Hosea Powers. The town established by Powers was located at the junction of four main roads: the old Military Road (which was to become the Butterfield Trail, named after a stage line that operated along that route from 1858 to 1861), the Duroc Road (entering from the south after crossing the Osage River), the Jefferson City Road (which led east to Jefferson City), and the Booneville Road (coming in from the north). This put the developing town in an advantageous position for growth, and hotels and businesses soon developed and thrived. In the ensuing years, emigrants from Kentucky, Tennessee, and northern Germany settled in the town and the surrounding area.

The Civil War saw a battle between the local Union home guard and the Confederate militia from Warsaw, which was the Benton County seat and a hotbed of southern sympathizers. The home guard was defeated, and the battle is the subject of a reenactment every two years.

After the war, Cole Camp saw further growth, and with the advent of the narrow-gauge railroad built from Sedalia to Warsaw in 1880, the old business district that had been centered on the square was moved nearer to the railroad right-of-way.

The early 20th century brought another railroad to the area. In 1904, the Rock Island Line, between St. Louis and Kansas City, built through Benton County two miles north of Cole Camp. The railroad spawned the towns of Crest and Ionia to the north and west of Cole Camp.

In the 1880s, lead mines were established three miles south of Cole Camp at a location known as Blaine. The name of the settlement changed as the mines expanded, and it eventually became know as Tahoma. Six mines were worked in the area. At one time, 80 men were employed at the Tahoma mine.

Until World War II, horse-drawn wagons and buggies were as common on the dirt and gravel streets of the town as were motorized vehicles. Most people kept a few chickens in the backyard, and some even kept a pig for butchering along with a cow for milk and butter. The Saturday streets were filled with local farmers who came to town for sustenance and gossip, while others gathered at the depot to witness the Missouri Pacific train loading cattle and switching cars of grain at the mill.

The town weathered the Great Depression with rural self-sufficiency and the application of a barter economy. While work and social programs of the New Deal did reach the town, they were looked upon with suspicion. The hard working and independent citizens of the area did not appreciate government-made work programs.

The advent of World War II saw the community give full support to the war effort, both financial and physical, by enlisting in the military and volunteering in other support services. The total commitment included working in faraway defense plants, buying war bonds, and complying with the ration laws.

After the war, the automobile became an integral part of American culture, and Cole Camp–area residents could easily access the shops and services beyond their city and county. In August of 1946, the Missouri Pacific branch line railroad was abandoned, and the town merchants saw a decline in local business. While some gave up their stores, others adapted to the new reality of a more mobile America and changed their business models to address the new markets. By the end of the 1960s, a thriving tourism industry was building, finding its base in a number of fine antique and craft shops that discovered a home in the town's many preserved and restored 19th-century buildings and homes.

Cole Camp residents had always clung to their German heritage and observed the festivals and holidays of the old country. This is evident in the many annual events that attract many visitors today. Christbaum, May Fest, Octoberfest, German choirs, and a yearly September Fair maintain the traditions of the Cole Camp area. It has become a mecca for day-trippers and vacationers seeking the quaint and quiet that the town now offers.

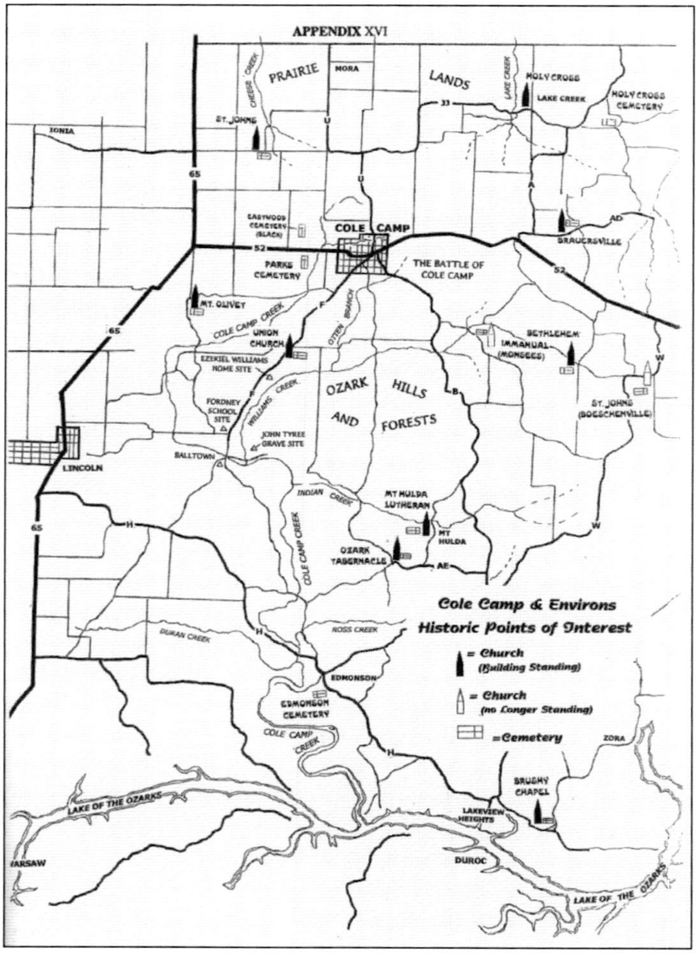

This map shows most of the Cole Camp, Missouri, area from the Osage River/Lake of the Ozarks in the south to the Pettis County line to the north. It includes the communities of Ionia, Lincoln, and Cole Camp. The c. 1898 Citizens-Farmers Bank is one of the 33 Cole Camp buildings listed on the National Historic Register.

One

City of Cole Camp

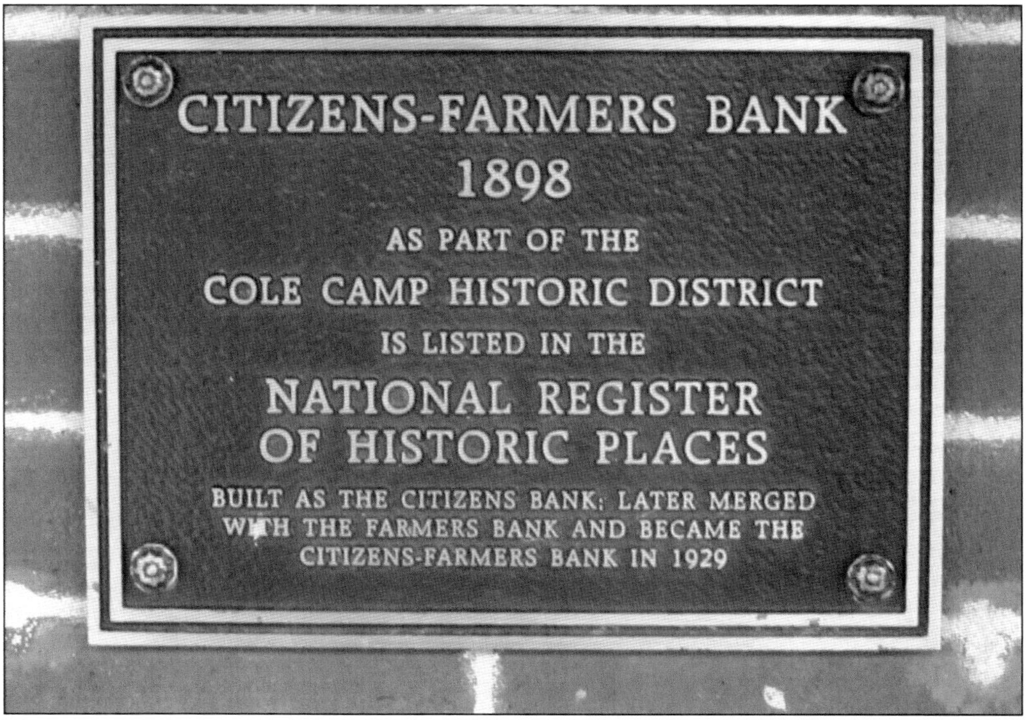

The c. 1898 Citizens-Farmers Bank is one of the 33 Cole Camp buildings listed on the National Historic Register.

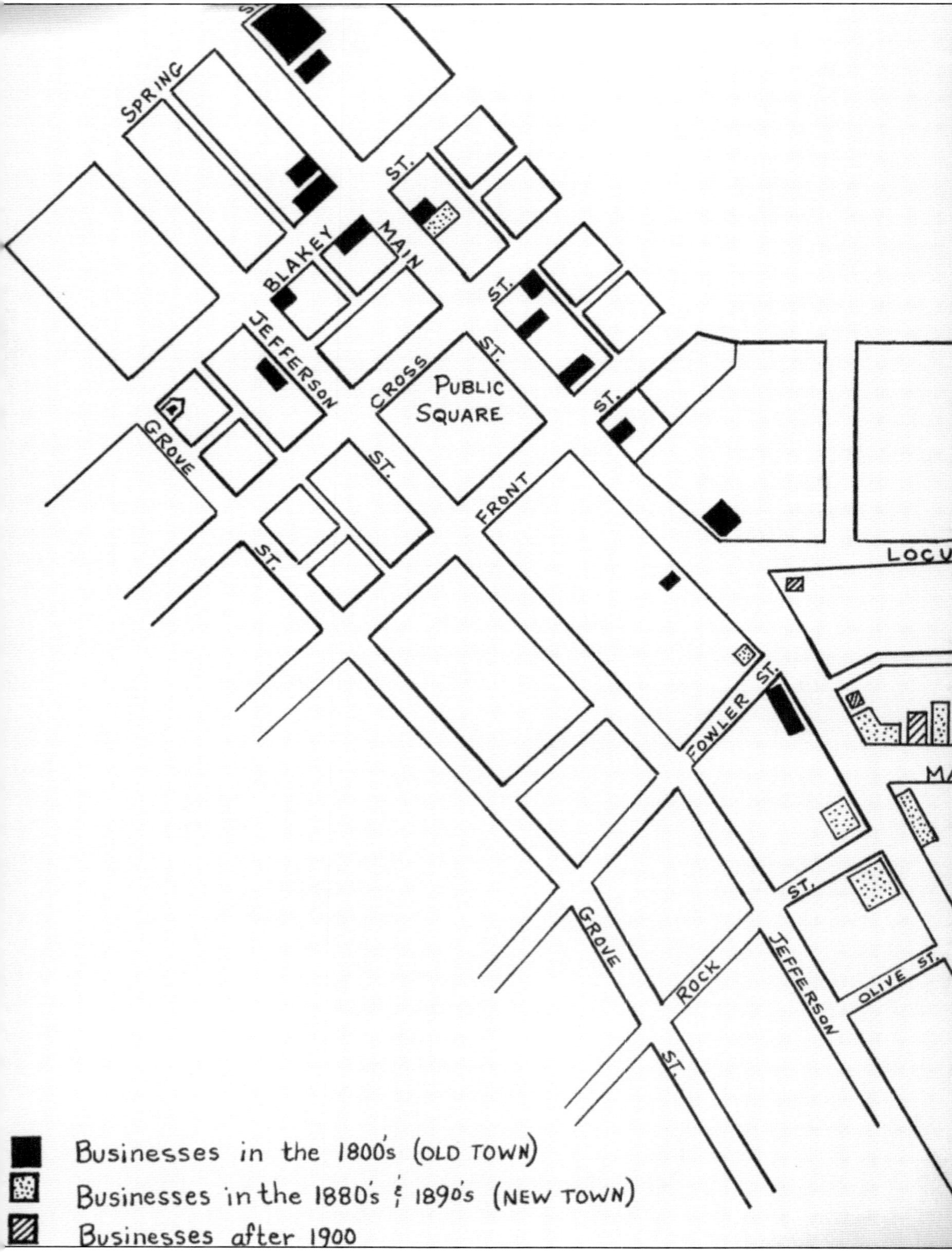
SPRING
ST.
BLAKEY
MAIN
ST.
JEFFERSON
CROSS
ST.
PUBLIC SQUARE
ST.
GROVE
ST.
FRONT
ST.
LOCU
FOWLER
ST.
MA
ST.
GROVE
ROCK
JEFFERSON
OLIVE ST.
ST.
Businesses in the 1800's (OLD TOWN)
Businesses in the 1880's & 1890's (NEW TOWN)
Businesses after 1900

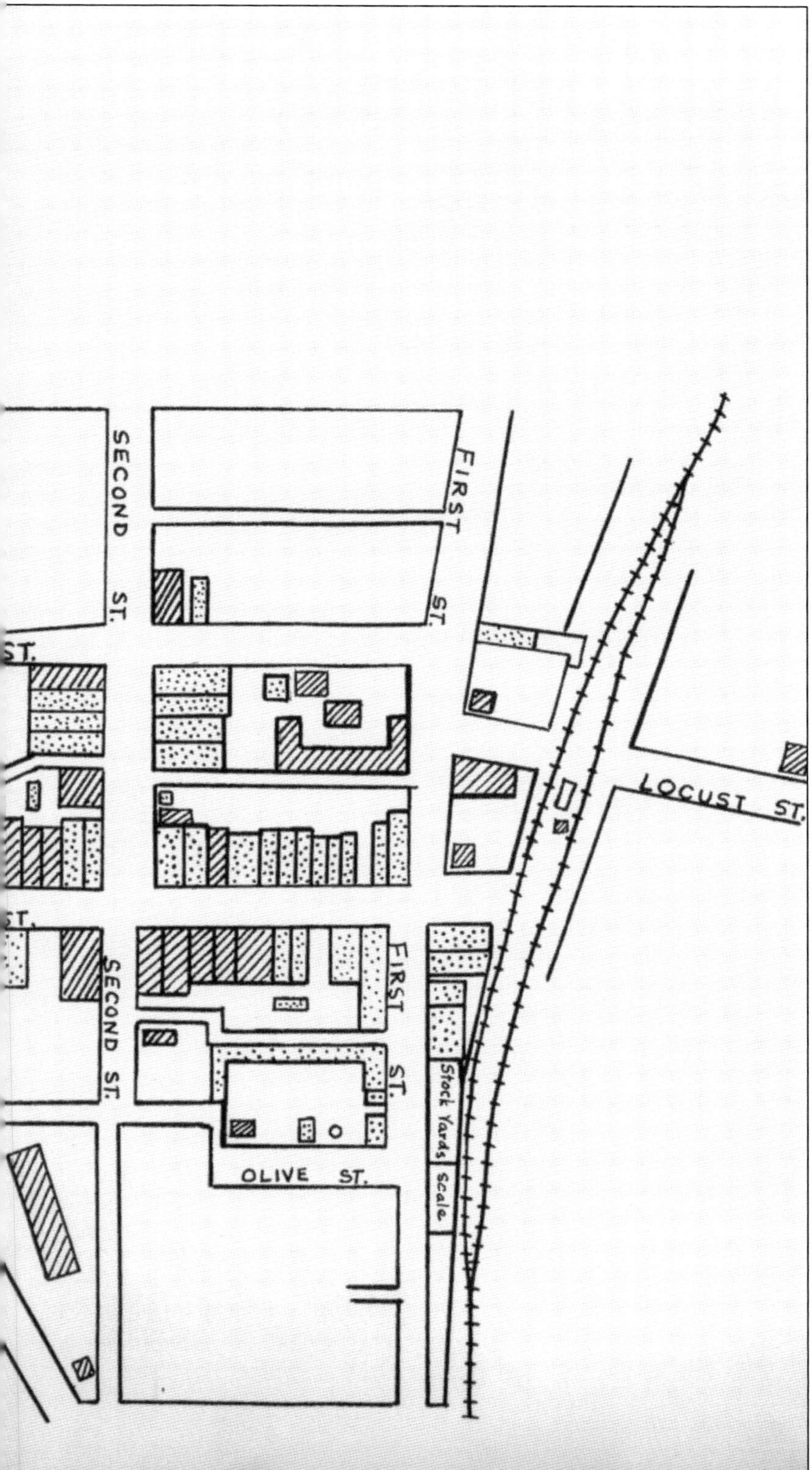

This sketch of the city of Cole Camp shows the "old town" centered on the old public square to the upper left and the "new town" built after 1880, when the narrow-gauge Sedalia, Warsaw and Southern Railroad reached the city.

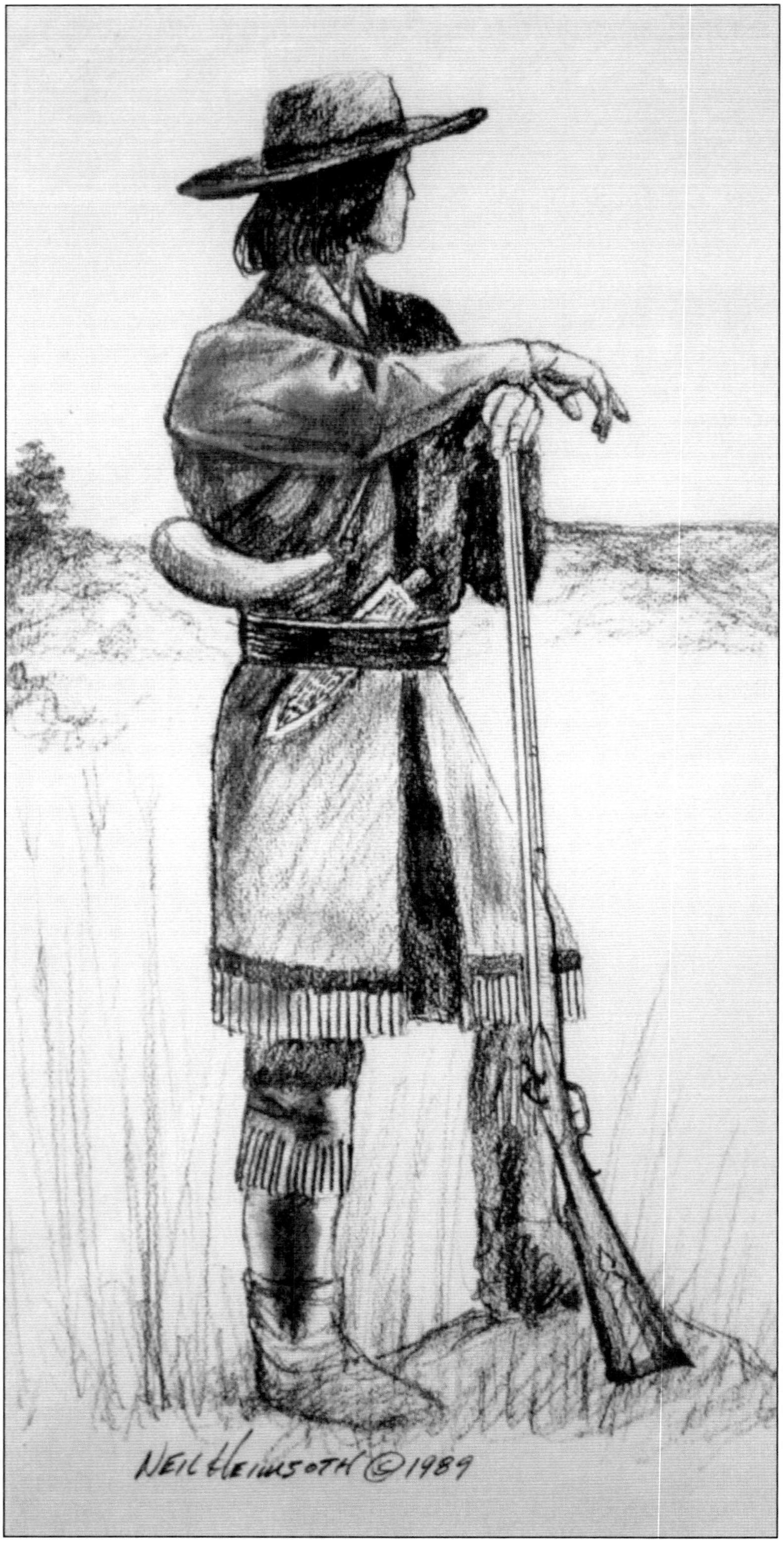

In 1839, Ezekiel Williams moved his post office two miles north on the Military Road to where a cluster of log cabins had been built around the home of Dr. Hosea Powers. The settlement adopted the post office name of Cole Camp. This drawing by Cole Camp artist Neil Heimsoth depicts Williams as he would have appeared exploring the area.

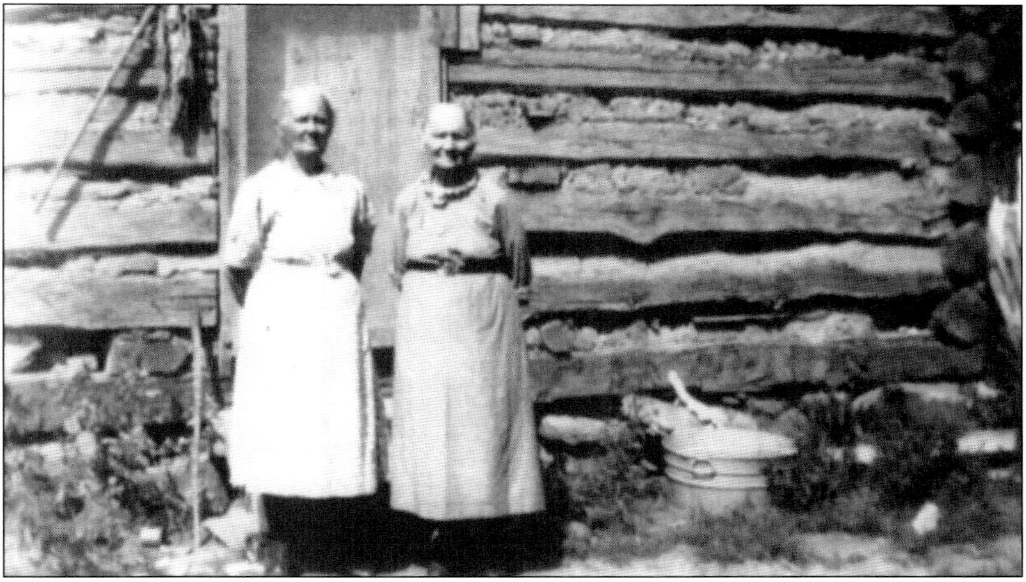

Log cabins were the norm in early-day Cole Camp but were soon replaced by the German settlers with more substantial homes situated around what would become the public square and the original business district.

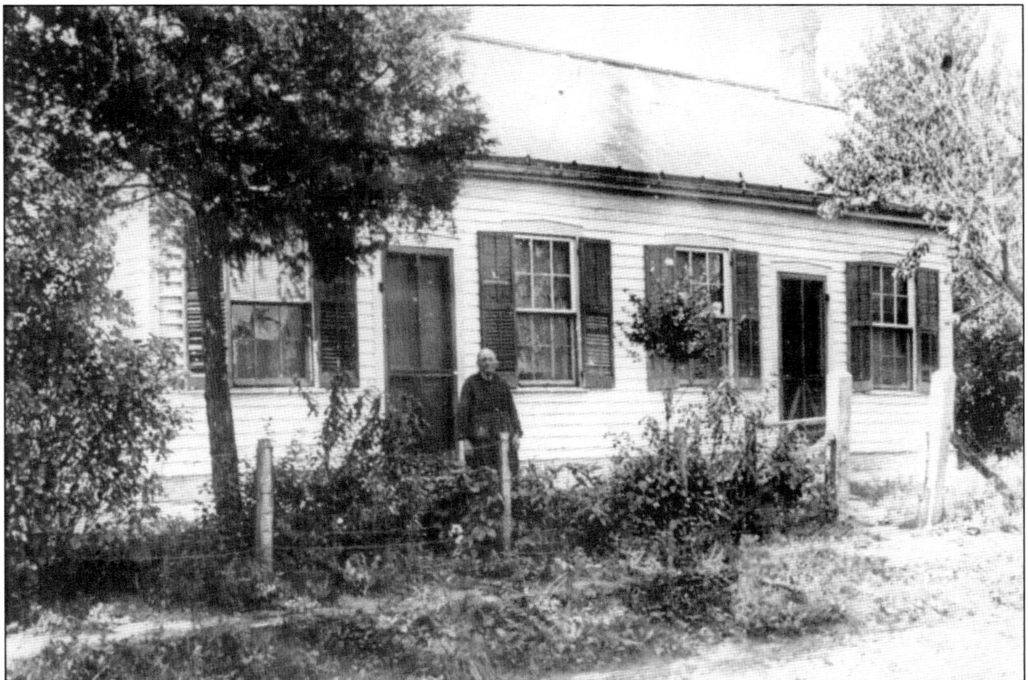

This example of an early Cole Camp home was built by Herman Postel in the 1840s. It is one of the oldest dwellings in Cole Camp. In the fall of 2010, it underwent a further restoration to be used as a bed-and-breakfast facility.

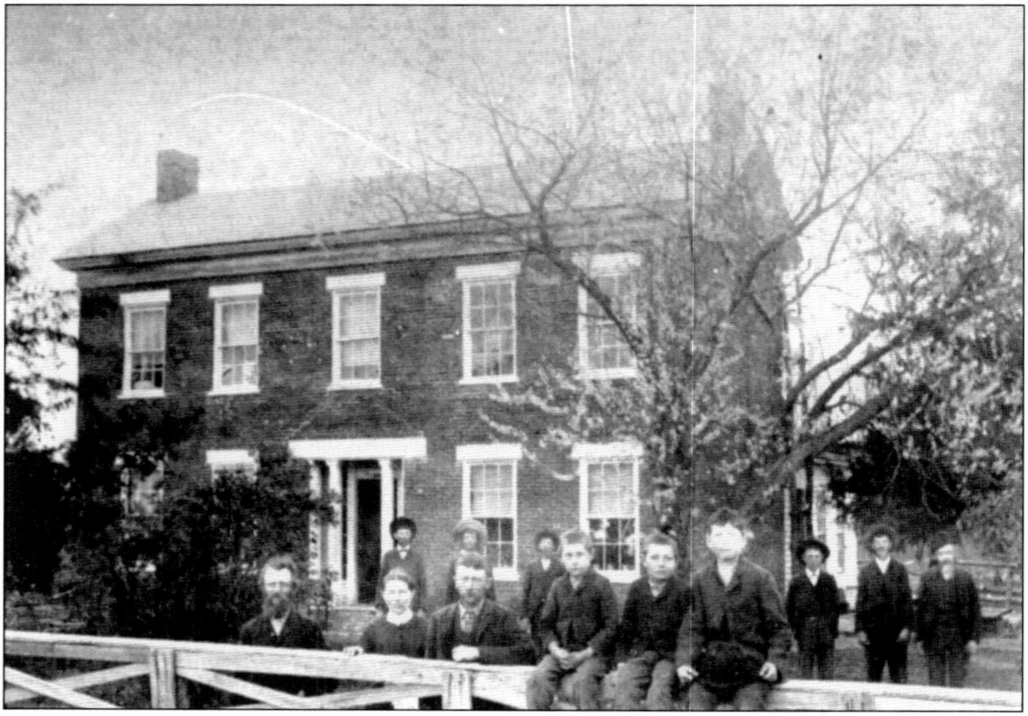

Built before the Civil War, the Renken home is an example of the early brick structures that make up much of the architectural heritage of the Cole Camp Area. Shown in this 1890 view are Anna and John Renken and their seven sons among the nine others.

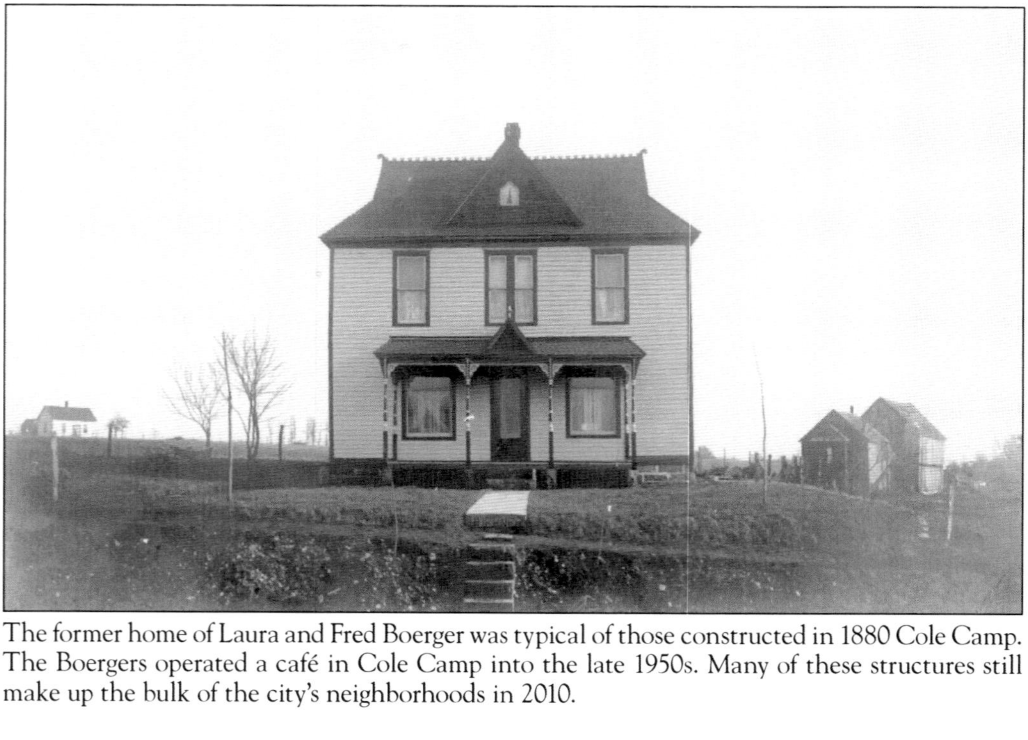

The former home of Laura and Fred Boerger was typical of those constructed in 1880 Cole Camp. The Boergers operated a café in Cole Camp into the late 1950s. Many of these structures still make up the bulk of the city's neighborhoods in 2010.

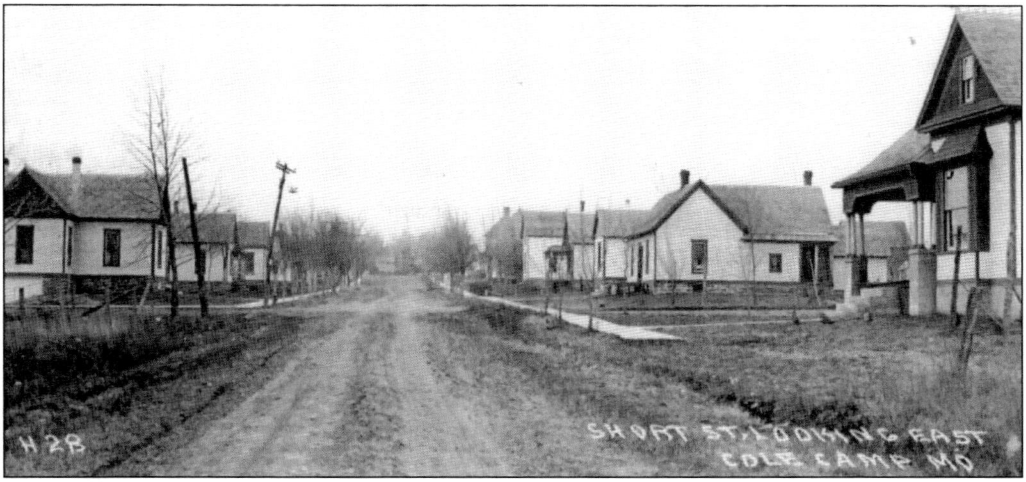

Short Street in west Cole Camp is only three blocks long, and most of it can be seen in this 1904 view.

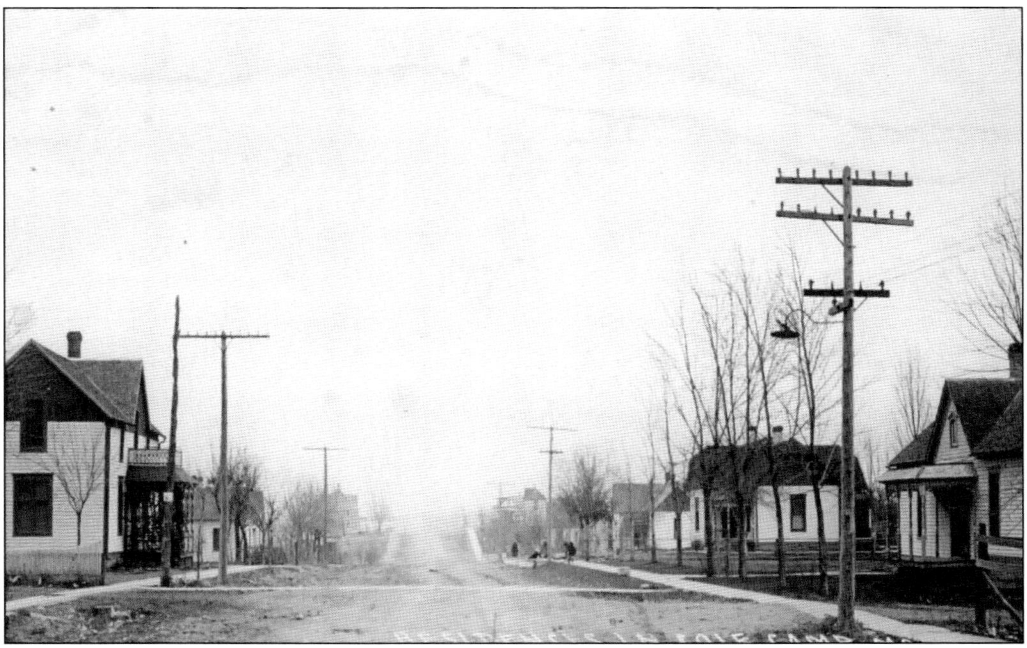

This view looks west on West Second Street in 1904. Second Street was renamed Main Street at the turn of the 20th century and later became present-day State Highway 52.

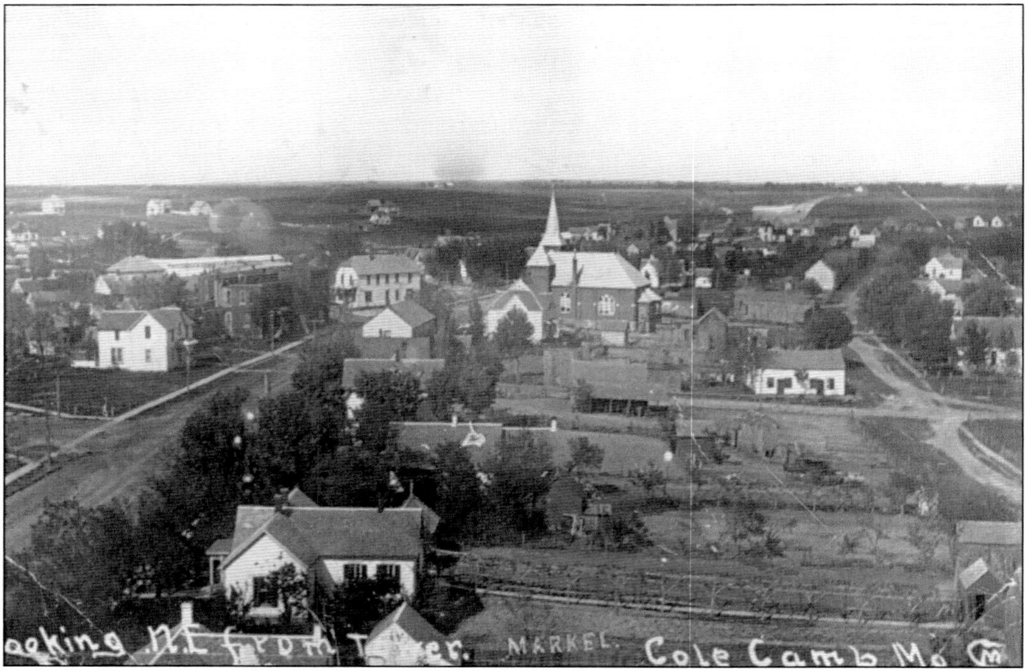

The photographer climbed the old water tower located in the center of the public square to capture this north-facing view. In the distance, Trinity Lutheran Church is visible. Directly across the street is where Maple Street intersects Butterfield Road, where the new business district was established in the 1880s.

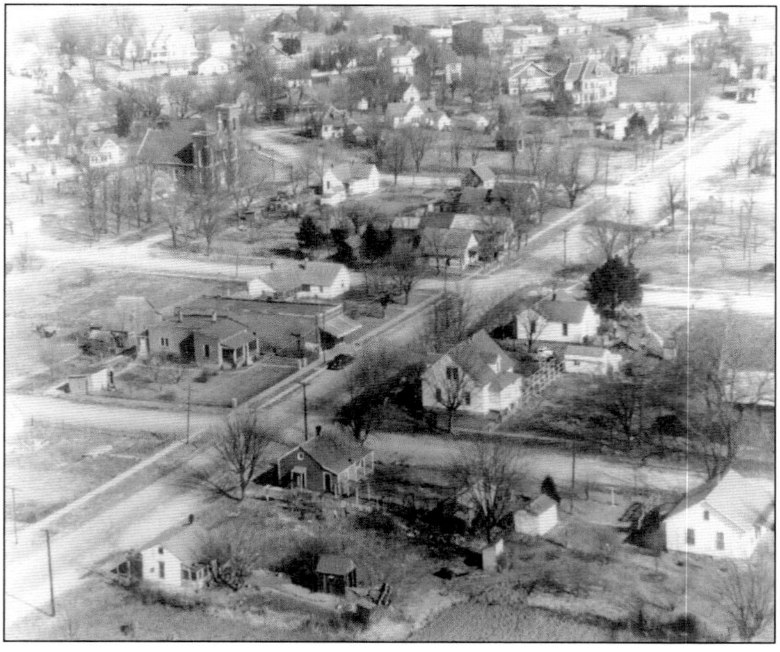

This 1920s aerial view of Cole Camp, the old Military Road (now Highway F or Butterfield Street) is seen running north to south. The building with the awning is the old Grother, and later, the Fagen Store. The Old Public Square can be located at the extreme upper right, identified by the leg of the town water tank. In the upper left is the Sts. Peter and Paul Catholic Church.

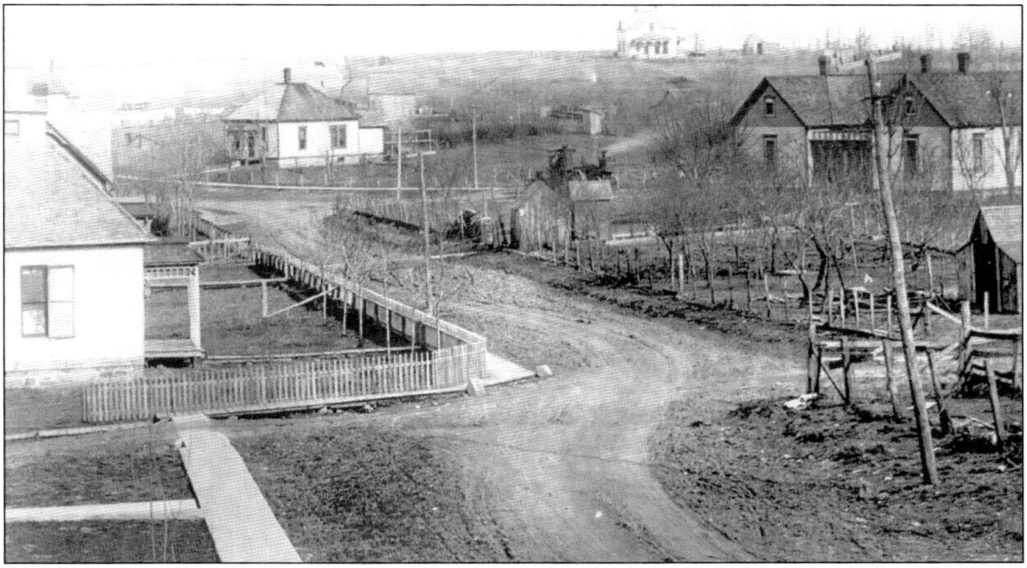

A late-19th-century panorama of the neighborhood east of Maple Street shows continuous progress in the new sidewalks and the work of a steam tractor grading the streets in the distance. Beyond the laundry hanging out on the left is the grade for the Missouri Pacific Railroad, the town's major connection with the outside world.

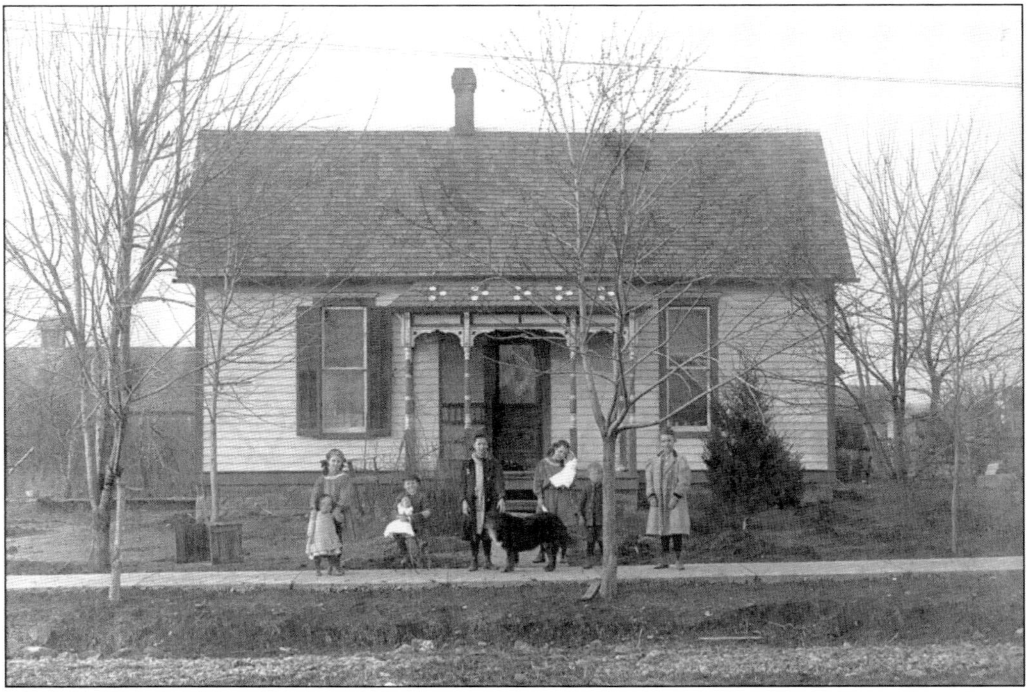

Identified as the A.E. Wright residence, this structure is typical of the housing that made up most of Cole Camp at the turn of the 20th century. Wright owned the downtown butcher store from 1895 to 1933.

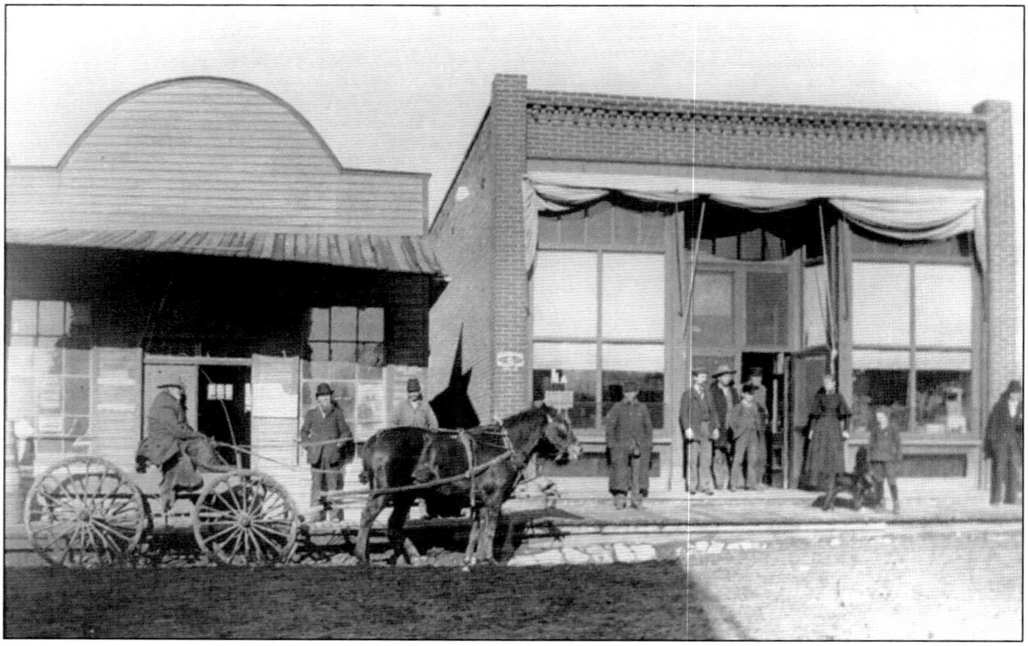

In this 1885 photograph is the Cole Camp General Store on Butterfield Road. The structure on the left is the Grother Drugstore. Louis Grother (1845–1925) built it of solid brick. He soon moved his store to the new business district that was created by the narrow-gauge railroad.

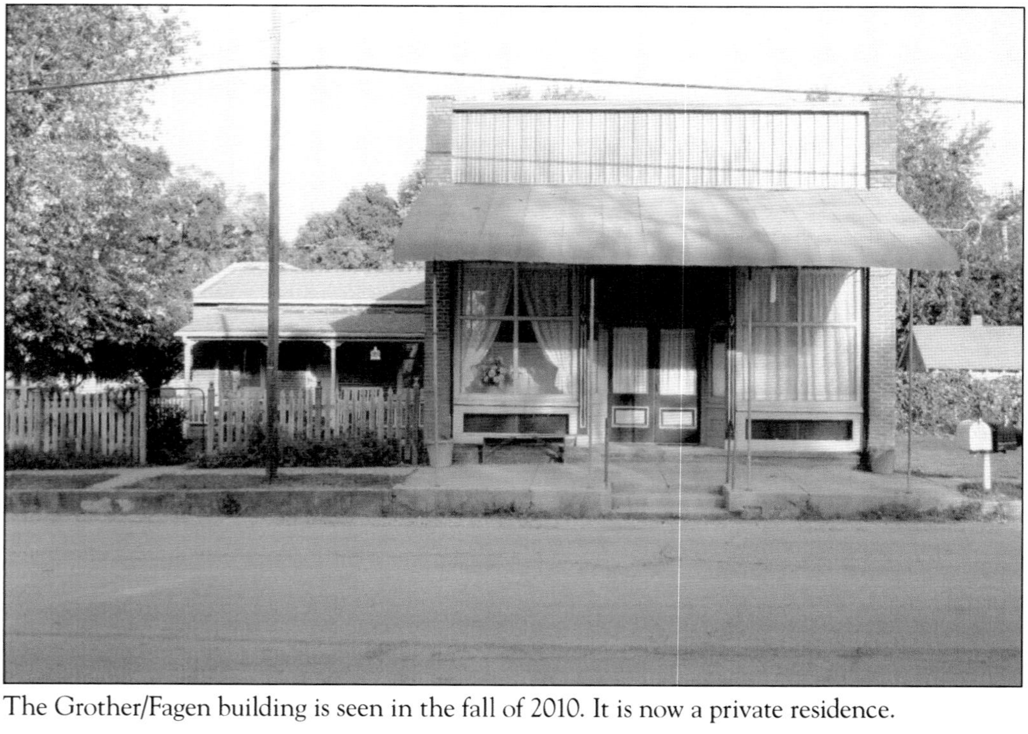

The Grother/Fagen building is seen in the fall of 2010. It is now a private residence.

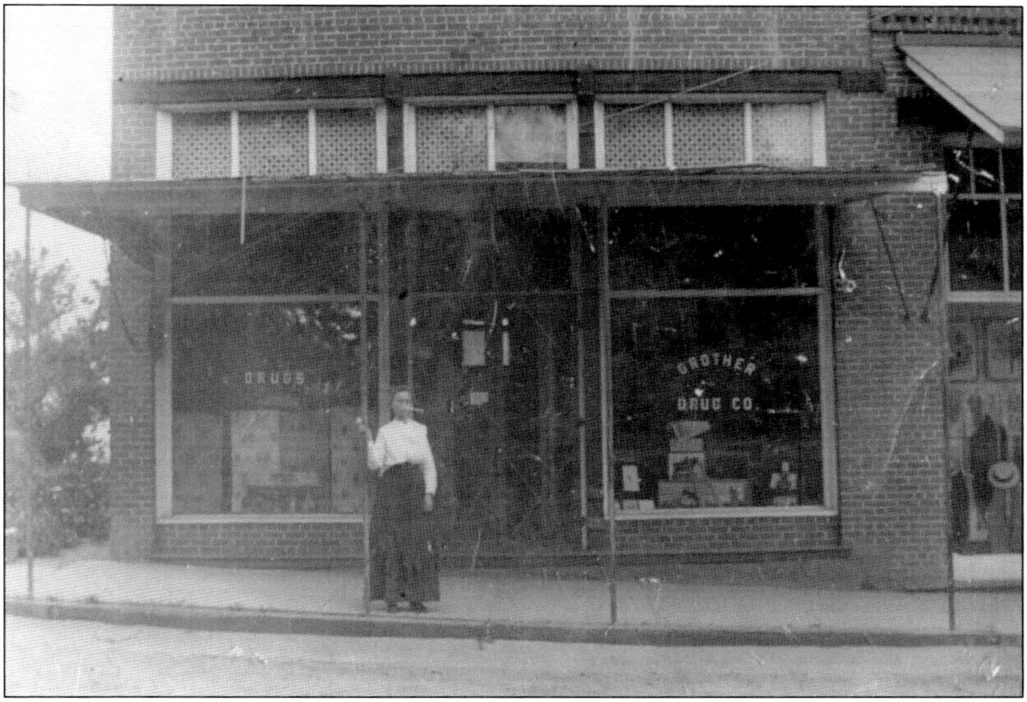

The Grother Drugstore was relocated to Maple Street. This building later housed the post office and the *Cole Camp Courier* newspaper.

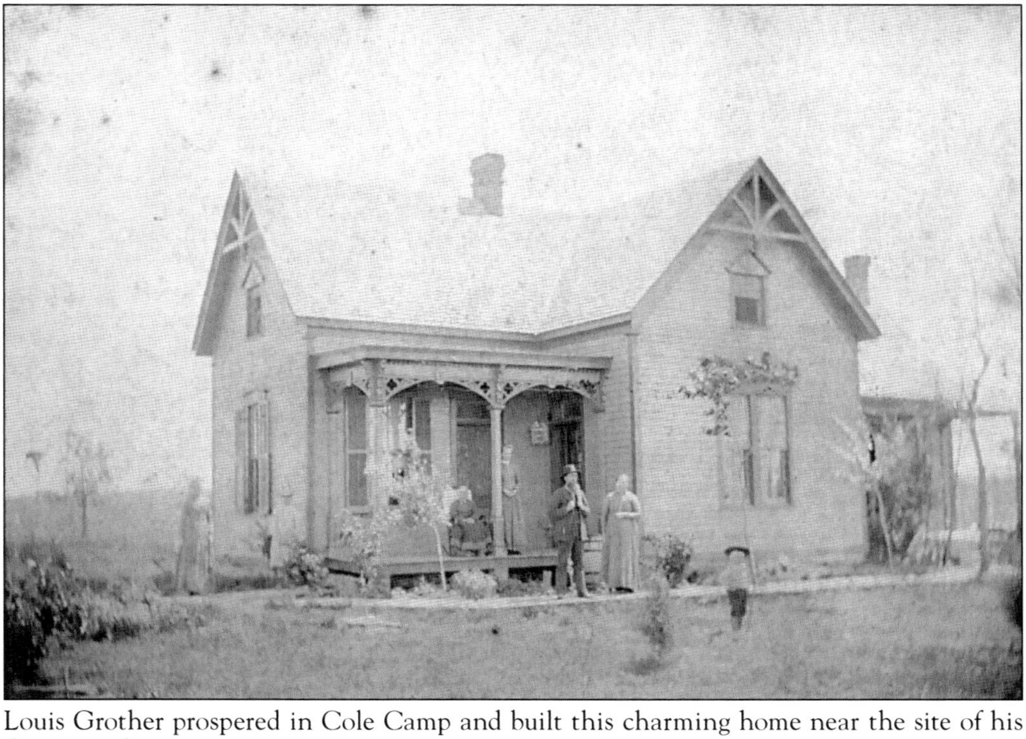
Louis Grother prospered in Cole Camp and built this charming home near the site of his downtown businesses.

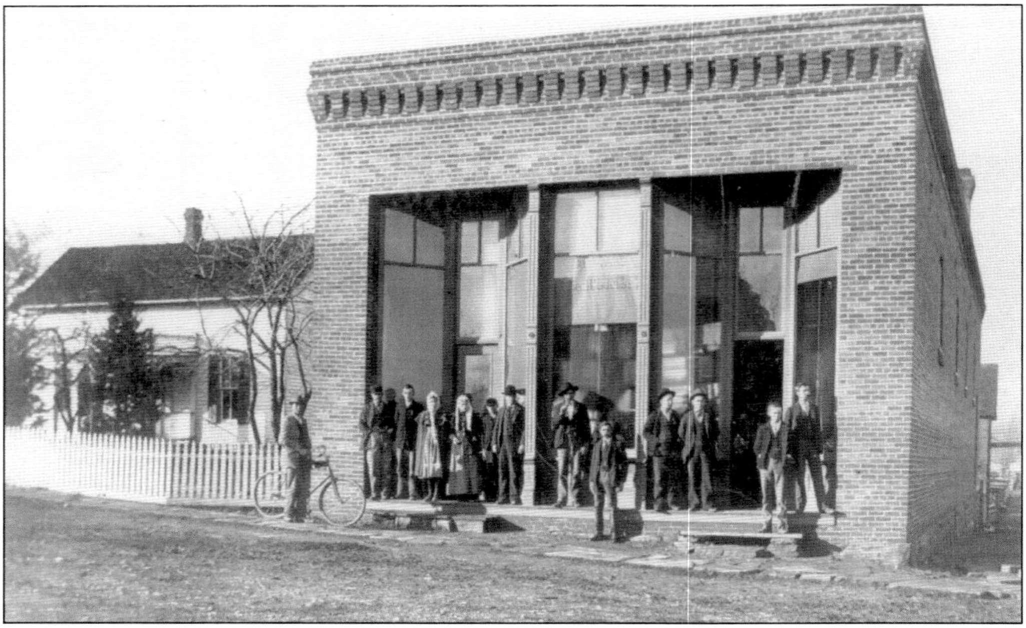

The new business district saw this building constructed in the 1890s by Joseph Schwald, who had originally established his general merchandise store on the old public square near the Grother Building. The pressure of business forced him to move to the "railroad addition." This handsome building, which still stands at Maple and Second Streets, includes some fancy brickwork and an iron window front with ornate columns.

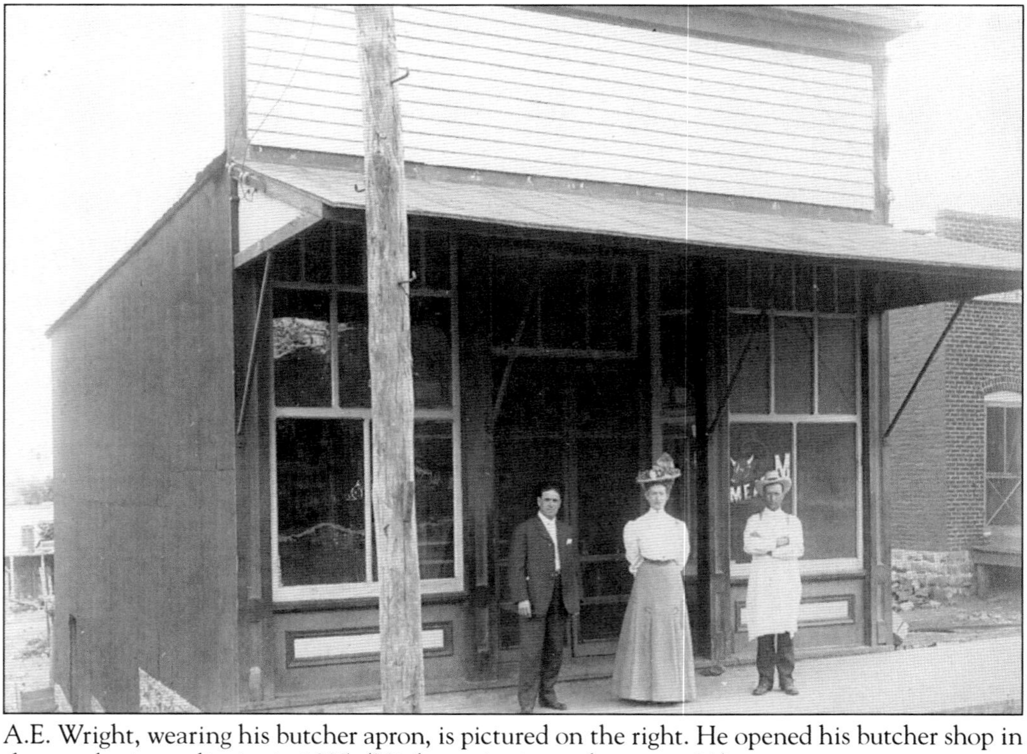

A.E. Wright, wearing his butcher apron, is pictured on the right. He opened his butcher shop in the new business district in 1895. (His home is pictured on page 16.)

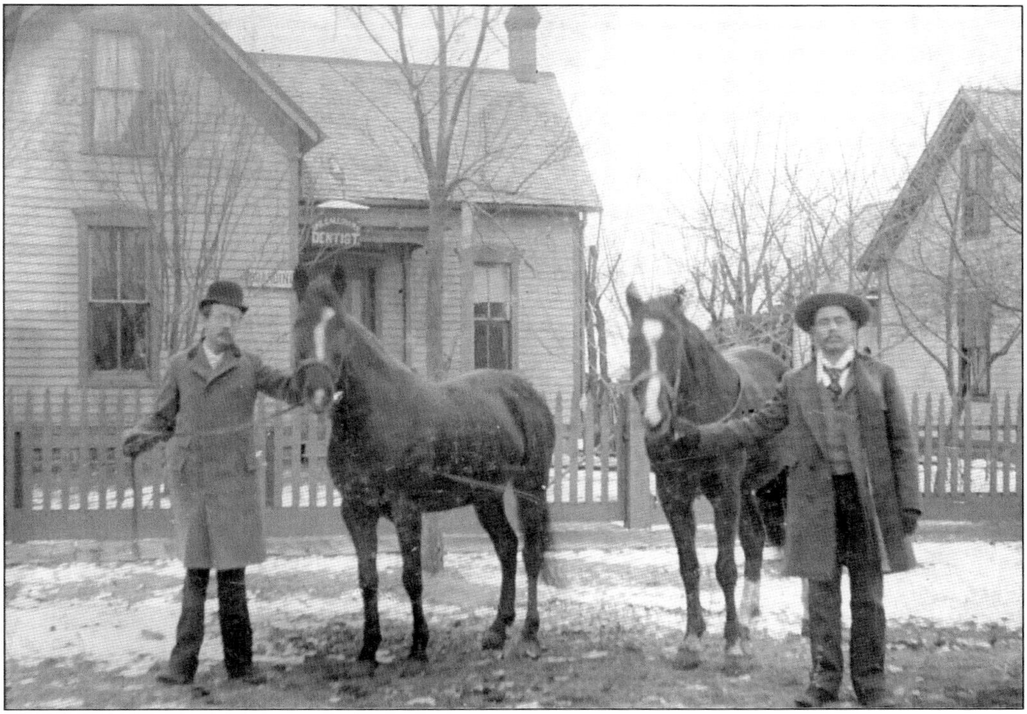

Physicians were a vital part of the early community. In this 1890s view, Dr. Schilling (left) and Dr. Melvin pose in front of the home of Dr. Galloway, the town dentist. The Galloway home also served as a local boarding house.

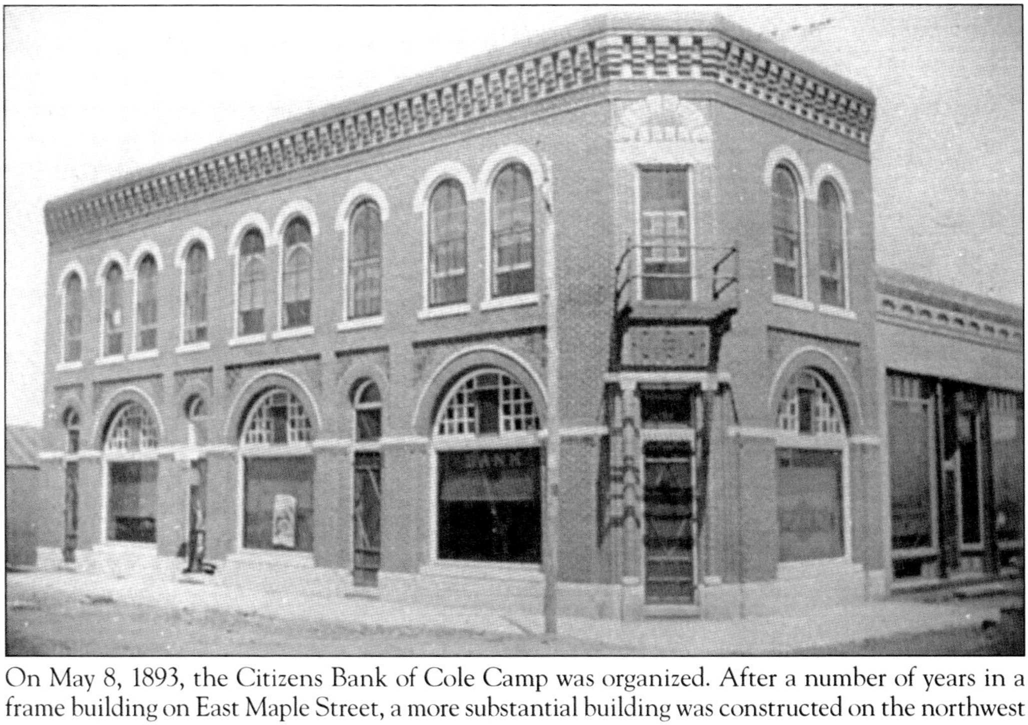

On May 8, 1893, the Citizens Bank of Cole Camp was organized. After a number of years in a frame building on East Maple Street, a more substantial building was constructed on the northwest corner of Main and Maple Streets.

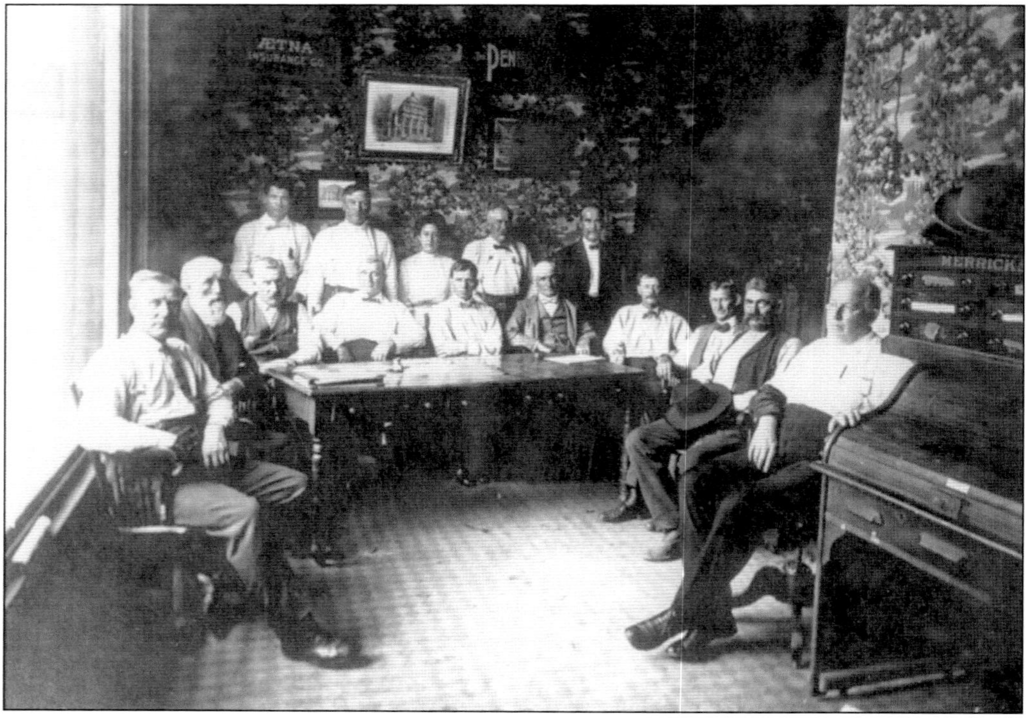

The board of directors of the Citizens Bank poses for its monthly meeting in 1907. The directors were selected from the local business and farming communities based on their deposits and stock ownership.

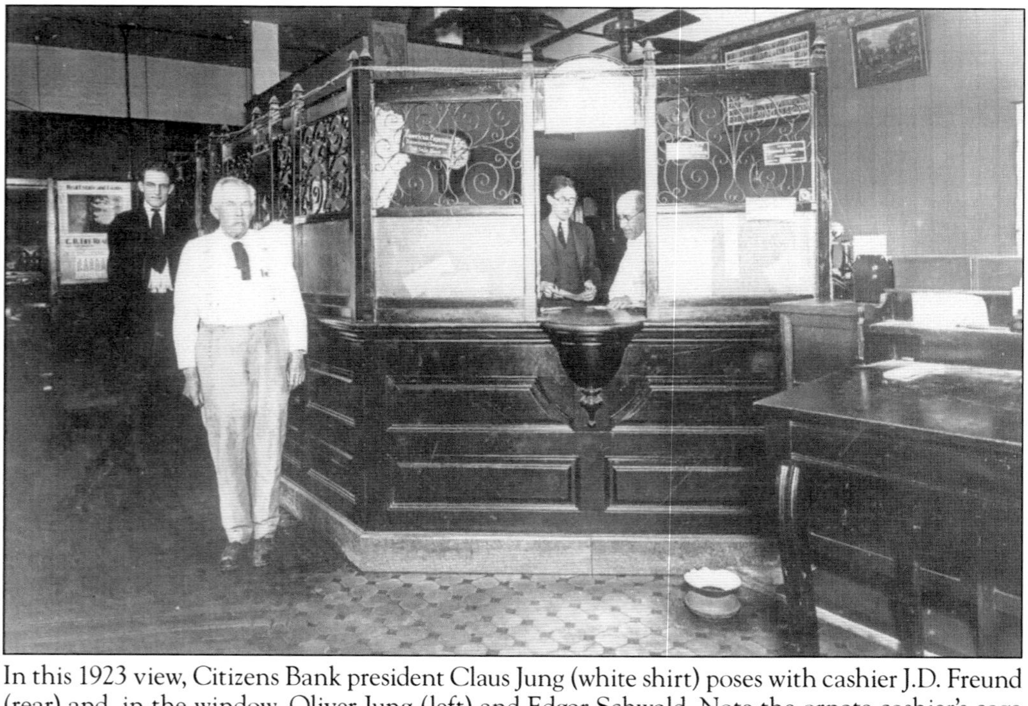

In this 1923 view, Citizens Bank president Claus Jung (white shirt) poses with cashier J.D. Freund (rear) and, in the window, Oliver Jung (left) and Edgar Schwald. Note the ornate cashier's cage and the porcelain spittoon, a common accessory of bank lobbies of the time.

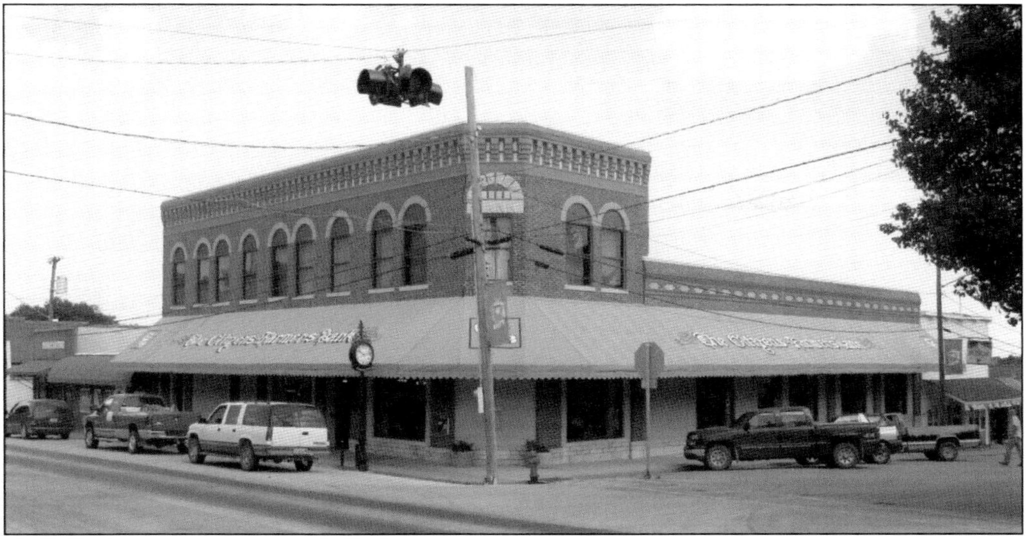

Now known as the Citizens-Farmers Bank, the original Citizens Bank building has changed little and remains a vital part of the Cole Camp historic district and economy.

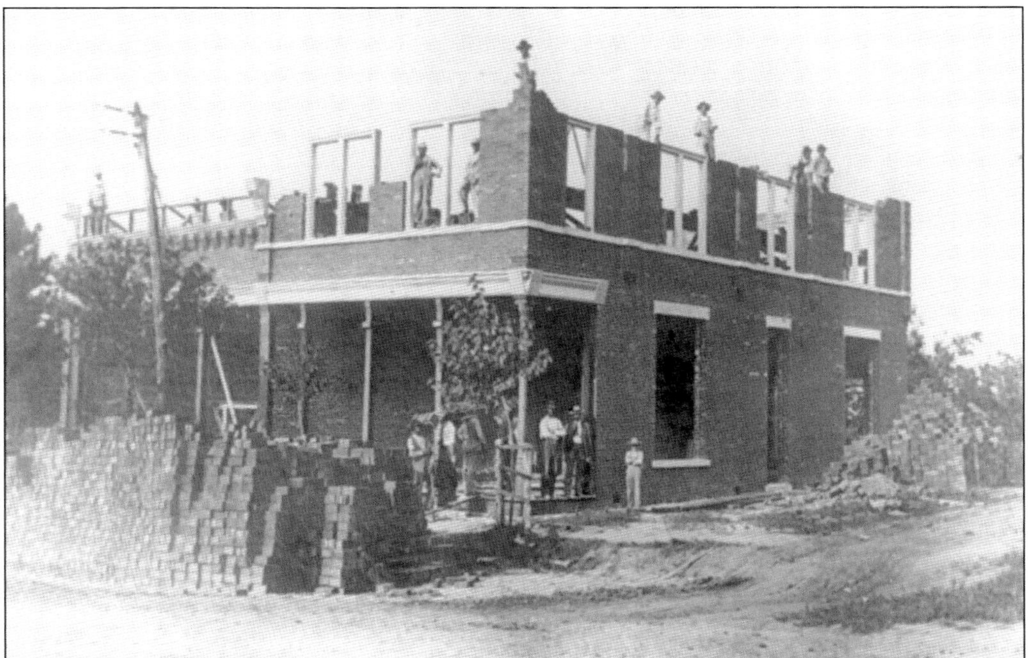

Early in the new century, a competing bank was constructed on Maple Street directly opposite of Citizens Bank. The Peoples Bank was chartered on March 1, 1906, with $15,000 capital, and soon the new building was under construction.

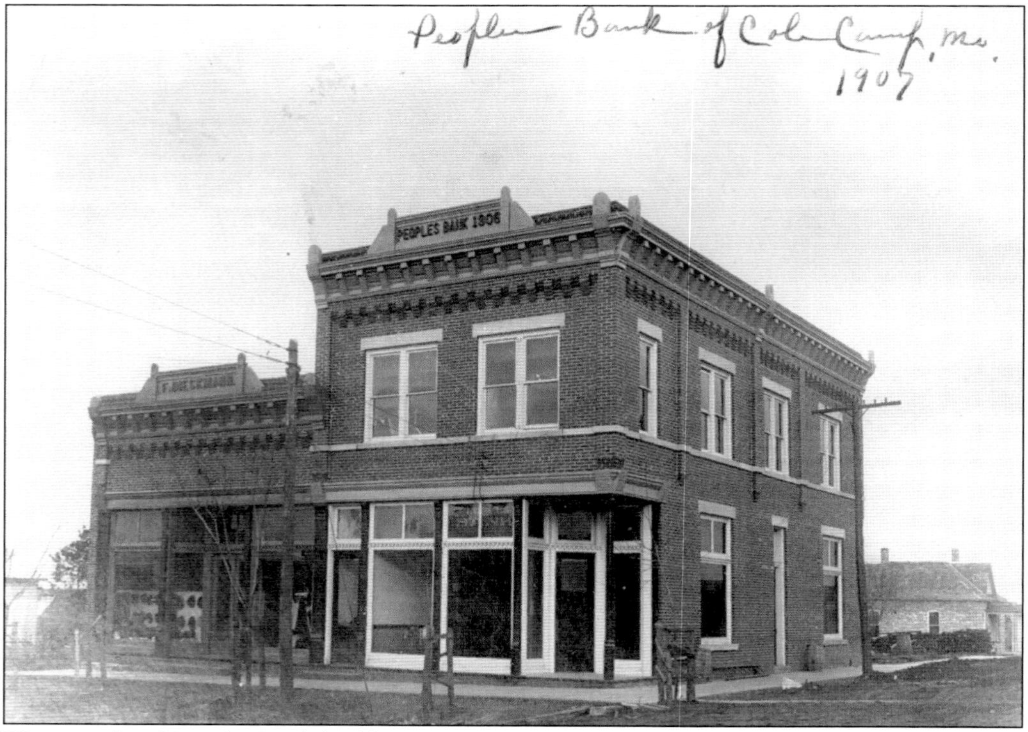

The completed Peoples Bank building is pictured in 1907.

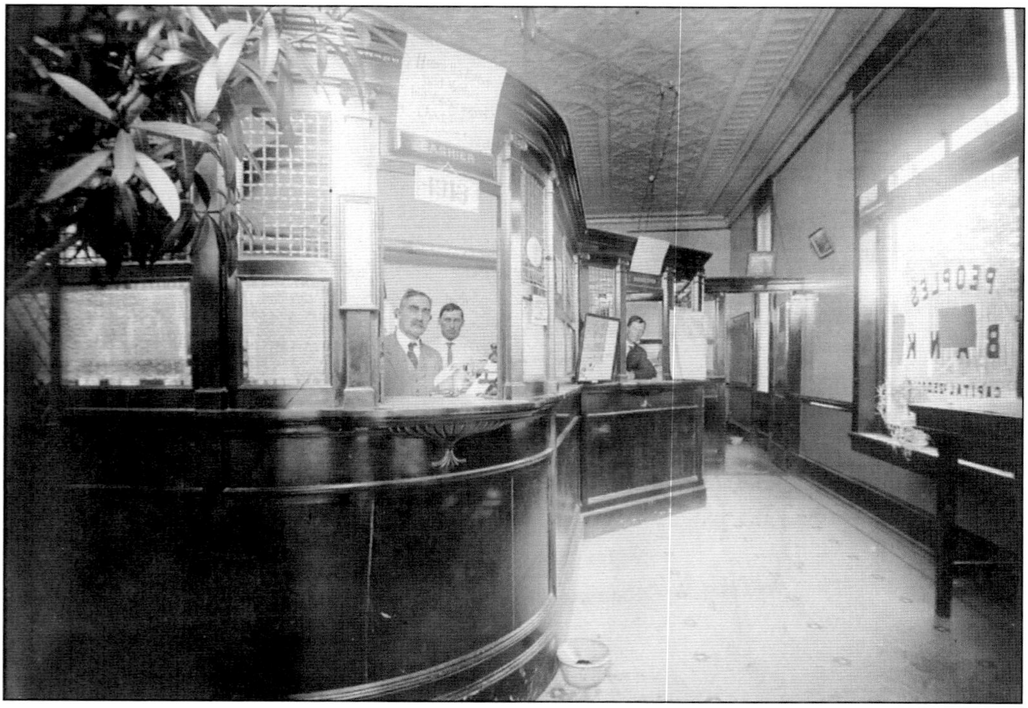

The interior of the Peoples Bank is pictured in 1908. The gentleman in the foreground is head cashier W.C. Nelson; his partner in the window is unidentified. Jim Freund, the assistant cashier, is in the rear window.

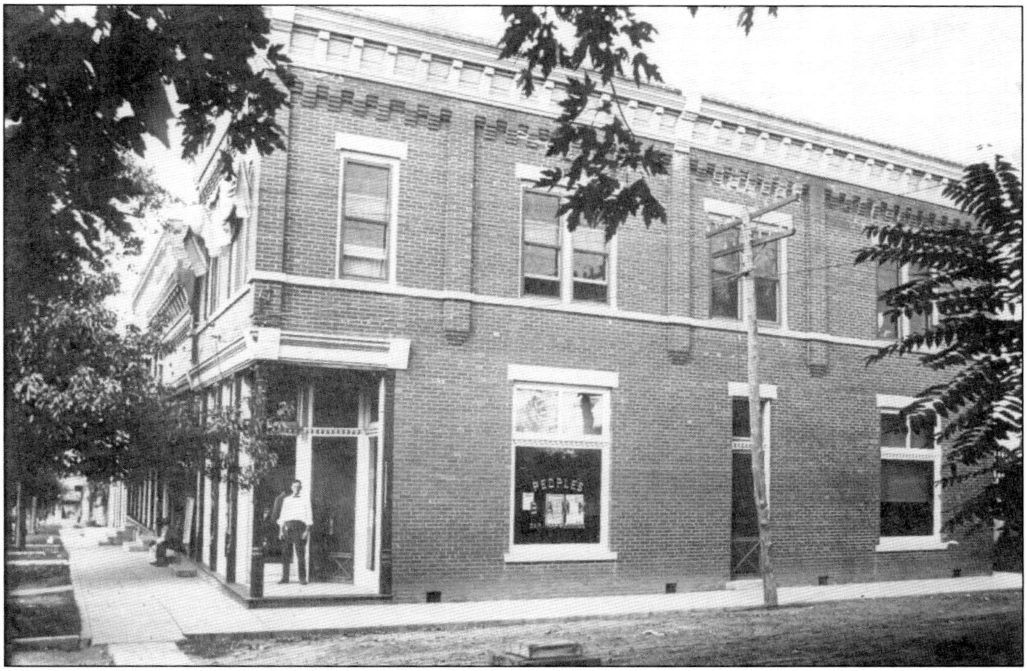

James D. Freund, the assistant cashier of the Peoples Bank, stands in the bank entrance on a summer day in 1918. In 1936, the bank succumbed to the Depression and was ordered closed by the Missouri finance commissioner.

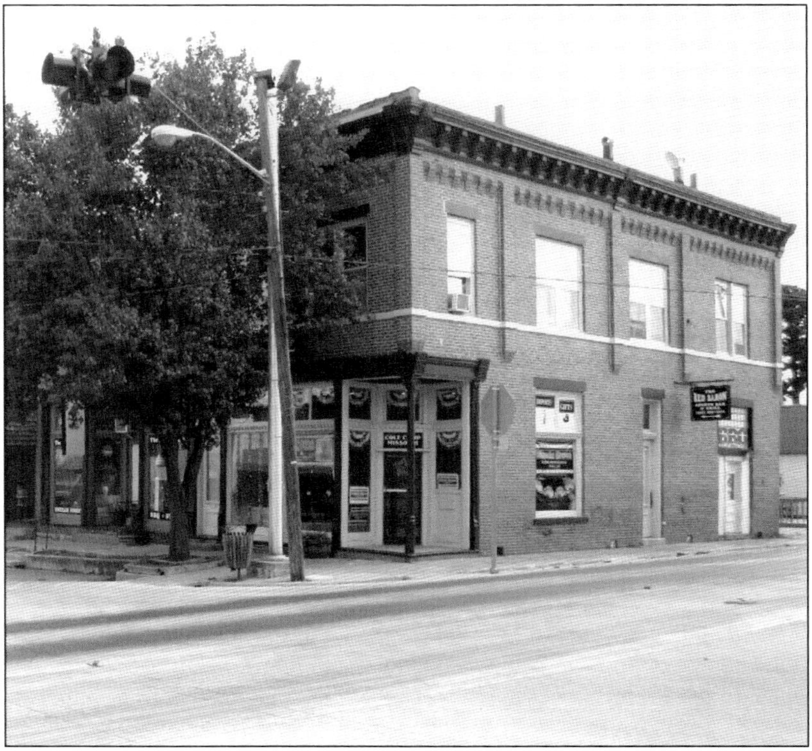

The Peoples Bank building has survived to become a major landmark in the Cole Camp historic district.

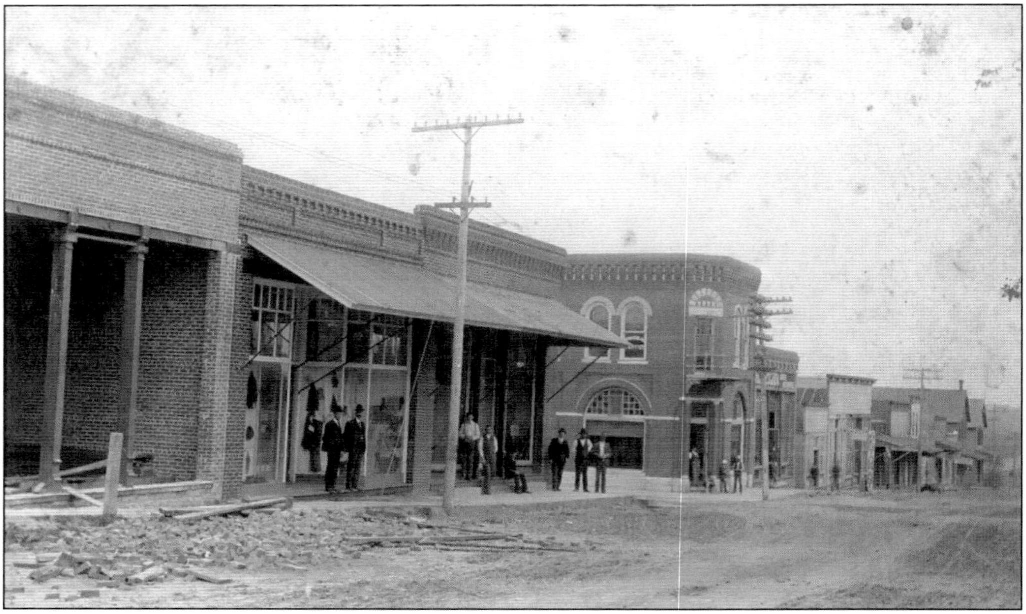

Construction in the new business district is illustrated in this late-19th-century photograph looking downhill and north on Maple Street. The building under construction is the third drugstore to be built in Cole Camp by Louis Grother. The Citizens Bank building and Boeschen's General Merchandise are visible, along with a variety of false-front frame buildings along North Maple Street.

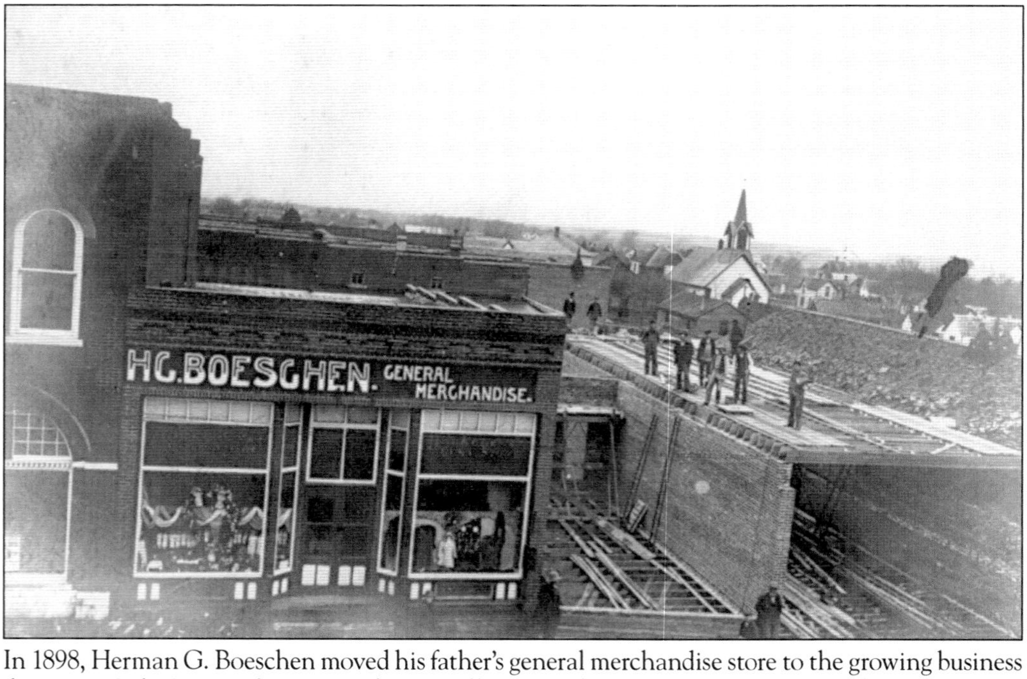

In 1898, Herman G. Boeschen moved his father's general merchandise store to the growing business district in Cole Camp. The store and a post office named Boeschenville had originally been located three miles southeast of Cole Camp. The new store was located on Maple Street adjacent to the new Citizens Bank building. Mr. Boeschen and his two sons, Lawrence and Amos, continued to operate the store until 1947. In the distance is the steeple of the Congregational Church.

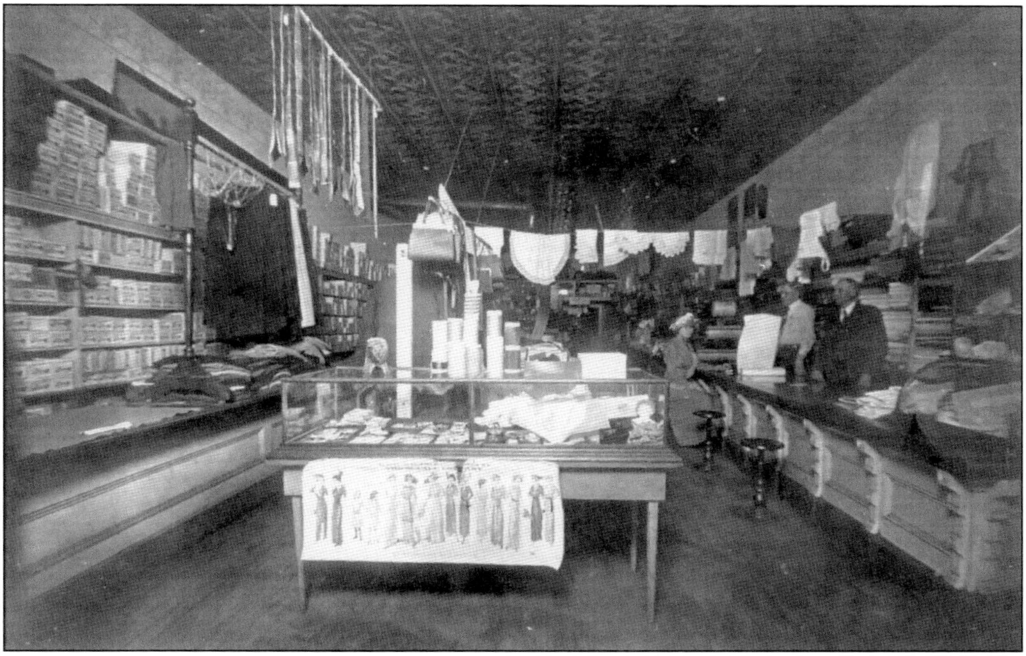

The pressed-tin ceiling, tall shelving, and sturdy counters of the Boeschen store were typical of early-19th-century emporiums. Note the ladies fashion patterns displayed in the center and the stacks of shoeboxes on the left. Ribbons, pocketbooks, bolts of cloth, and men's ties are among the many offerings of the store. The gentleman to the right is proprietor Herman Boeschen.

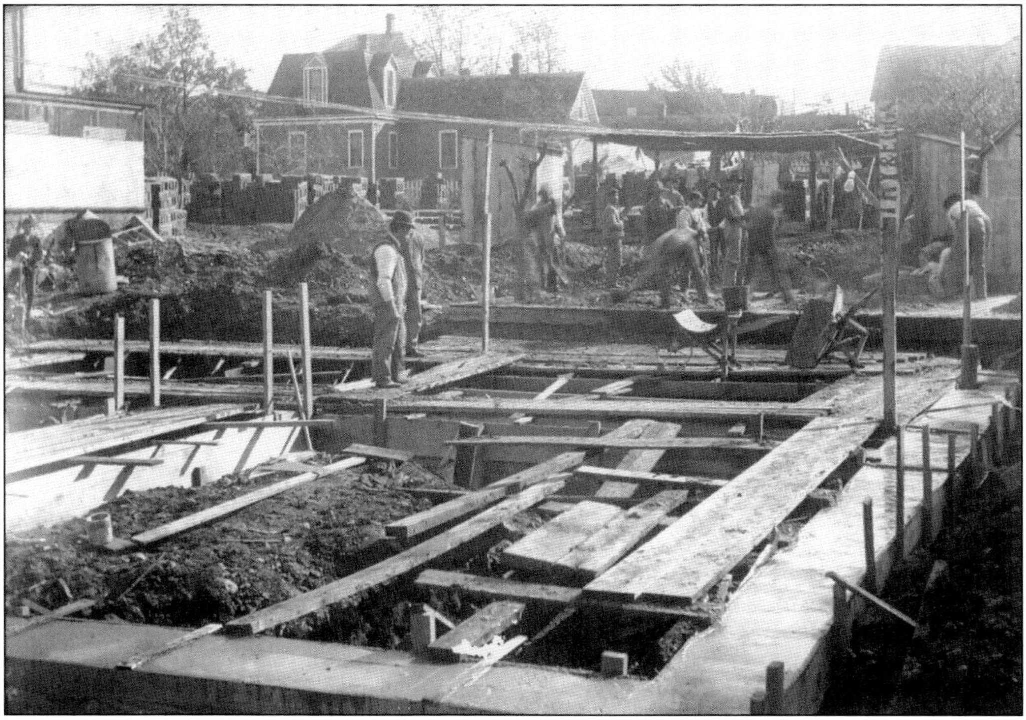

In 1907, workmen in bowler hats pour the foundation of what would be known as the "cement block building," located on Second Street, now Main Street, across from the Citizens Bank building.

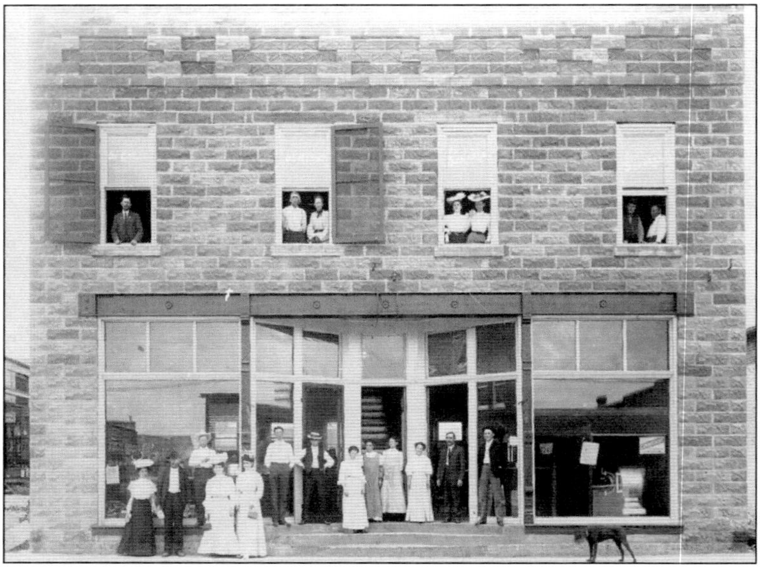

The cement block building on West Second Street is being inspected by a group of Cole Camp residents. A.E. Wright moved his butcher shop to the east portion of the building, which had a confectionery on the first floor and professional offices for doctors and dentists on the second floor. From 1912 to 1946, the second level also housed the telephone company office.

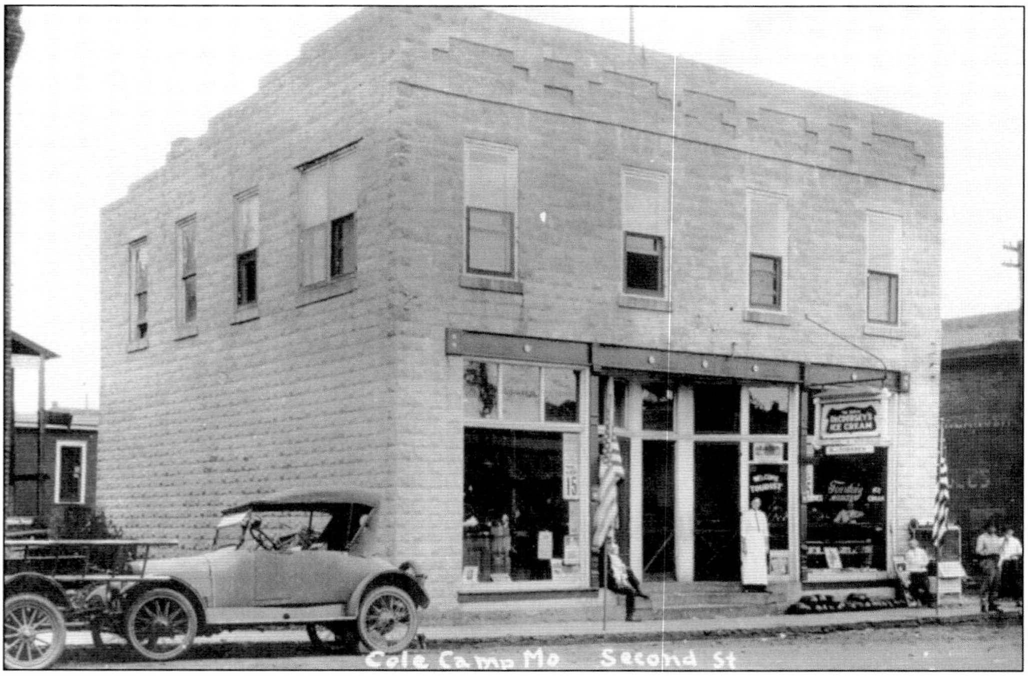

Rufus J. Tobaben is standing on the steps of the cement block building in this 1919 image. The flags would indicate a holiday, possibly the Fourth of July. Tobaben operated his confectionery here from 1916 into the 1930s. The aging cement blocks became difficult to maintain, and the building was torn down in 1972. Today, it is the site of the Cole Camp bandstand.

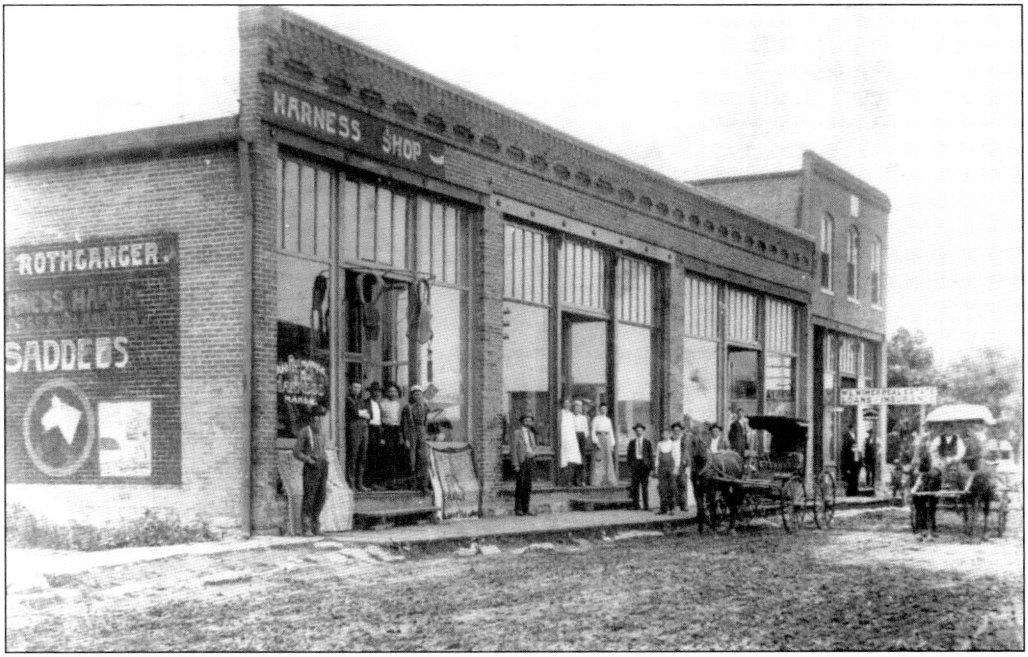

This c. 1905 view is looking west on what was then Second Street (now Main Street). The shops include the Rothganger Harness Shop, the C. F. Berry Store, Eickhoff Furniture Store, and the Wimer Real Estate office. The upstairs was the Woodman Hall, where town meetings and band rehearsals were held. In 2010, this entire block is intact, and the Eickhoff Furniture Store is still in operation by the third generation of owners, Betty and E.L. Eickhoff.

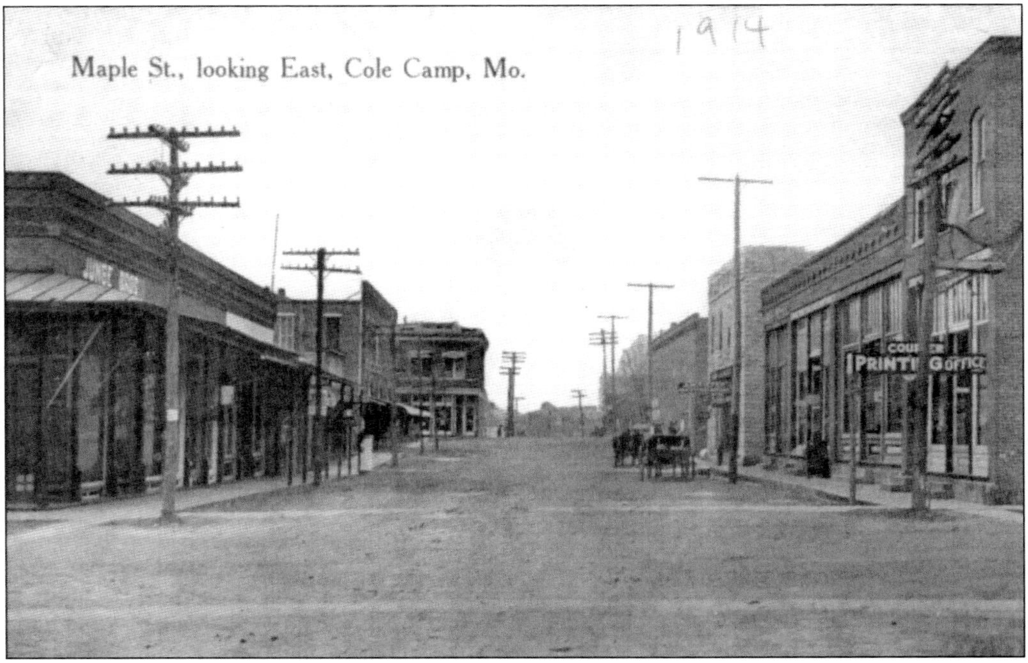

This postcard view looking east on Second Street is dated 1914. The Woodman Building, on the right, was occupied by the *Cole Camp Courier*, and Eickhoff Furniture Store was next door. Across the street is the Jung Brother store.

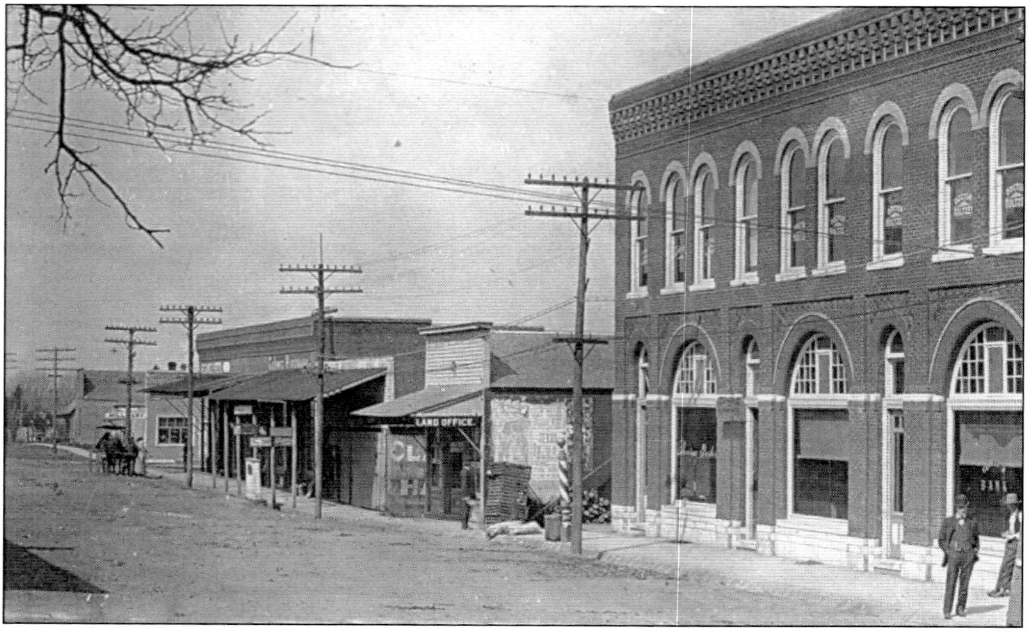

This 1900 image was shot looking west on Second Street. The Citizens Bank is on the right, and the west portion of the building is occupied by Henry Postel's barbershop, as indicated by the sidewalk-mounted barber pole.

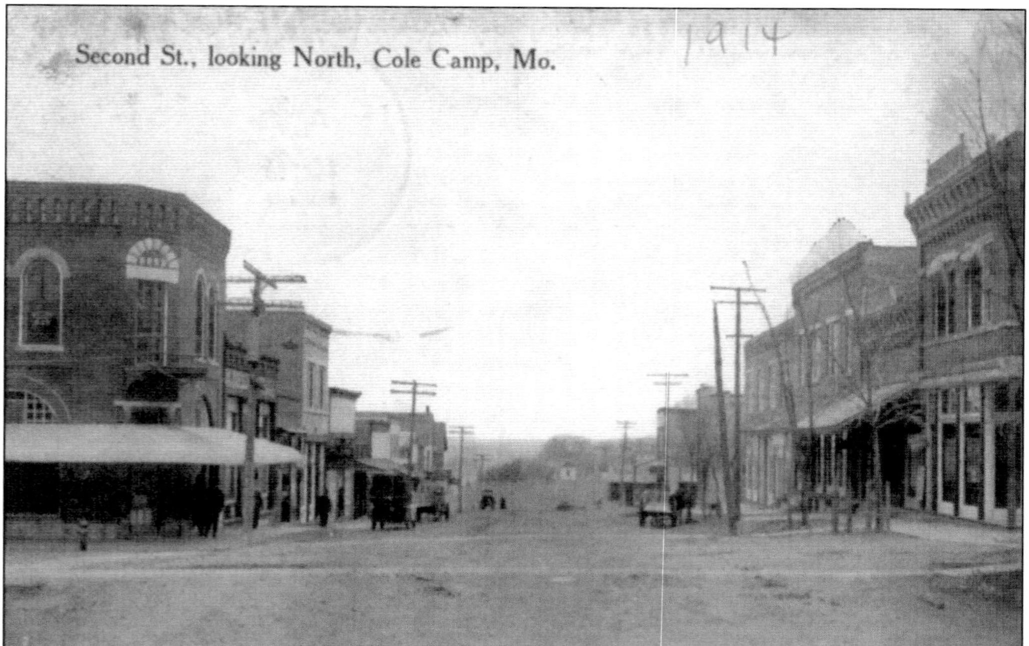

This 1914 view looks north on Maple Street. The Citizens Bank building is on the left, and the rival Peoples Bank is on the right. The Missouri Pacific Railroad branch line is at the very end of Maple Street.

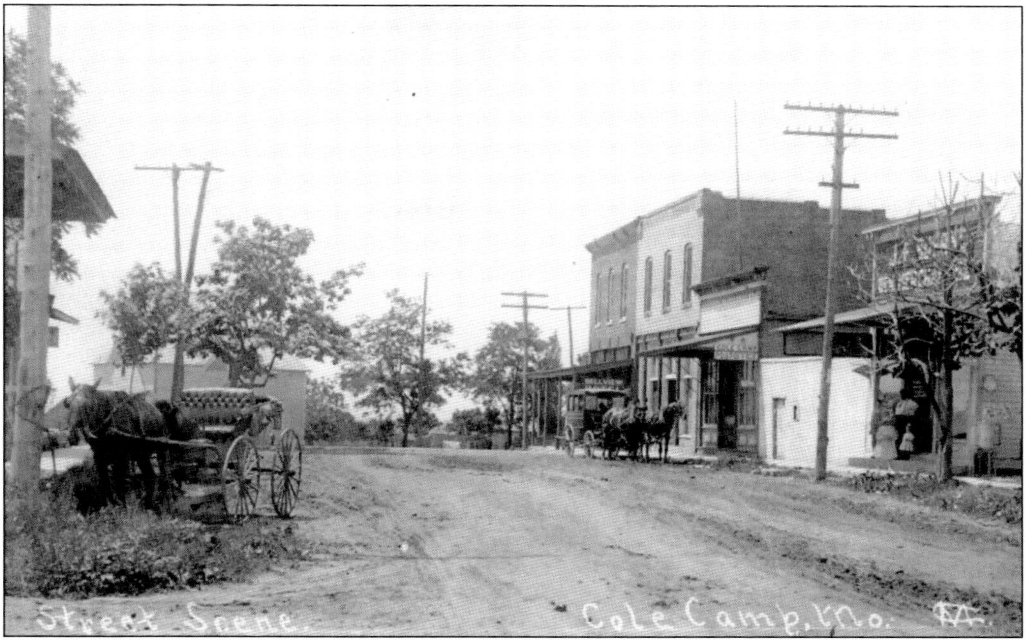

This 1913 view looks south on Maple Street. The building at the far corner of Booneville and Maple Streets is the Belleview Hotel. Two doors down from the hotel are the post office and the J.F. Berry General Store. In 2010, the Belleview Hotel was in operation as a restaurant.

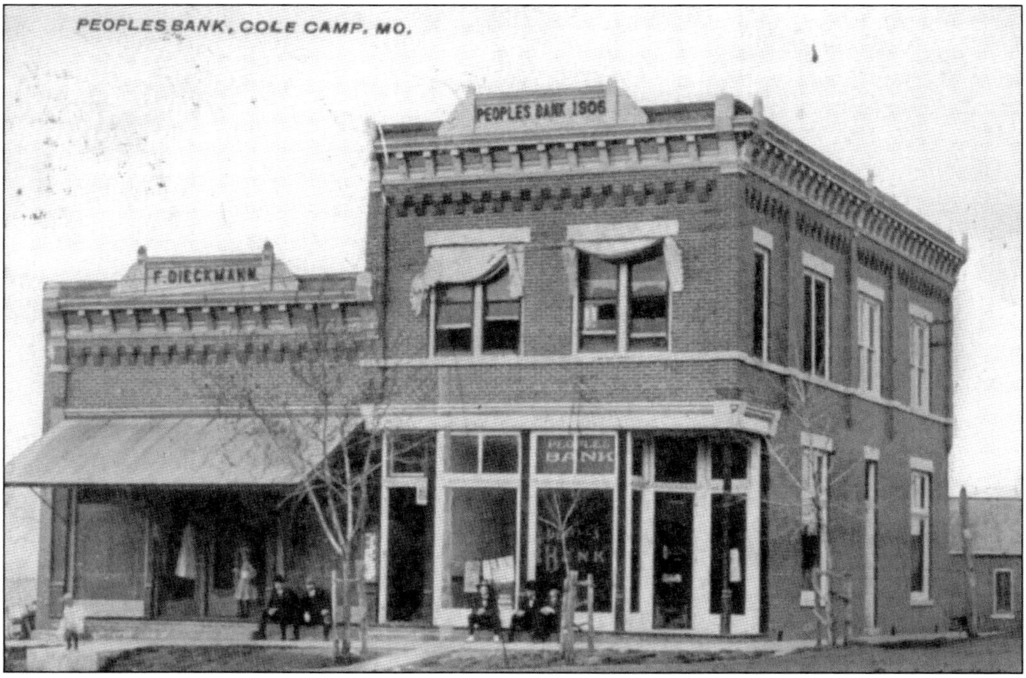

Situated next to the Peoples Bank building was Fred Dieckmann's store that opened in 1907. The Dieckmann building still exists and has housed a number of businesses, including a hardware store, shoe store, radio repair shop, and a Western Auto store. In 2010, the Red Baron restaurant continues to occupy the building and the old Peoples Bank lobby next door.

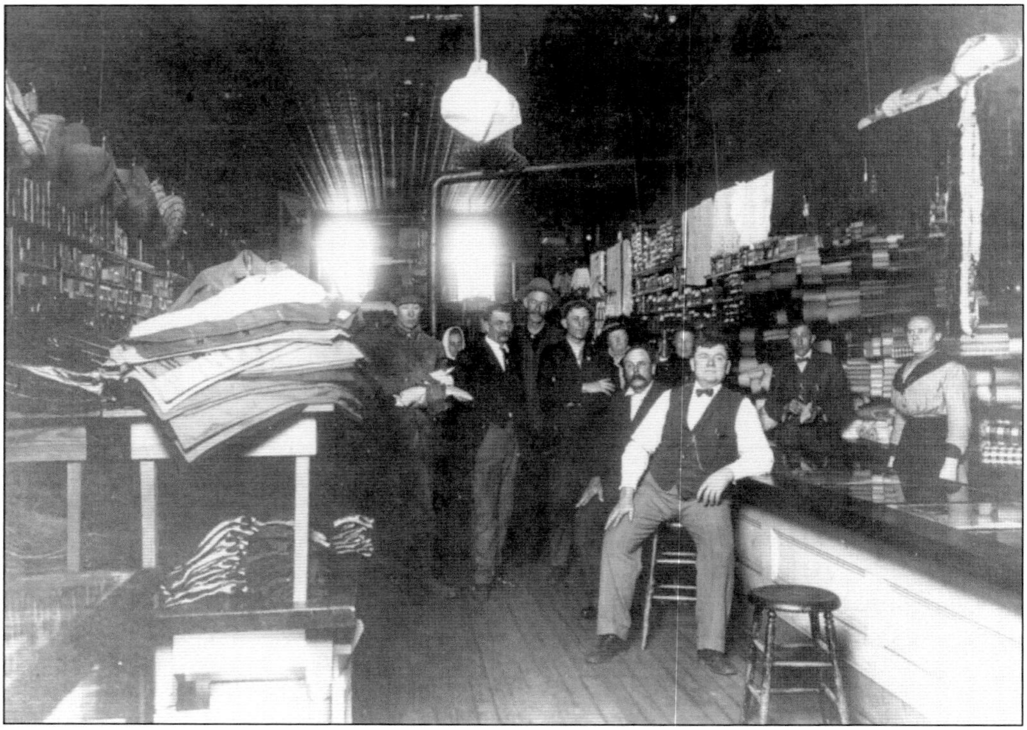

In this photograph is the interior of the Dieckmann store in 1910. The seated gentleman is Bill Harms, Dieckmann's partner. The clerks behind the counter are Hulda Harms Dieckmann and Henry Riegers. The mustached gentleman behind Harms is Otto Viets.

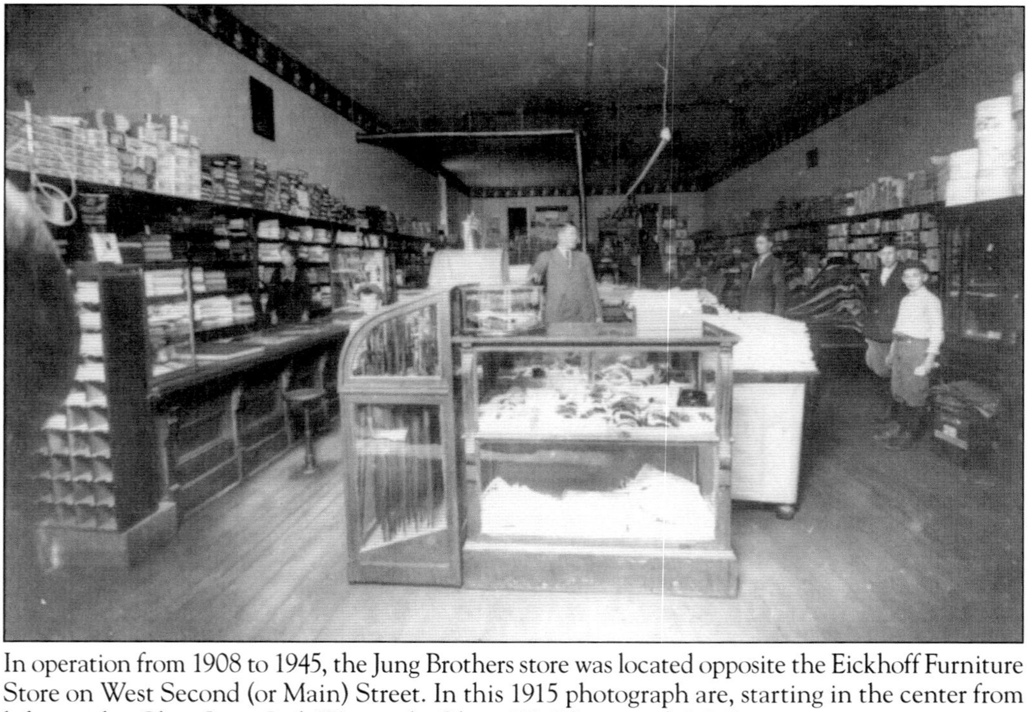

In operation from 1908 to 1945, the Jung Brothers store was located opposite the Eickhoff Furniture Store on West Second (or Main) Street. In this 1915 photograph are, starting in the center from left to right, Claus Jung, Jack Weymuth, Oliver "Cy" Jung, and C.P. Jung.

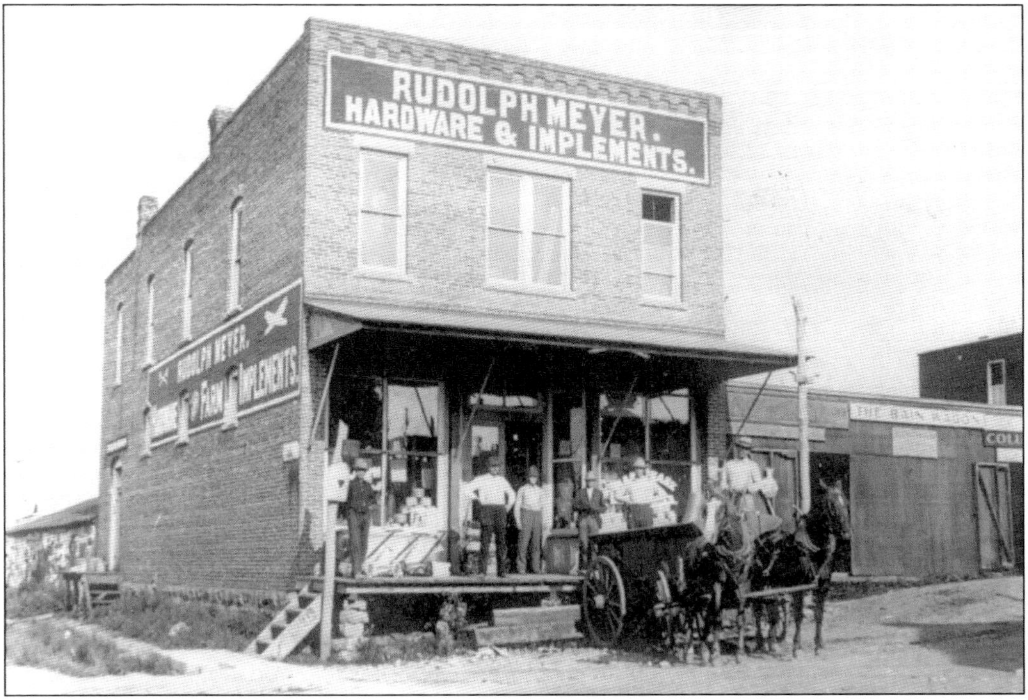

Situated at the southeast corner of First and Maple Streets, Rudolph Meyer established his hardware store in a building originally constructed by August Kreisel in 1898. Kreisel operated both a hardware store and wagon and implement business until his death. Family members ran the business until it was sold to R. Meyer in 1910.

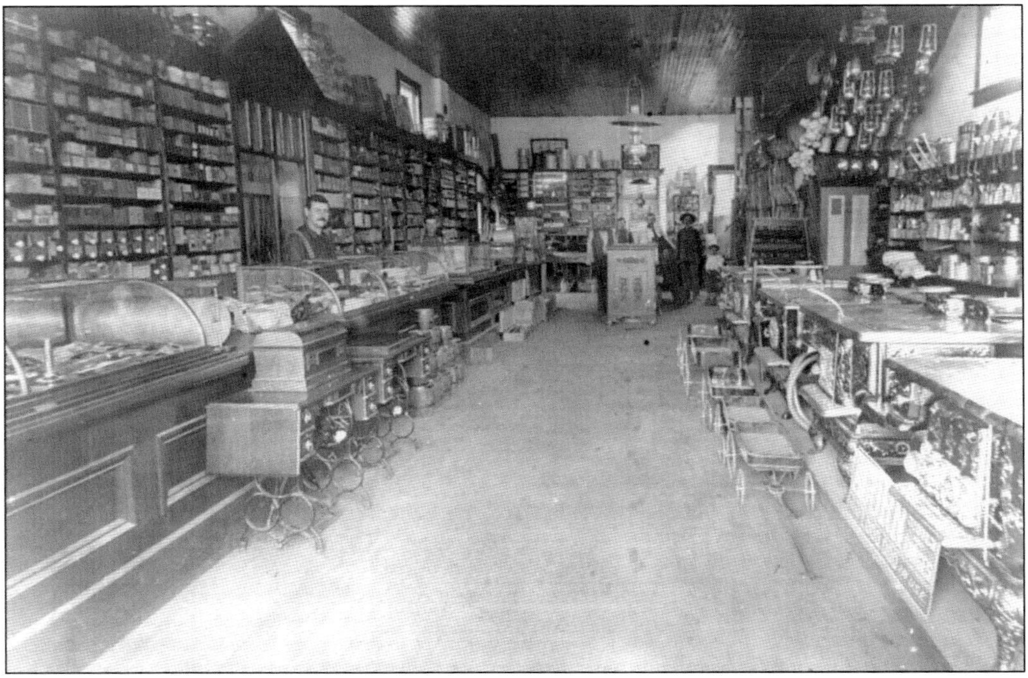

August Kreisel (left) poses in his well-stocked hardware store. Sewing machines, children's wagons, coal oil lanterns, and a large variety of cast-iron cook stoves are among the items on display.

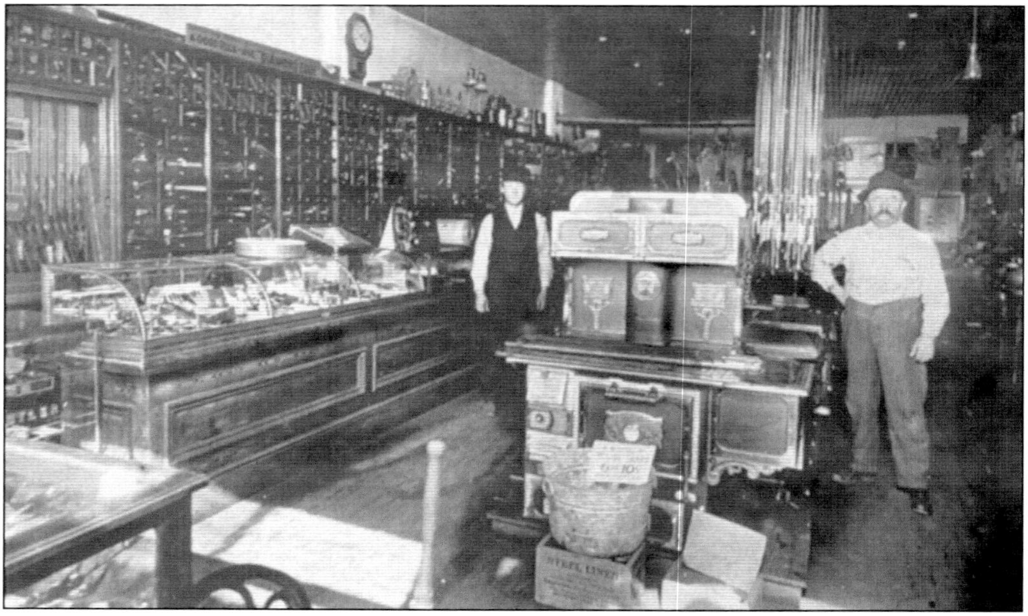

Rudolph Meyer (left) poses next to a hanging display of buggy whips. Firearms can be seen to the right of the curved glass display cases, and drawers along the wall are adorned with the tools that make up their contents. The iron cook stove would please anyone of the period, and an ample supply of mousetraps could be had for only 10¢.

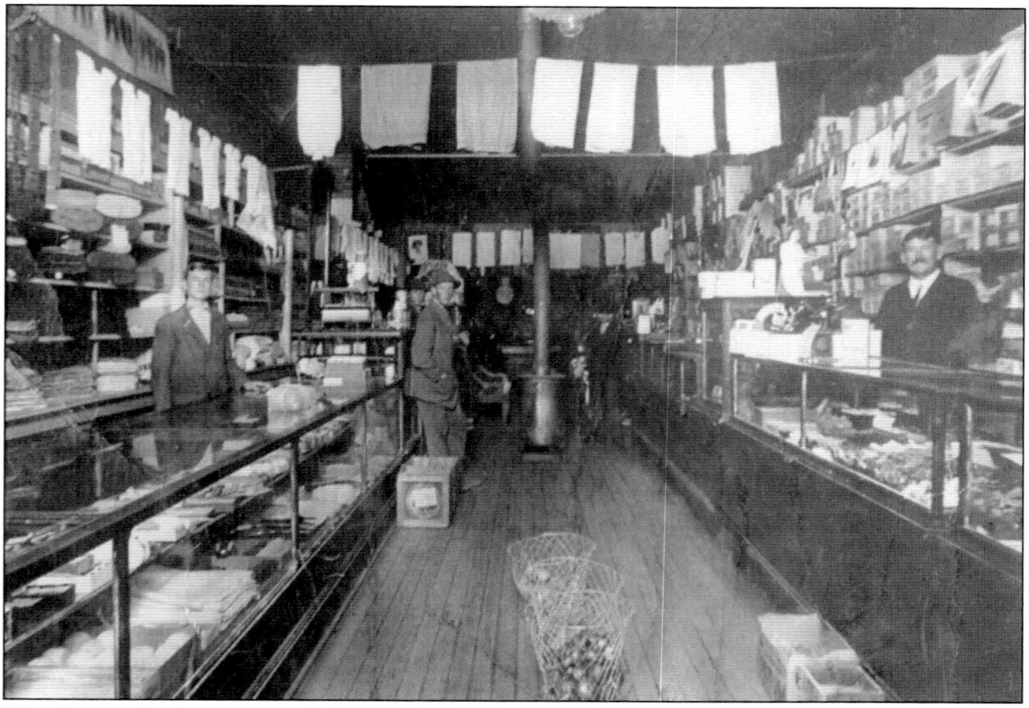

The shopper had a variety of choices in early-day Cole Camp, and the store of John Fred Burke was another example of a general merchandise business. Burke, who moved to Cole Camp from Boeschenville, opened his store on Maple Street in 1906. The classic potbellied stove provided central heating. Burke is pictured on the left behind the counter.

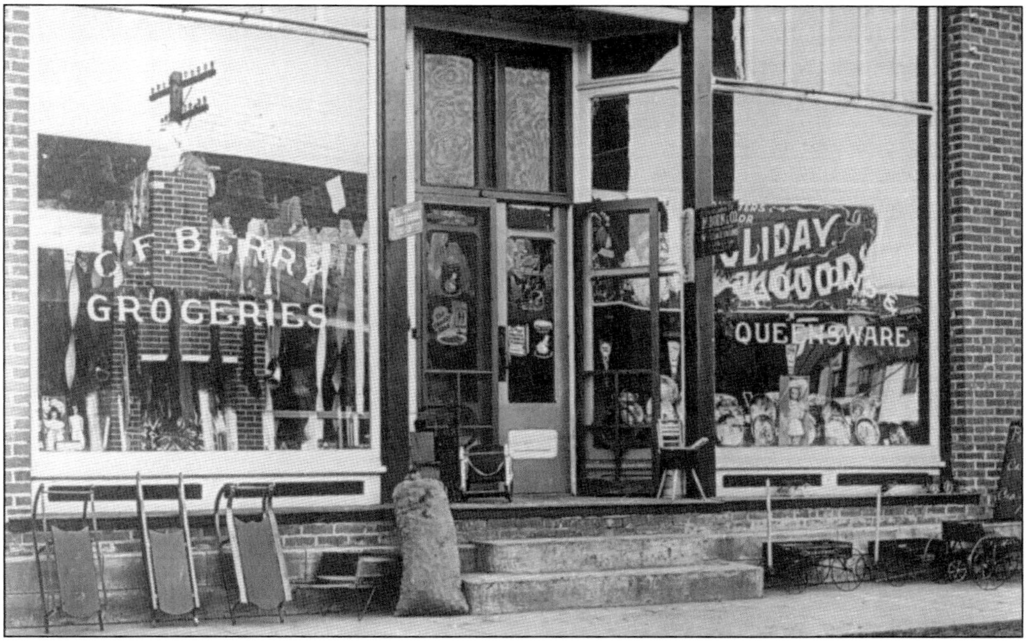

In 1898, C.F. Berry constructed a two-story building on East Second Street. The upstairs became the Woodman Hall. He operated a café downstairs until 1910, when he converted it to a store. In this pre-Christmas view, both sleds and wagons are on display.

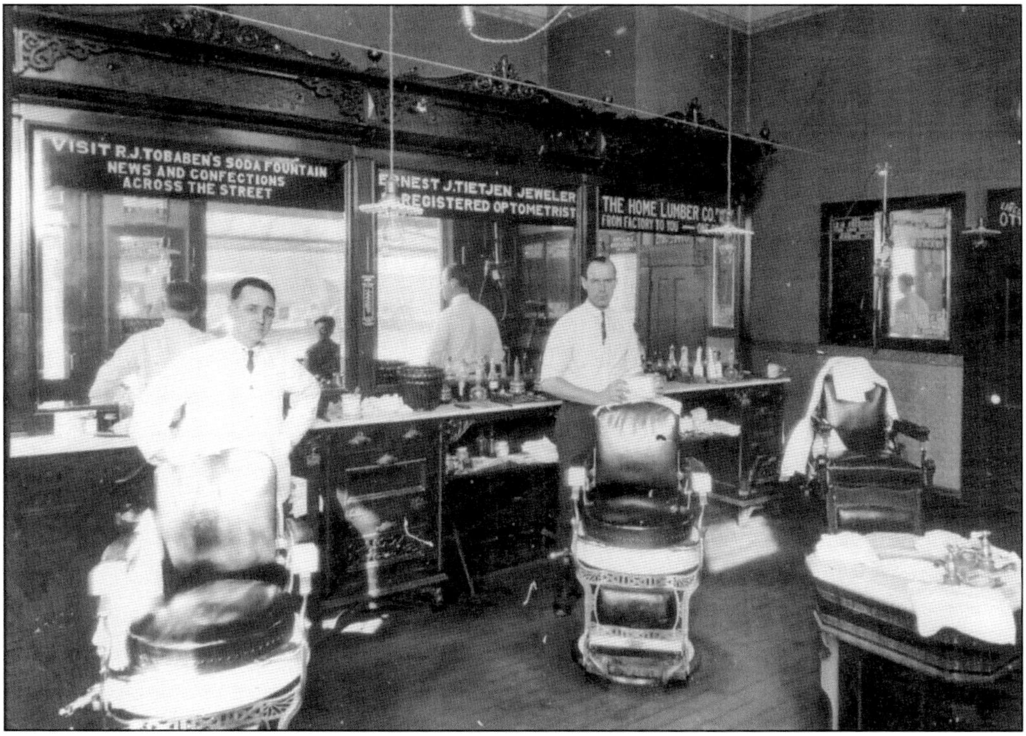

Barbers Nerge Parks (left) and Ed Monsees await customers in their barbershop, located in the Citizens Bank building. Henry Postel was the first barber in 1898. The shop was occupied until 1956, when the bank remodeled the space.

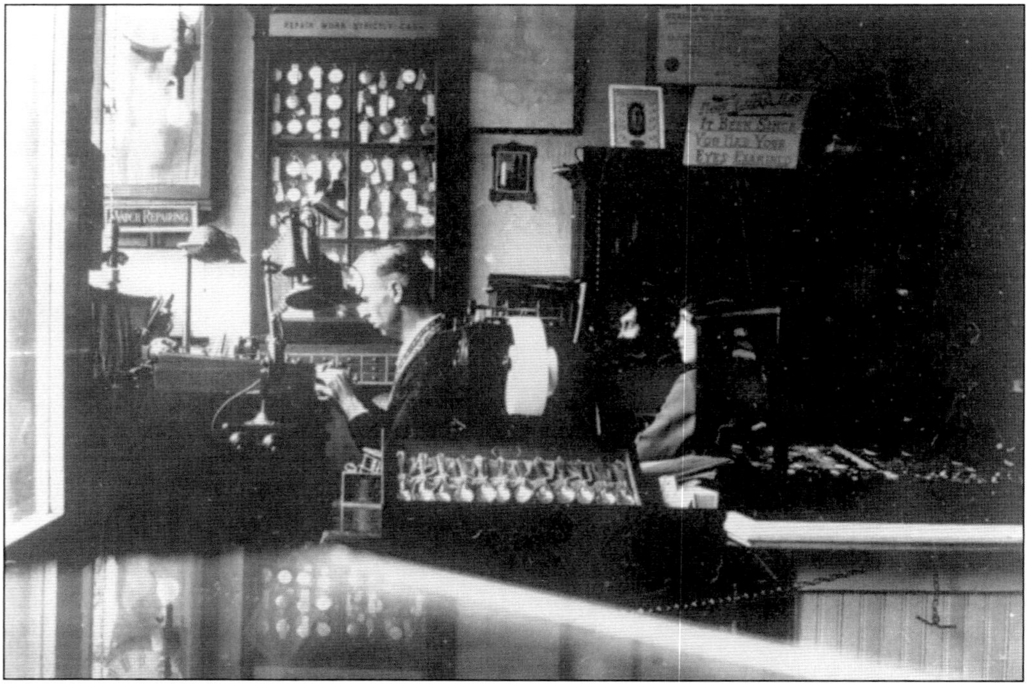

In 1919, J. Tietjen and Judge Bohling opened a jewelry store next to Boeschen's General Store on North Maple Street. Upon the death of Bohling, Tietjen continued the business and added optometry to his offerings. He was in business until 1931, when he sold the store and moved to Jefferson City, Missouri.

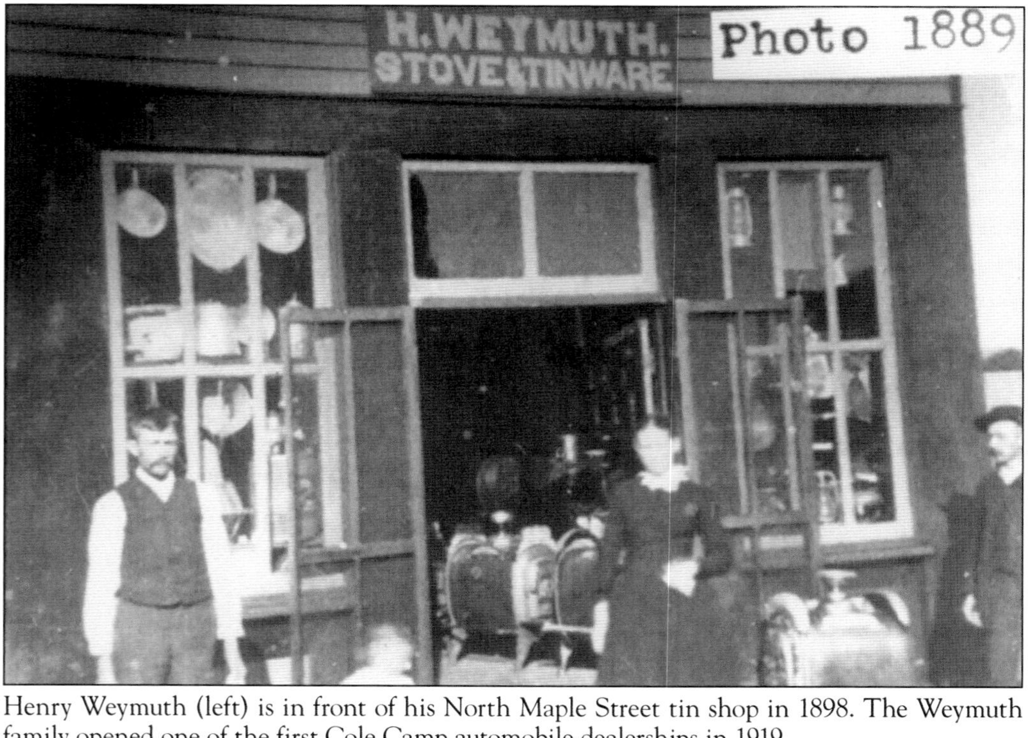

Henry Weymuth (left) is in front of his North Maple Street tin shop in 1898. The Weymuth family opened one of the first Cole Camp automobile dealerships in 1919.

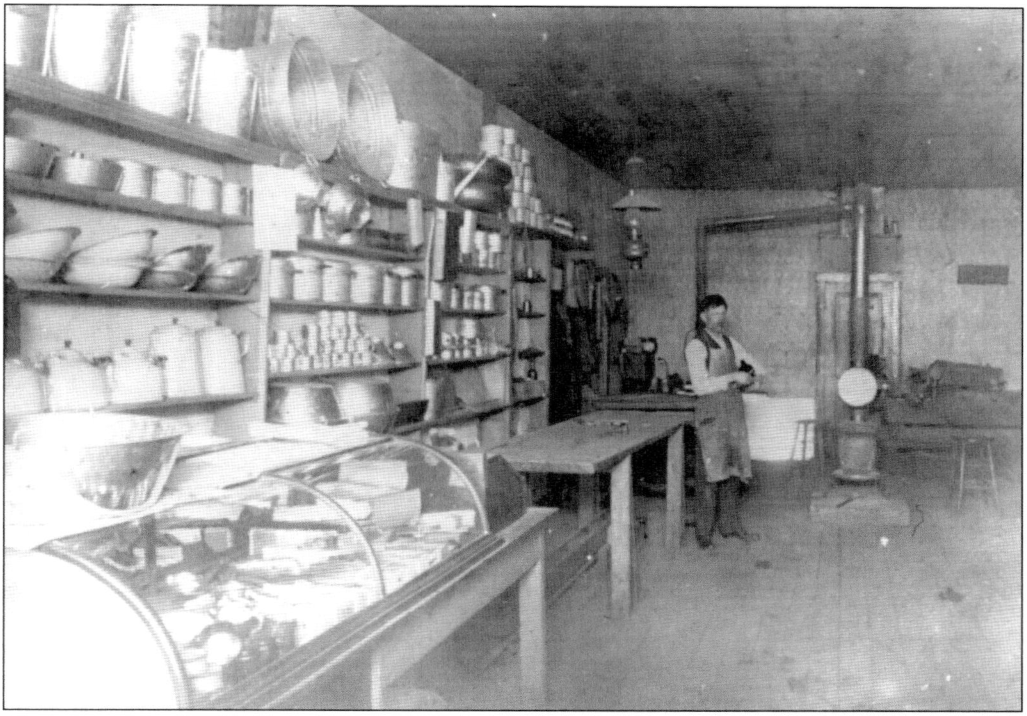

Washtubs, cups, bowls, pots, pans, and buckets made up the stock of Mr. Henry Weymuth's 1898 tin shop.

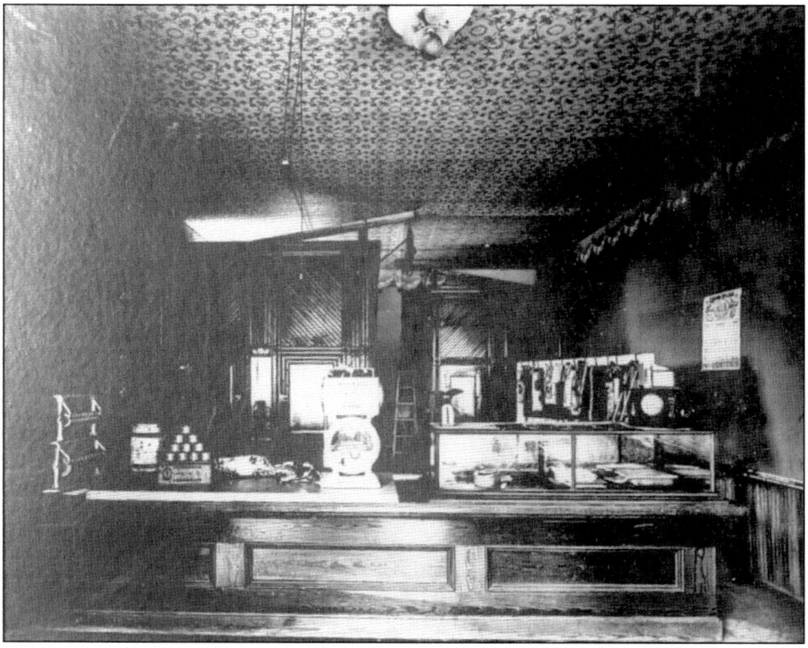

In 1908, Adam and Frank Smasal purchased A.E. Wright's butcher shop. In later years, it became the location of a produce business, restaurant, and in 1975 a hobby shop. Note the printed ceiling and the early knob-and-tube electrical wiring.

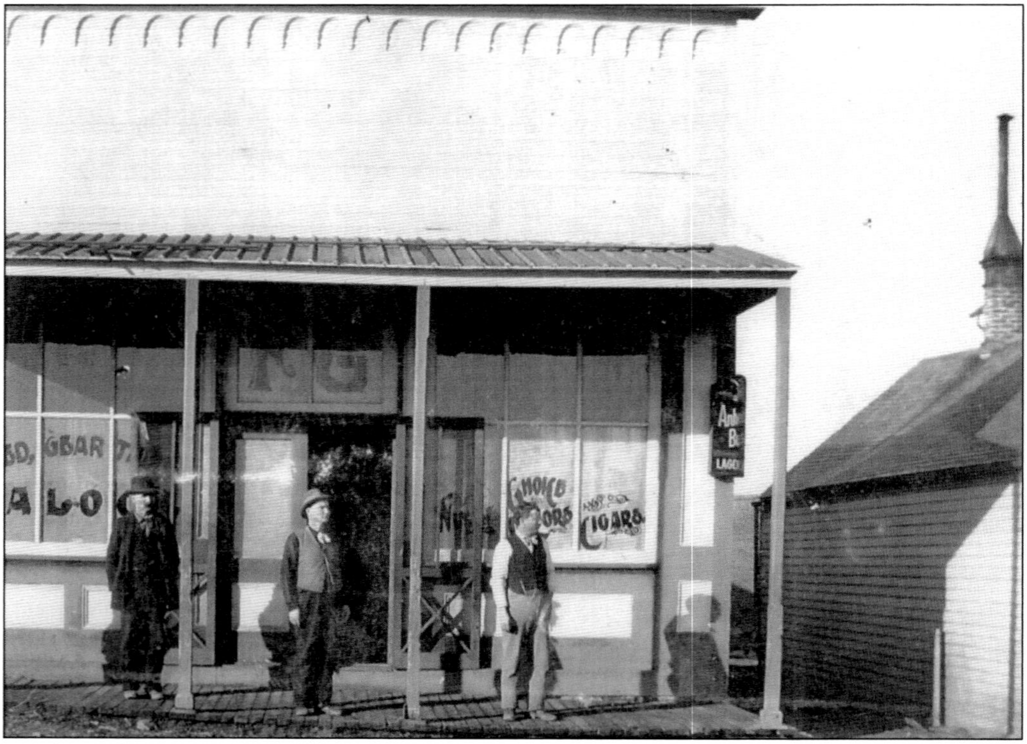

North Maple Street was once known as Battle Row due to the number of saloons that dominated the block. In 1899, the Gartner Brothers Saloon was offering Anheuser-Busch lager to its clientele.

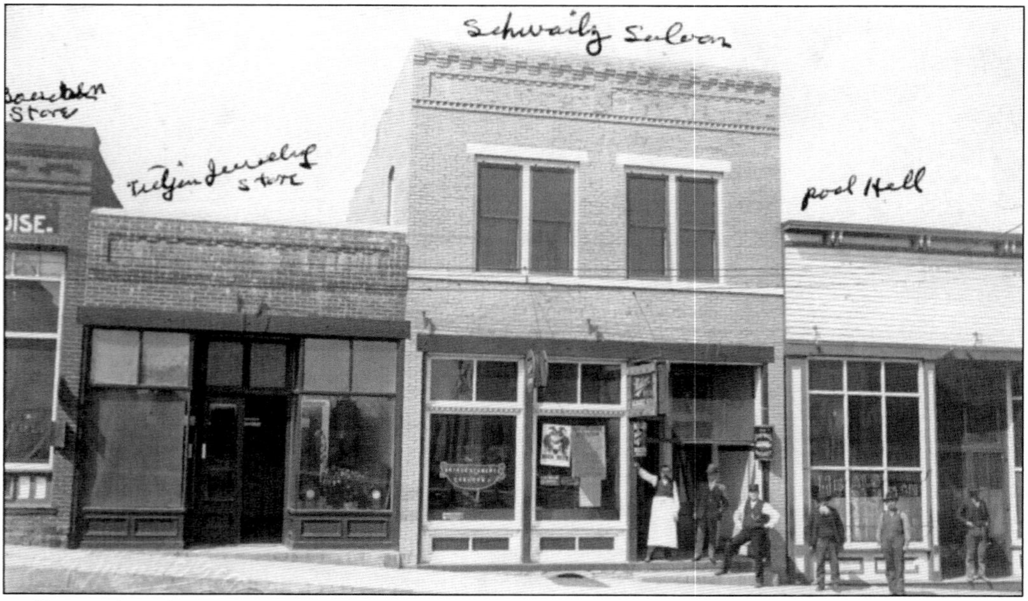

Miller High Life was on tap at Schwartz's Saloon on Battle Row in 1904. Railroad employees, like the man with the vest and watch chain, were prohibited by "rule G" from drinking while on duty. Boeschen's store and Tietjen's jewelry are on the left, and the notorious pool hall is on the right. Railroad workers from the under-construction Rock Island Railroad were often customers of Battle Row saloons.

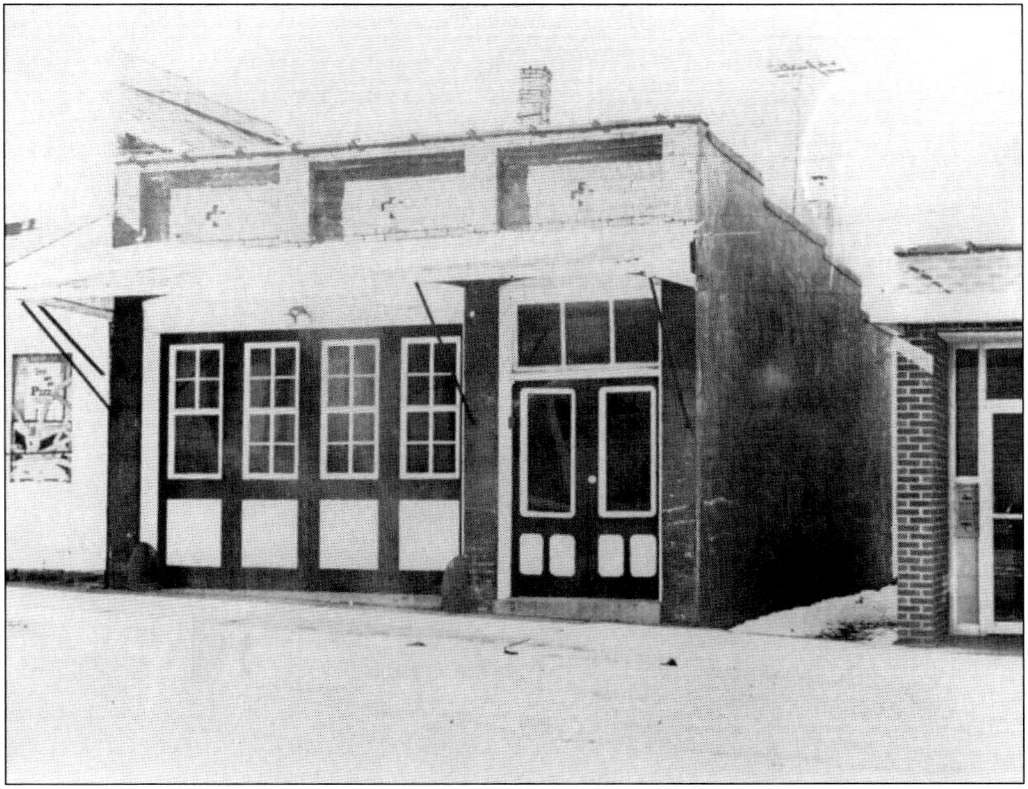

The old Cole Camp Fire House was located in the middle of Battle Row on South Maple Street. The occasional sounding of the fire siren provided a short diversion for the local saloon patrons.

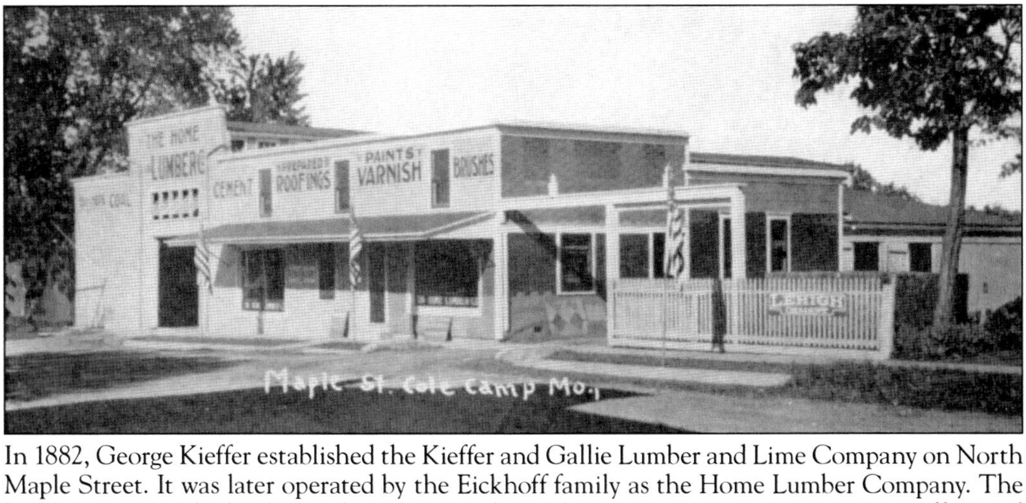

In 1882, George Kieffer established the Kieffer and Gallie Lumber and Lime Company on North Maple Street. It was later operated by the Eickhoff family as the Home Lumber Company. The building remained a lumberyard until 1967, when it became a construction company office and storage yard.

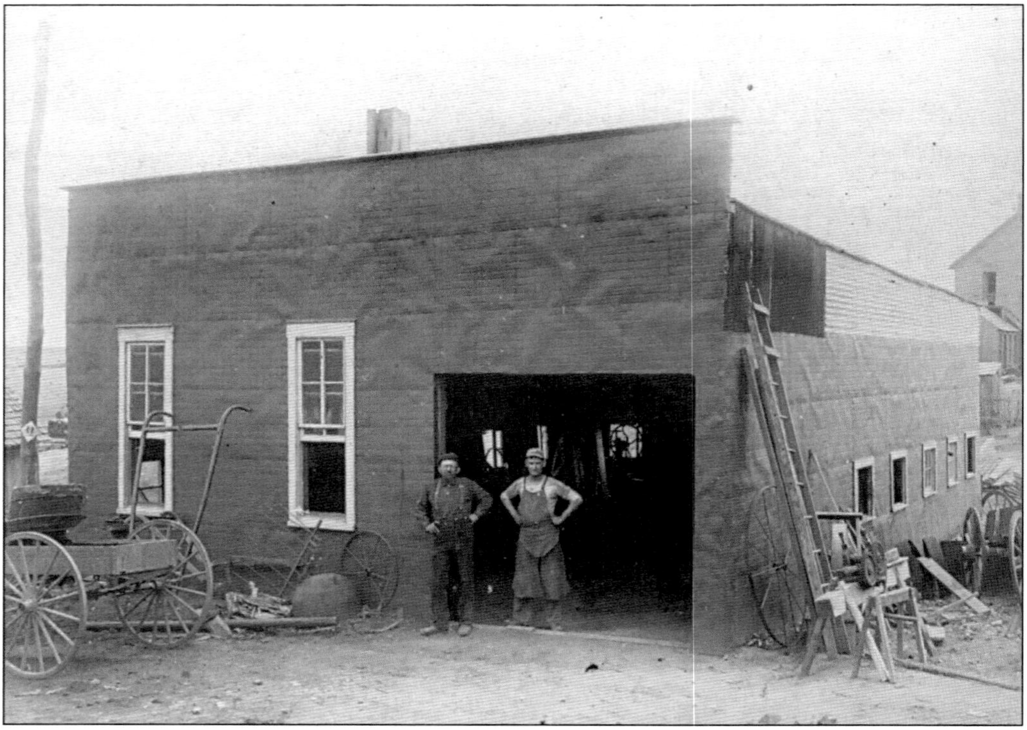

John Stadtherr (1859–1951) established his blacksmith and machine shop in Cole Camp in 1878.

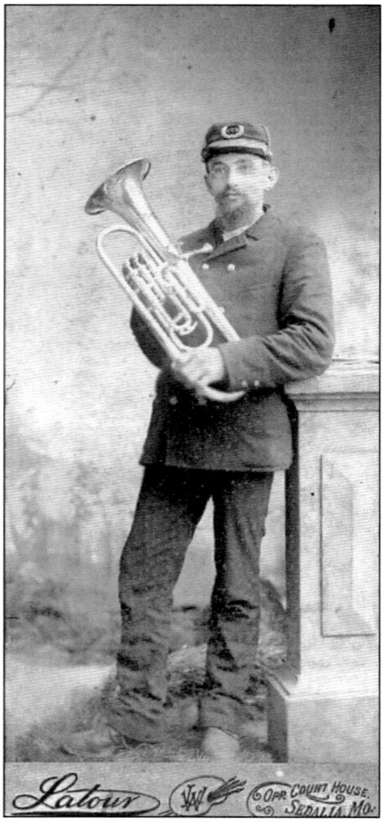

When not pounding hot iron, John Stadtherr was a member of the Cole Camp Band. He was also instrumental in the establishment of Sts. Peter and Paul Catholic Church in 1878.

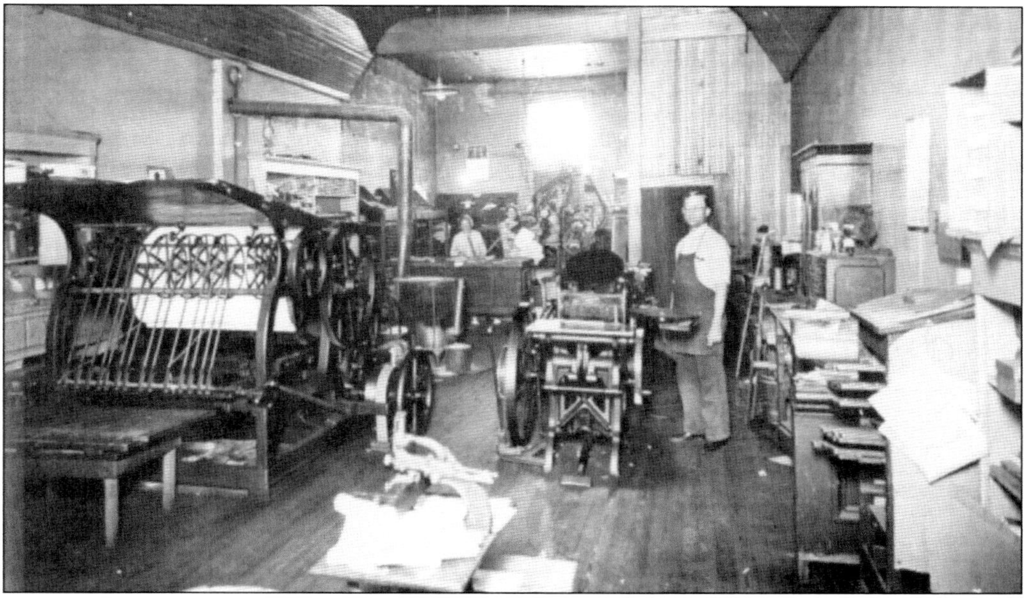

The weekly *Cole Camp Courier* newspaper has been published continuously since 1893 when N.H. Robinson started the publication. Over the years, the ownership has changed hands, and it is currently owned by Standard Publishing of Carrolton, Missouri. In this 1935 photograph, owner and publisher Edwin Wilkens is seen standing near his press.

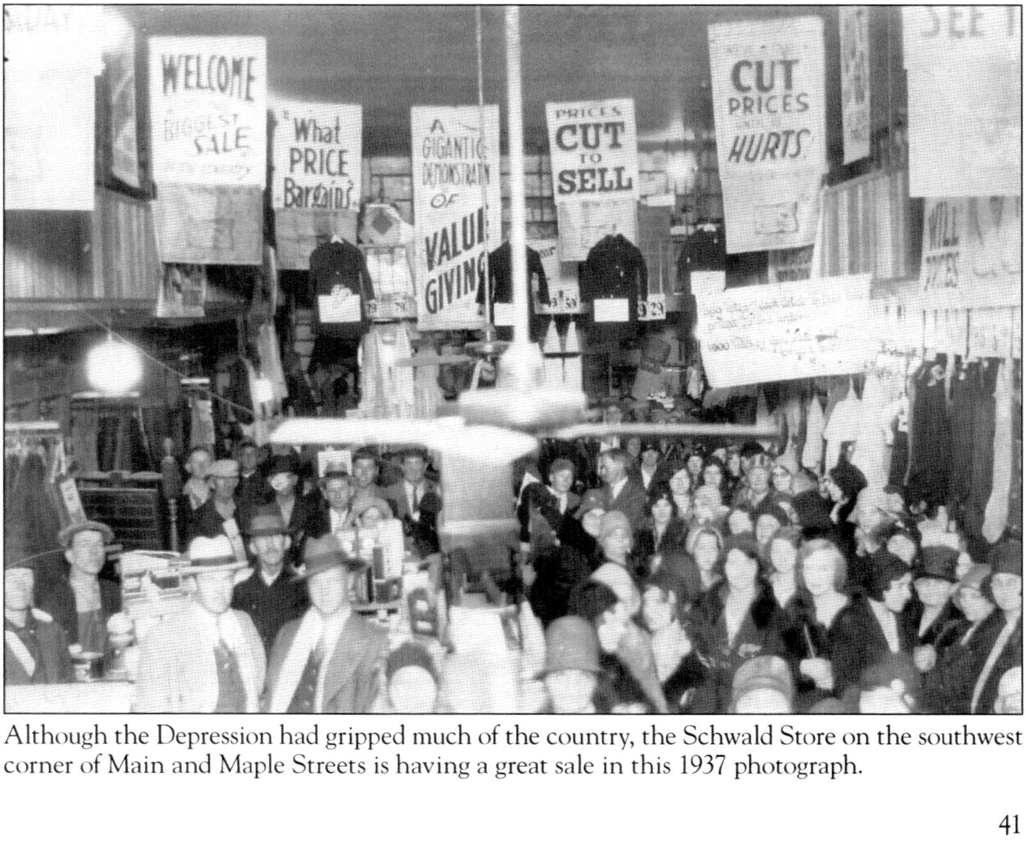

Although the Depression had gripped much of the country, the Schwald Store on the southwest corner of Main and Maple Streets is having a great sale in this 1937 photograph.

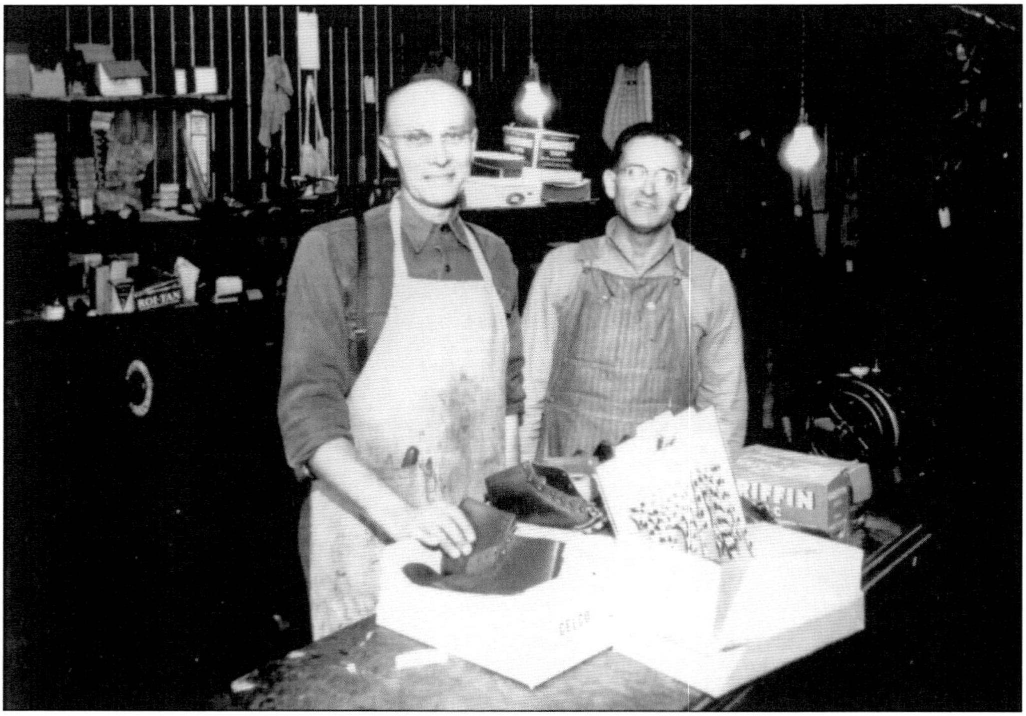

William Hink (left) and Sherman Brown are in their cobbler shop in this 1930s photograph. They offered shoe repair and sold boots and shoes. Hink operated the shop until his retirement in 1960.

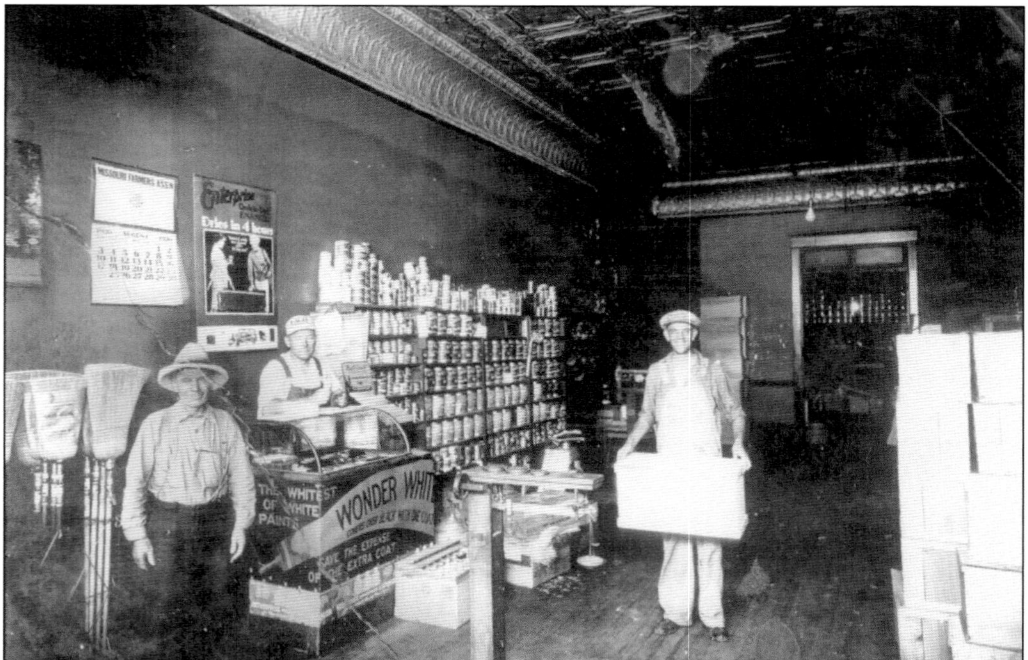

Henry Semon operated a produce business in his former saloon on North Maple Street. In this 1930 view are, from left to right, Herman Pritzel, Otto Zimmerschied, and Henry Intelmann Jr.

Two

City of Lincoln

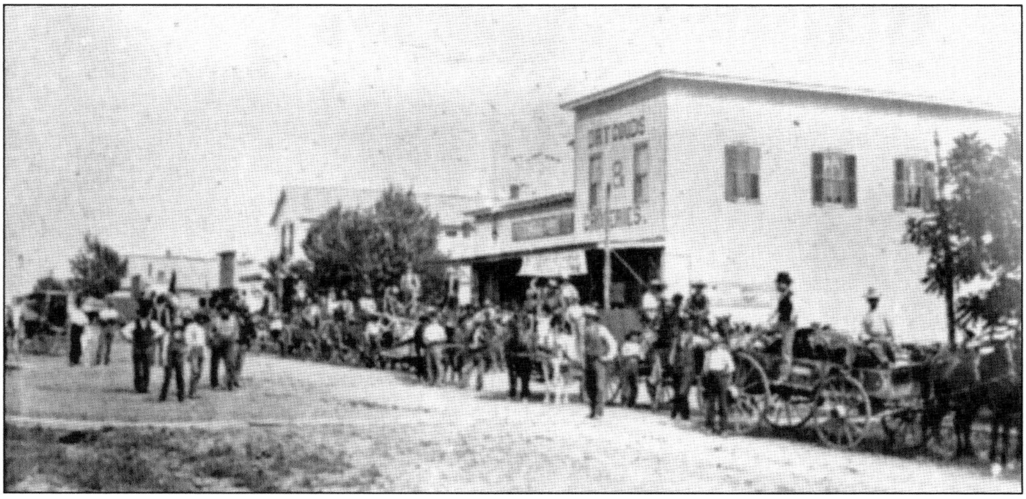

Lincoln is located eight miles southwest of Cole Camp. It was named after the martyred president and incorporated in 1869. The area was settled in 1860 by Wiley Vincent, who operated a tavern on the road from Lexington to Warsaw. The town moved northeast when the narrow-gauge railroad was built through the area in 1880. This 1890 photograph shows the Main Street in Lincoln. Unlike Cole Camp, few of Lincoln's historic building have survived into the 21st century, with the exception being the Lodge Hall, the building with the peaked roof down the street on the right.

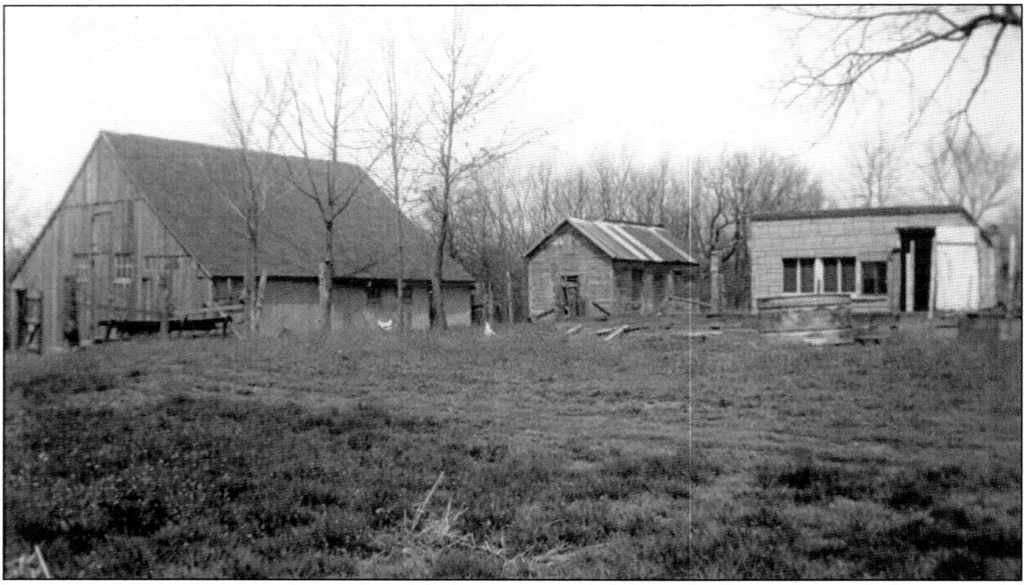

The building on the far right, photographed here in 1956, once housed a drug store and was located at the original site of Wiley Vincent's 1860 tavern. (Courtesy of Earl Meyer.)

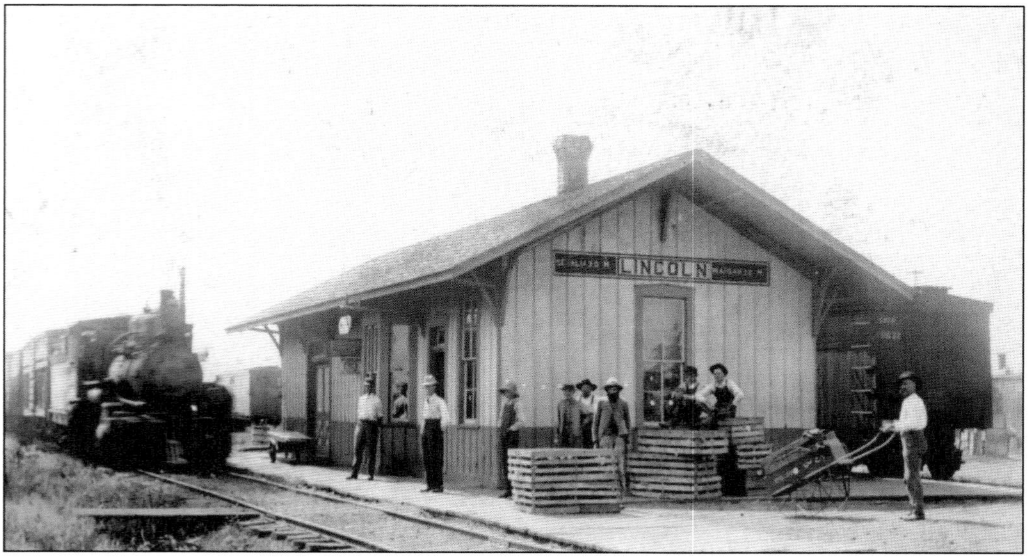

In 1880, the Sedalia Warsaw and Southern Railroad built a 42-mile narrow-gauge railroad from Sedalia, Missouri, through Lincoln, that terminated at the Benton County seat of Warsaw. The line was standard gauged in 1902, and in this view from 1909 the northbound train is entering Lincoln. The postmaster has the mail cart ready and the usual gang of station gadflies is on hand for the daily ritual of the train's arrival.

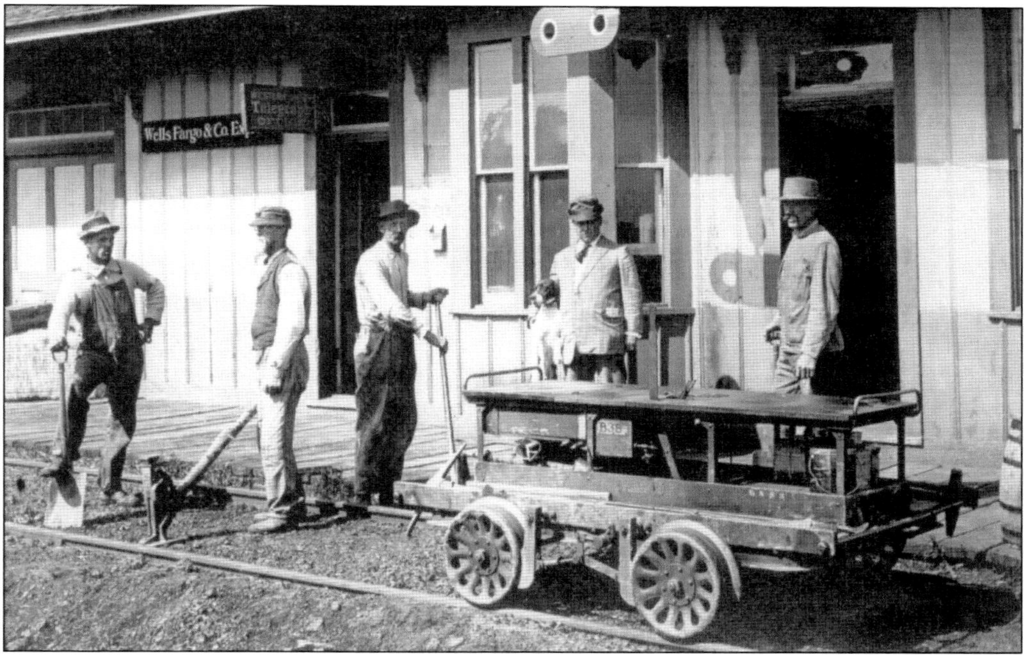

In this view from 1910, the railroad section crew is about to depart for a day's work on the line. John Jack Reeves, the station agent at Lincoln from 1906 to 1939, holds the station mascot.

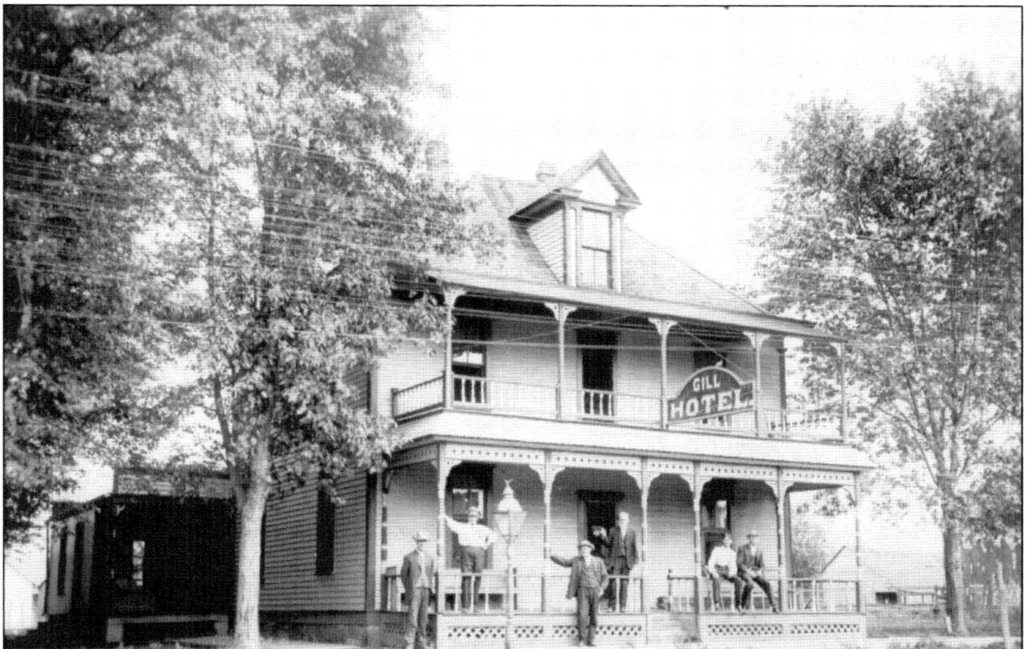

The Gill Hotel was one of two that offered rooms to the traveler as well as showrooms for the traveling salesmen of the day. The building was torn down in 1967 and is now the site of a small park on Main Street.

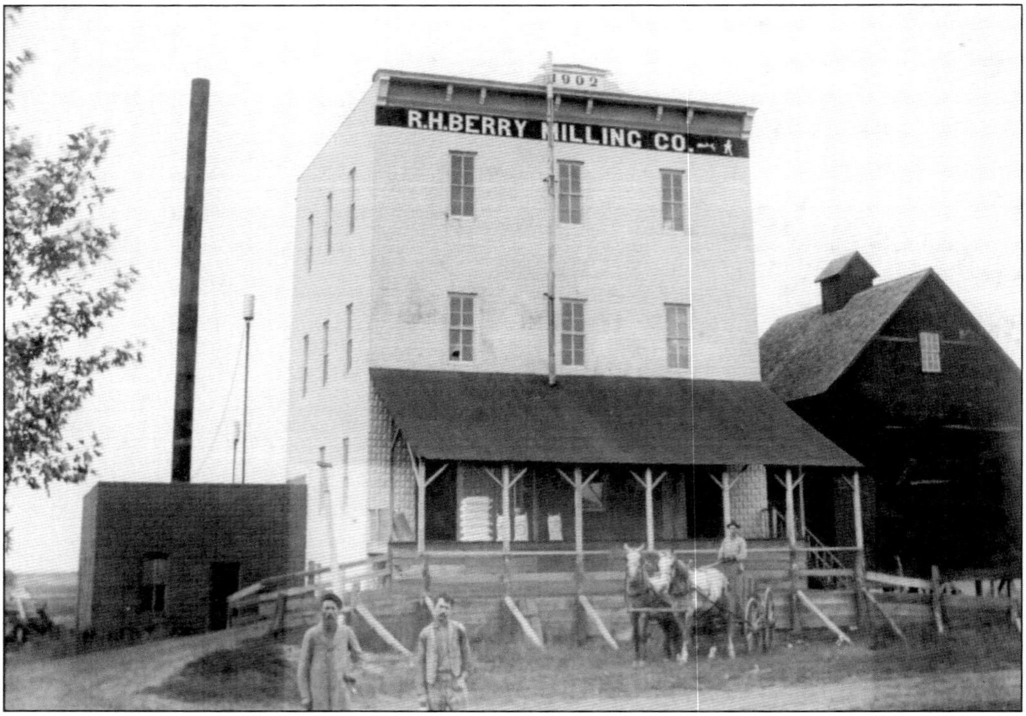

Agriculture has always been the main economic activity of Lincoln, and the R.H. Berry Mill was a major economic asset in 1910. The building was replaced in later years with a new mill, which continues to operate in 2010 under the ownership of the Producers Exchange, based in Ionia.

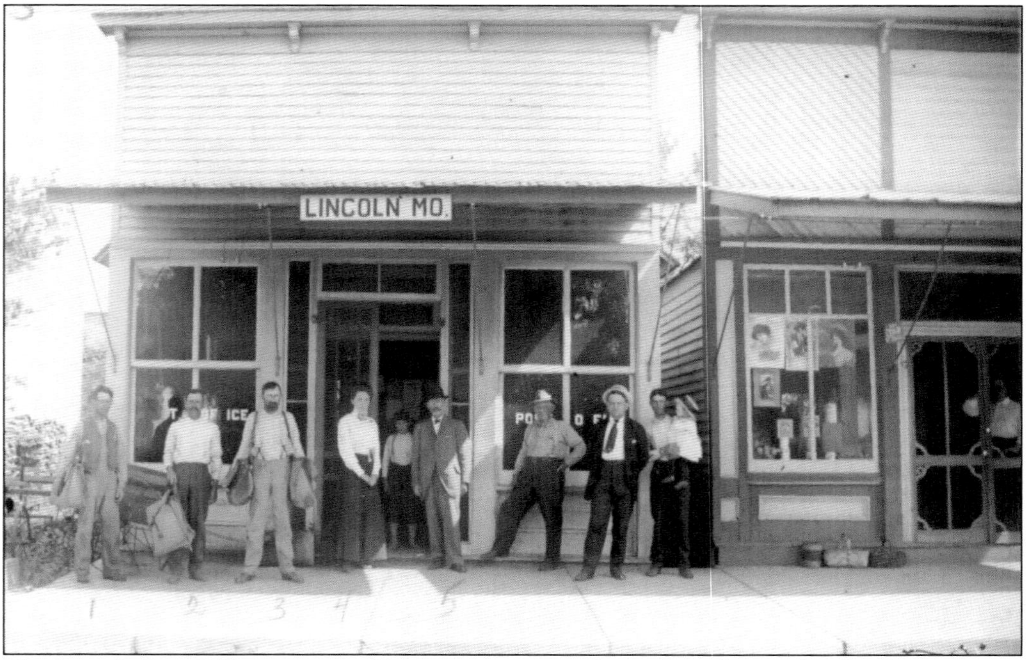

The Lincoln Post Office is pictured here in 1911. It was located on the north side of Main Street next to the Brill and Wisdom General Store.

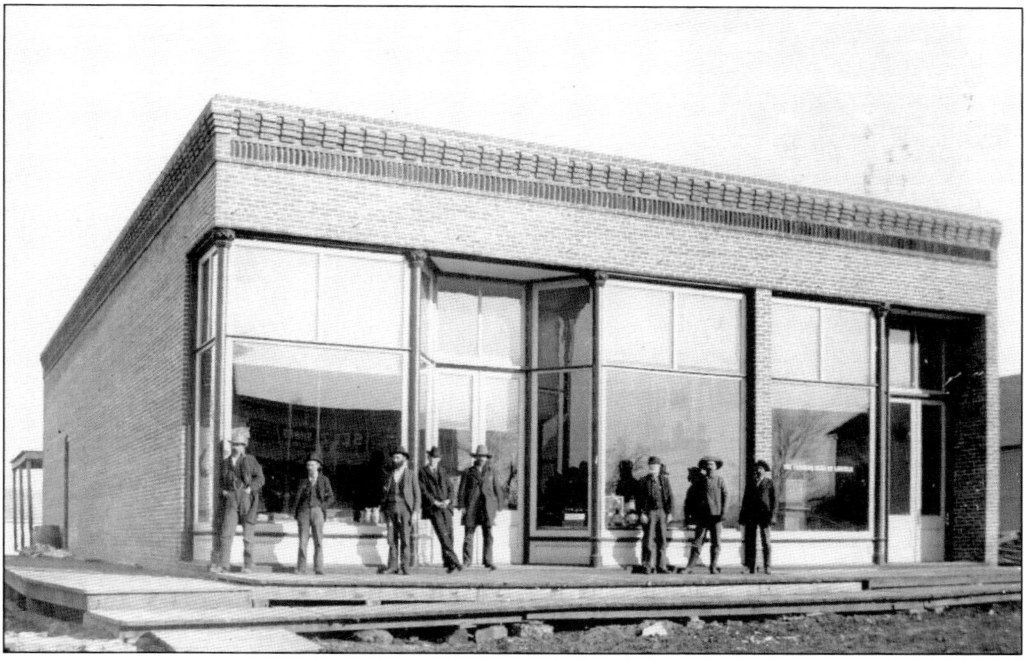

In 1898, William Wisdom and Charlie Brill opened the Brill and Wisdom General Store at the northeast corner of Main and Market Streets. In this photograph, taken shortly after the building's construction, the right side is occupied by the Farmers Bank of Lincoln. The building was demolished and is presently a parking lot.

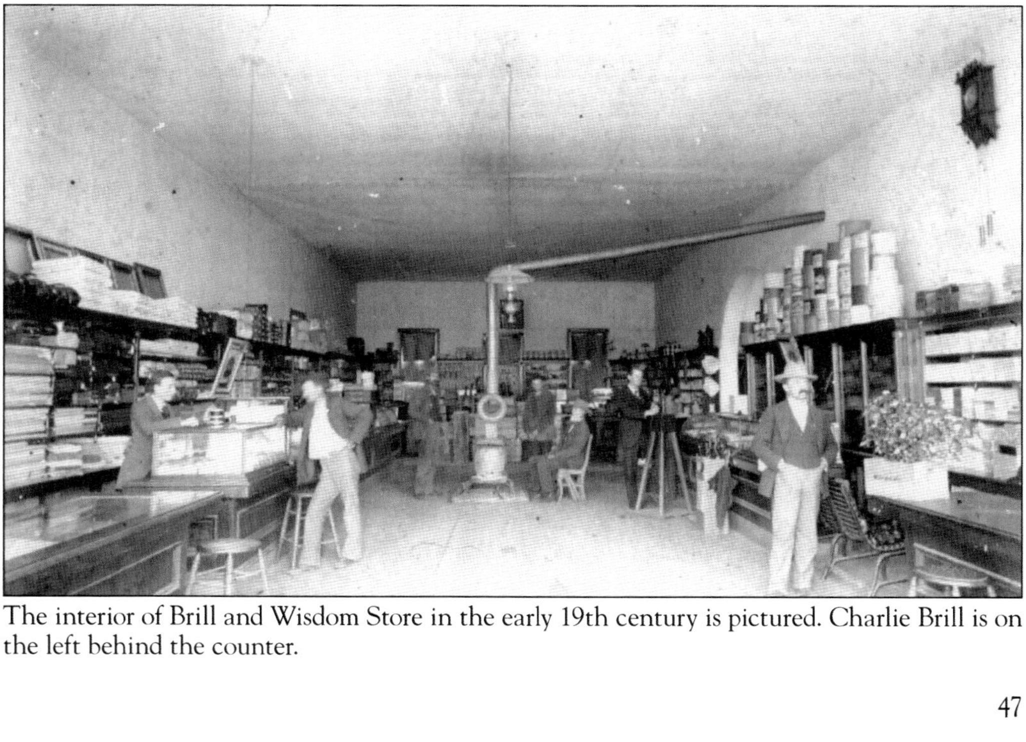

The interior of Brill and Wisdom Store in the early 19th century is pictured. Charlie Brill is on the left behind the counter.

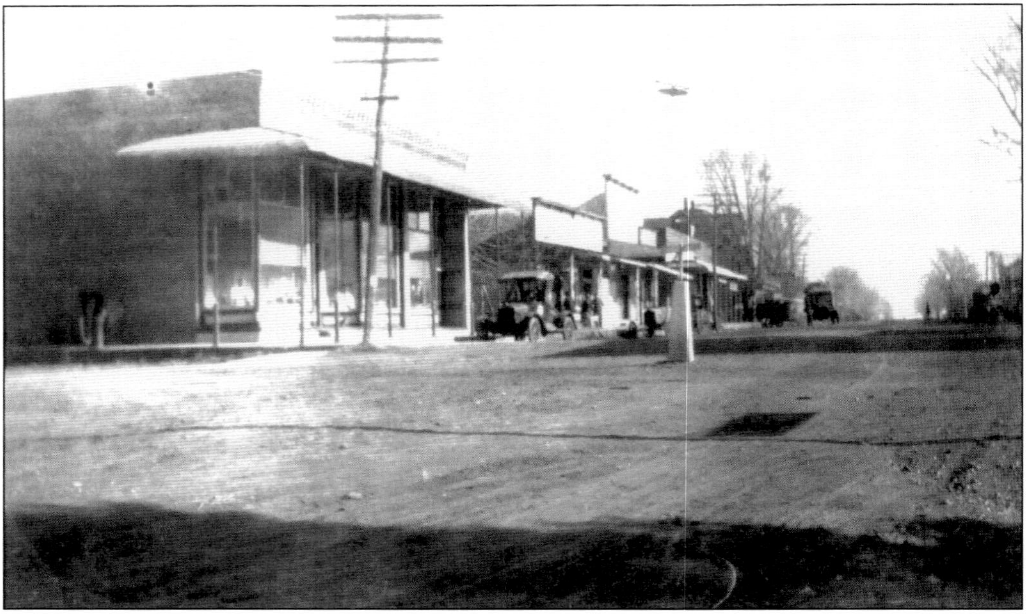

The corner of Main and Market Streets is pictured, looking east. The Brill and Wisdom Store is on the left.

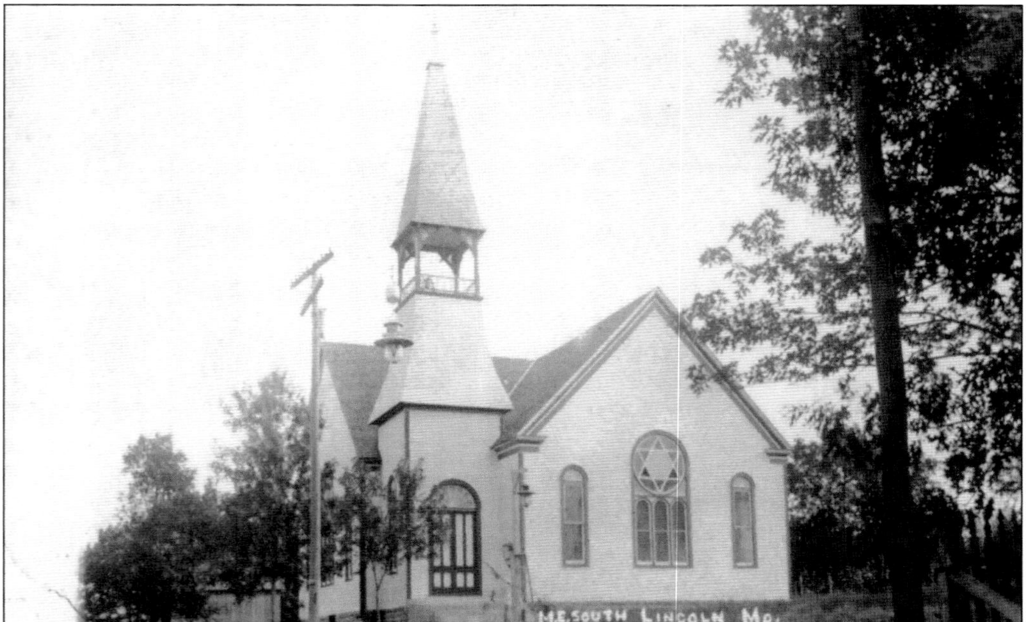

The old United Methodist Church on Main Street was established in 1882. The building is still in use, although it lost its steeple during remodeling some years ago.

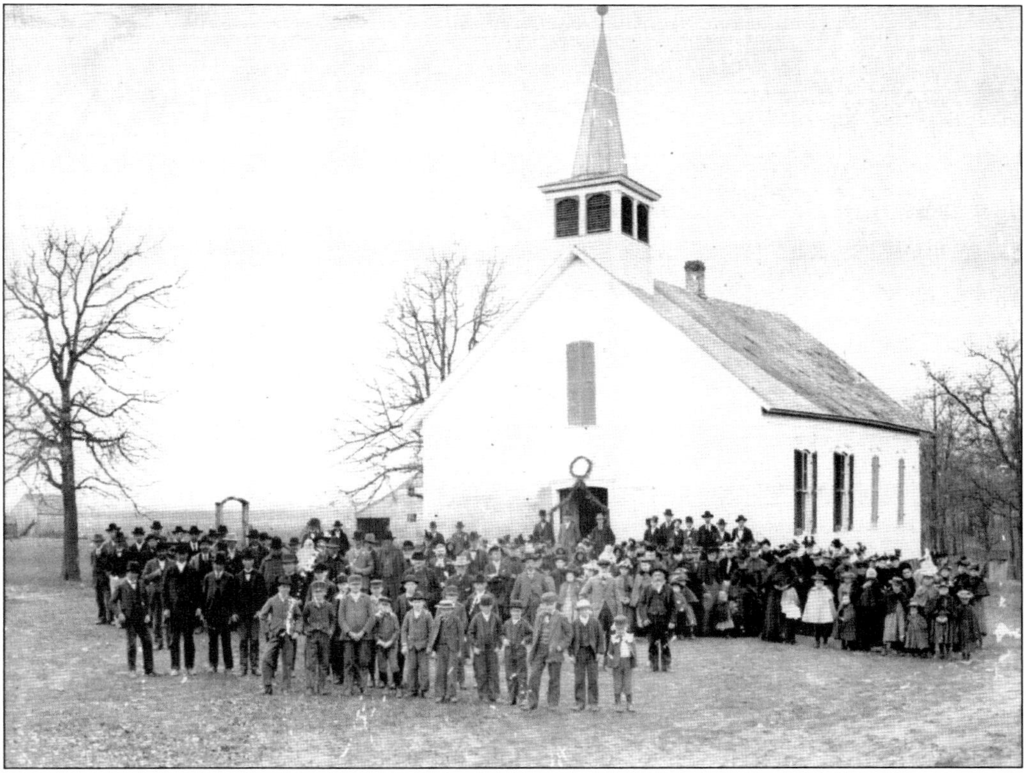

This 1878 view shows Zion Lutheran Church, established in 1859, ten years before Lincoln was incorporated. The second church on this site, it was replaced with a newer church in 1925 (see chapter six).

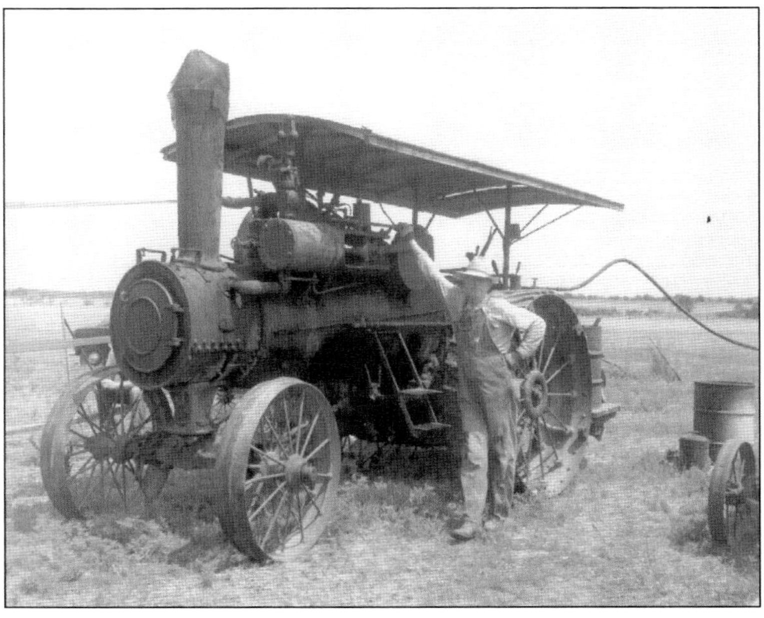

Herman Rotermund (1883–1965) of Lincoln continued to use his steam tractor and horses into the 1950s to work his fields. (Courtesy of Flora Rotermund.)

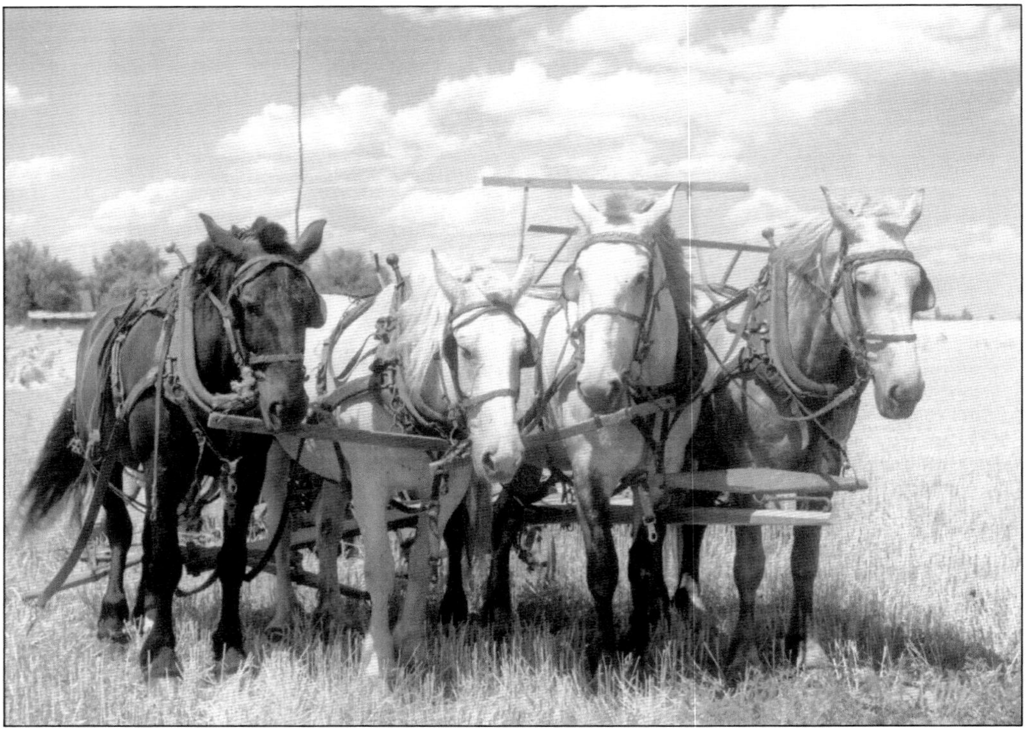

On his farm near Lincoln in 1953, the prized Percheron horses of Herman Rotermund aid in cutting wheat with this late-19th-century mowing machine. (Courtesy of Flora Rotermund.)

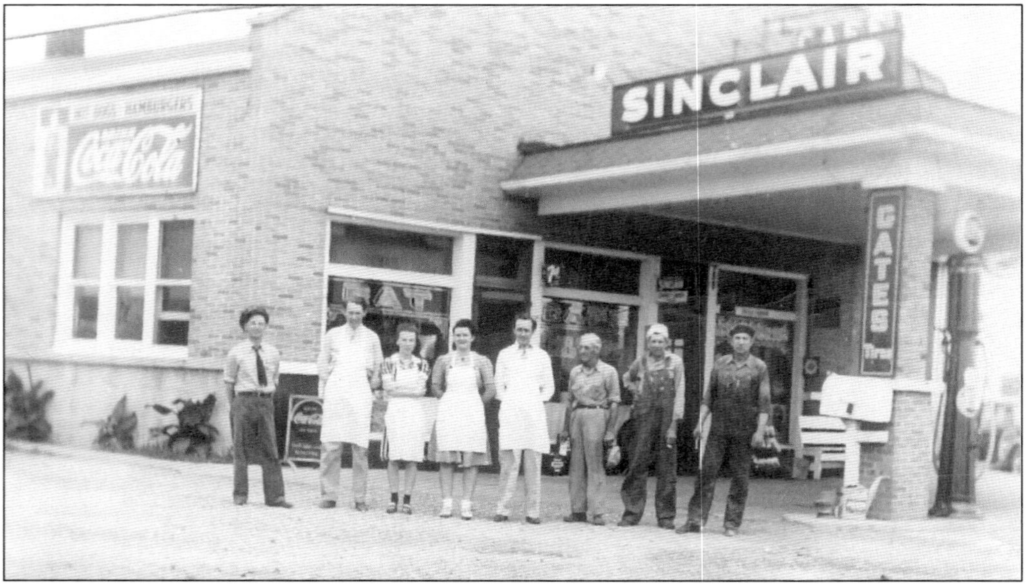

US Highway 65 was completed through Lincoln in 1930, and the Highway Café was a major stop for truckers and motorists in the 1930s. Posing a few months after the opening in 1935 are, from left to right, owner Leo Hare, Amos and Mary Owen, Irene Henry, Hap Yeager, Charles Carpenter, and George and Lester Roark. The building was demolished in the 1970s to make way for a new Farmers Bank building. (Courtesy of Robert Hare.)

Three

City of Ionia

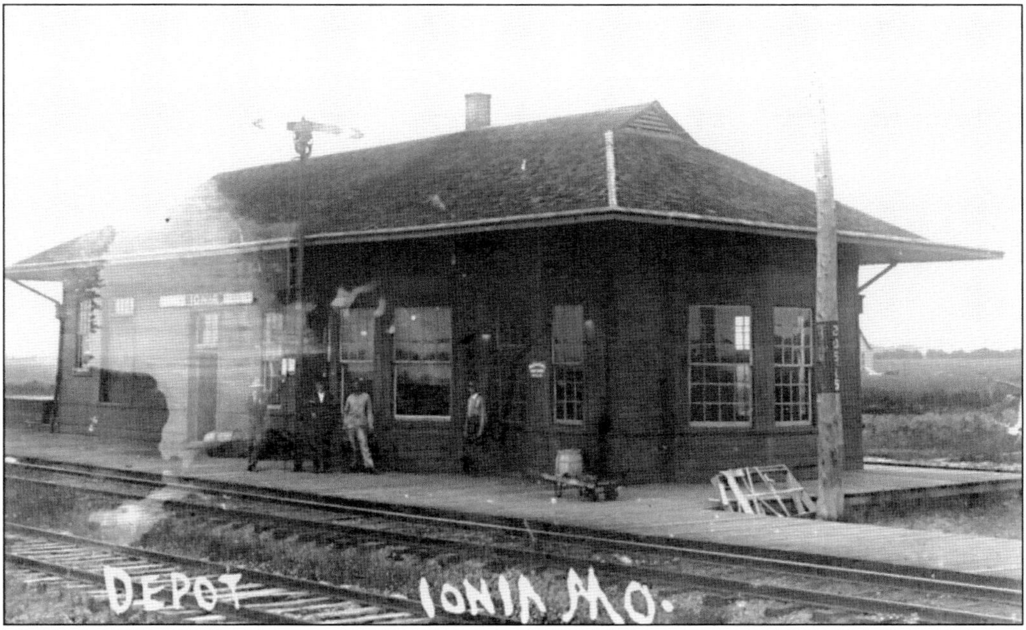

Portions of the city of Ionia are in southern Pettis County and northern Benton County, 12 miles north of Lincoln. While the area was settled earlier, the town was not formally established until January 26, 1904, when the Rock Island Railroad completed its line from St. Louis to Kansas City. The Rock Island Depot is pictured in 1910. The telephone pole on the right indicates that it is 215.15 miles from St. Louis.

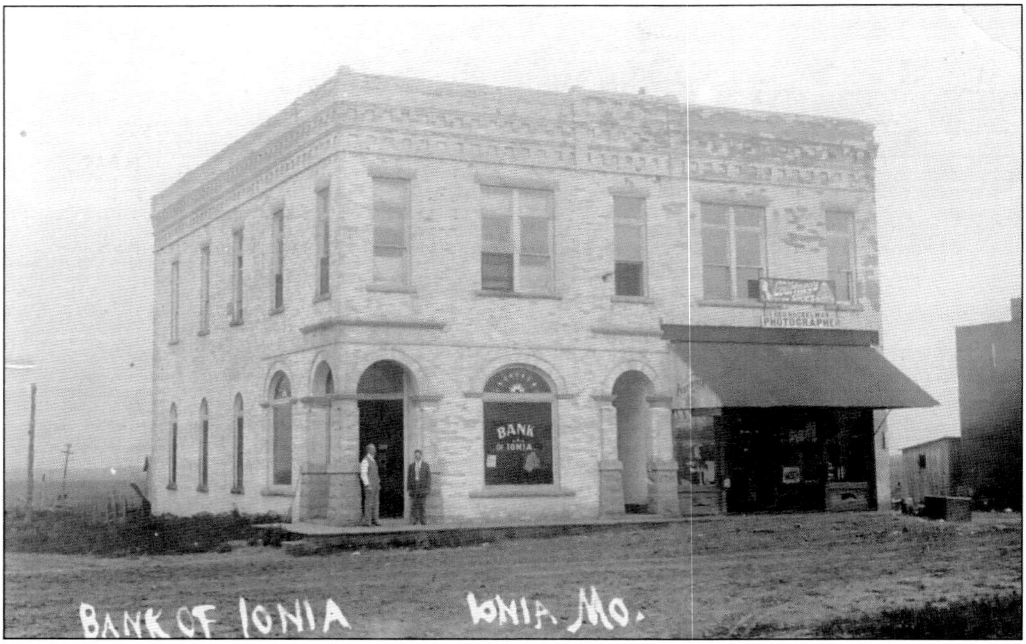

The Bank of Ionia opened in 1905 and served the community for 99 years. (Courtesy of J.D. Williams collection.)

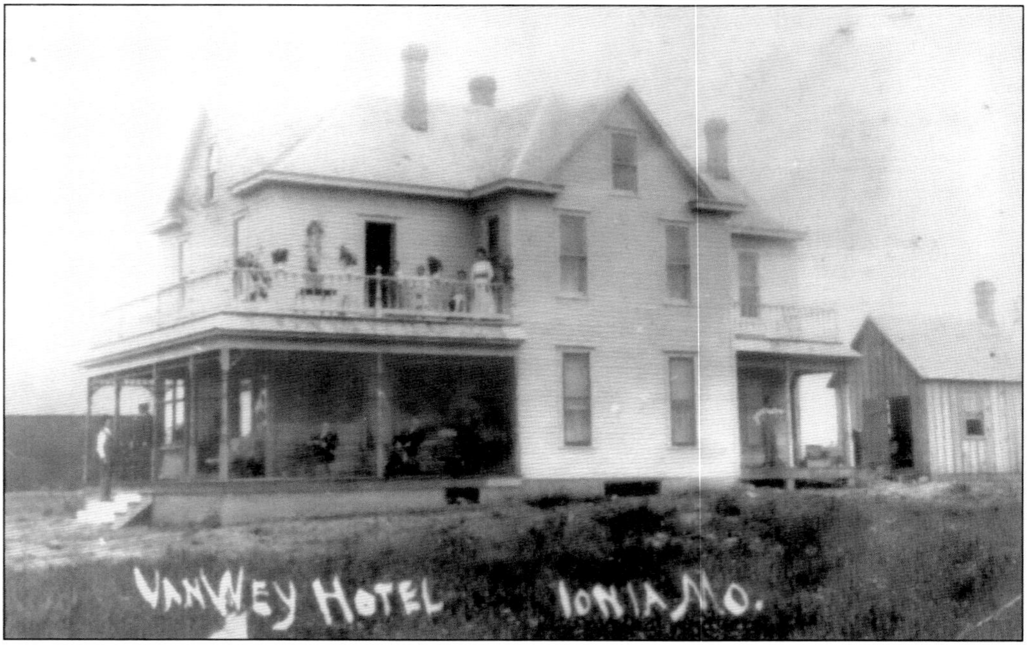

Built by Oliver Van Wey in 1906, this hotel was a stopping place for drummers and visitors who arrived by the Rock Island Railroad. (Courtesy of J.D. Williams collection.)

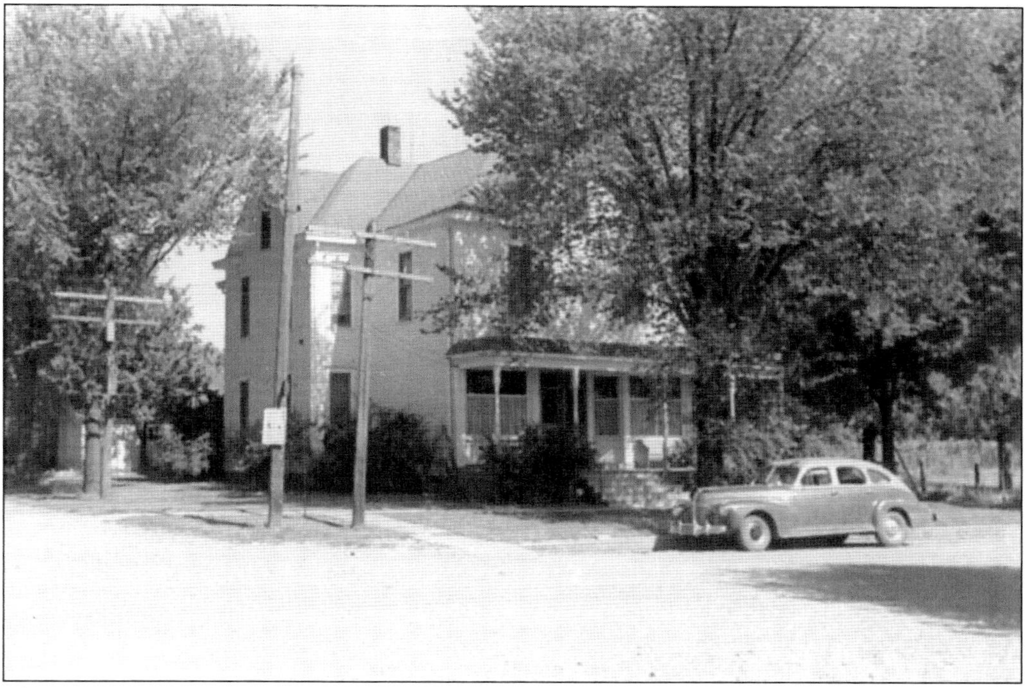

The Van Wey Hotel continued to serve travelers until the 1950s, when it became a residence. It is pictured here in the 1940s. The post office was also located in the building at that time. The structure survived as a residence until it was demolished in 2004. (Courtesy of J.D. Williams collection.)

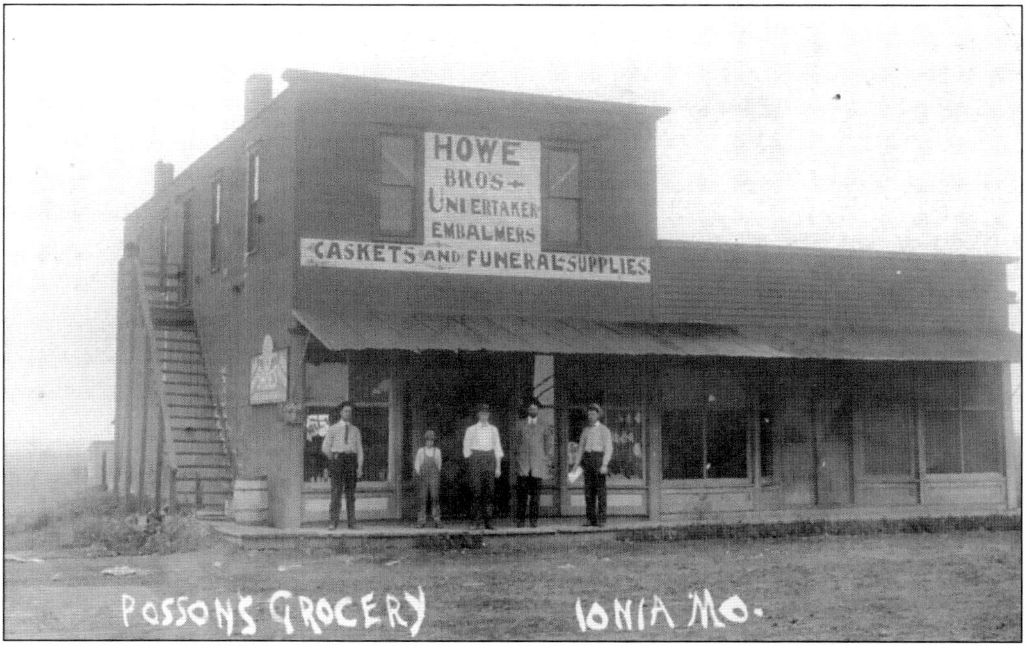

Passon's Grocery shared quarters with Howe's undertaker business on Main Street in Ionia. (Courtesy of J.D. Williams collection.)

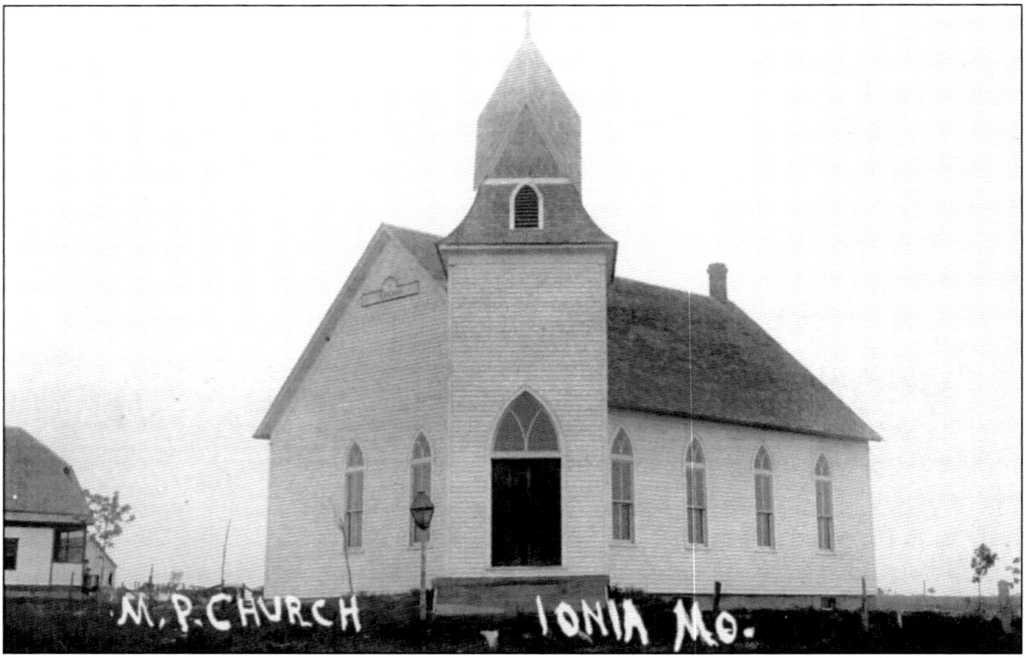

The Methodist Church was established in 1882. It continues to serve the Ionia community in 2010 and features a massive public Harvest Dinner each November. It is so popular that numbered reservations are required to enjoy the feast. (Courtesy of J.D. Williams collection.)

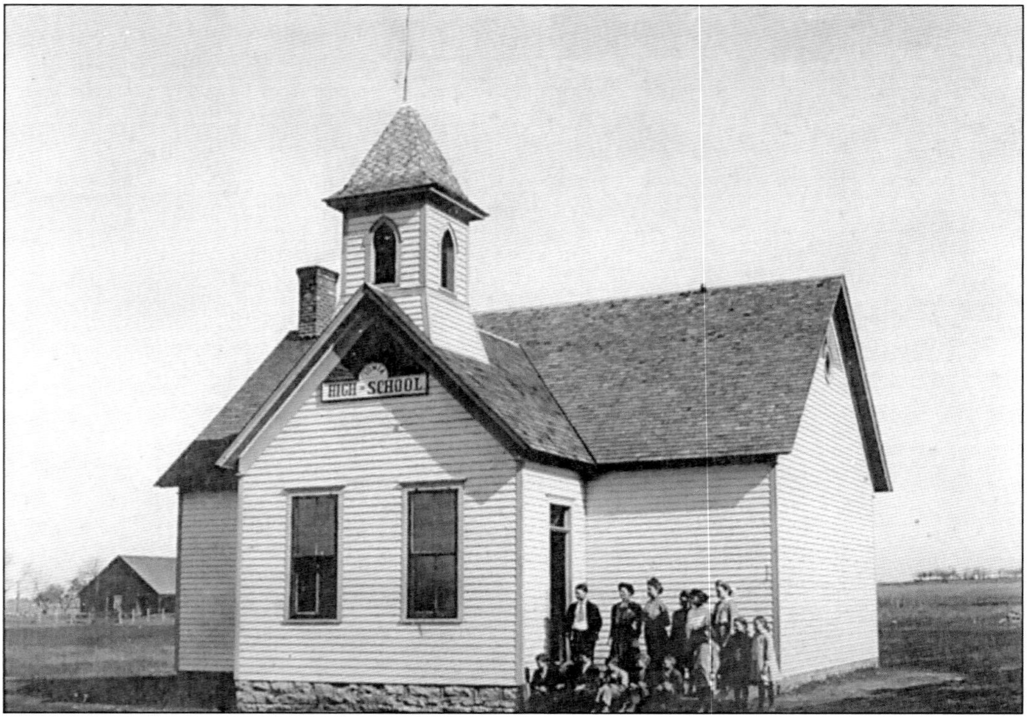

The Ionia High School is pictured in 1917. In later years, the high school became the grade school, and students went to Cole Camp High School. (Courtesy of J.D. Williams collection.)

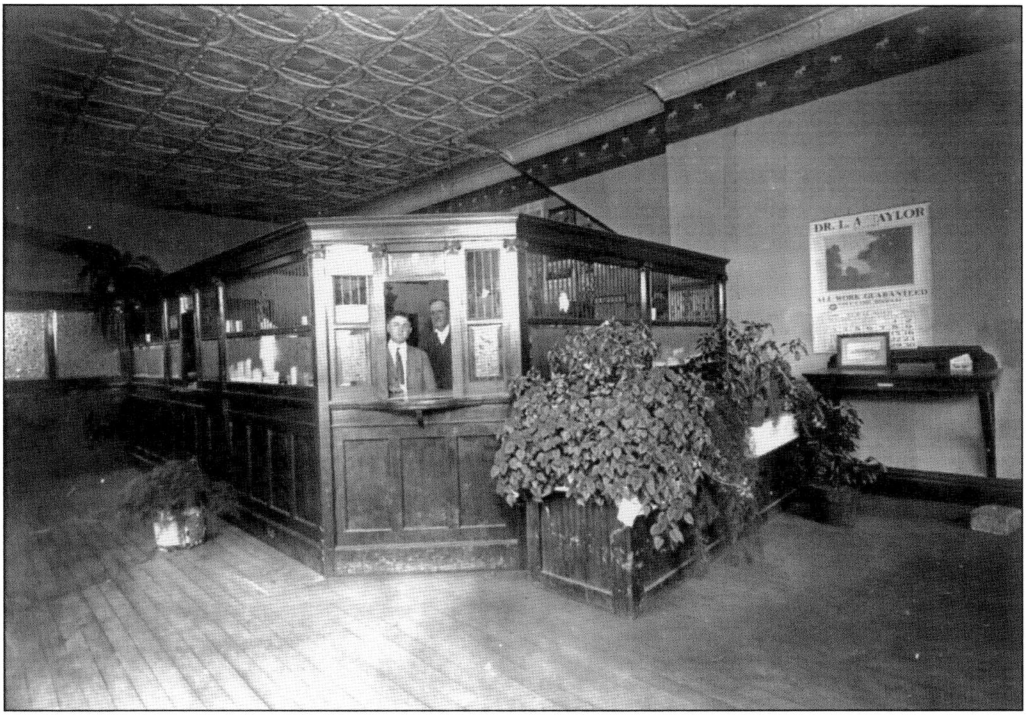

Ionia bank cashier J.F. Howe (left) and Clarence Schnabel peer out the teller window in September 1916.

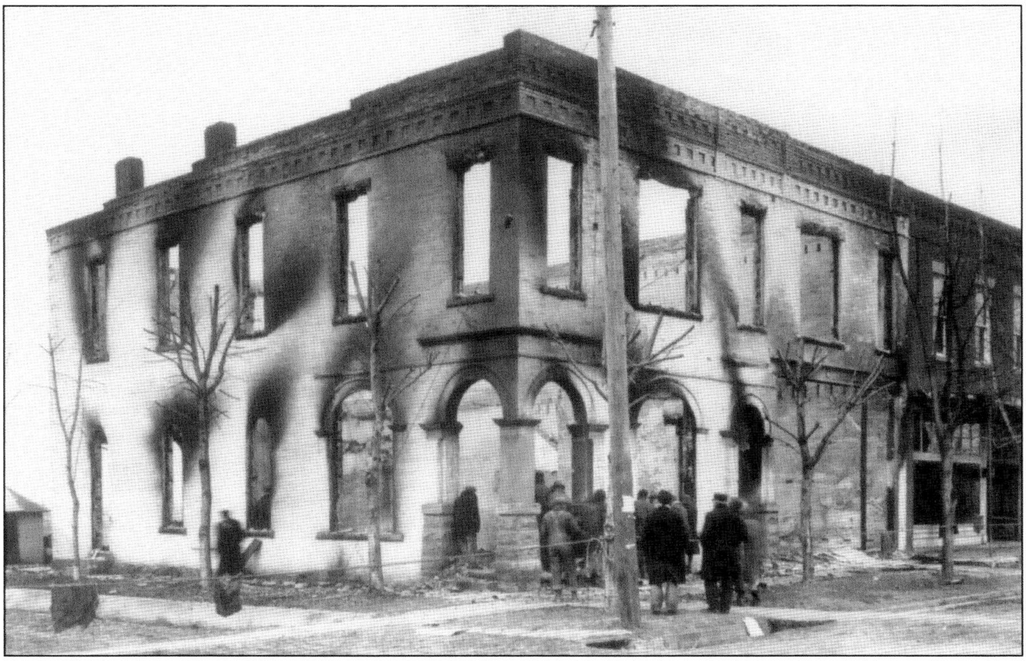

On February 1, 1929, the Ionia Bank suffered a major fire. It was rebuilt and reopened in August of that year. While it changed ownership over the years, the bank served the community until 2004, when it closed. It had the distinction of being held up five times, the first time in 1931 and the last in 1987. (Courtesy of J.D. Williams collection.)

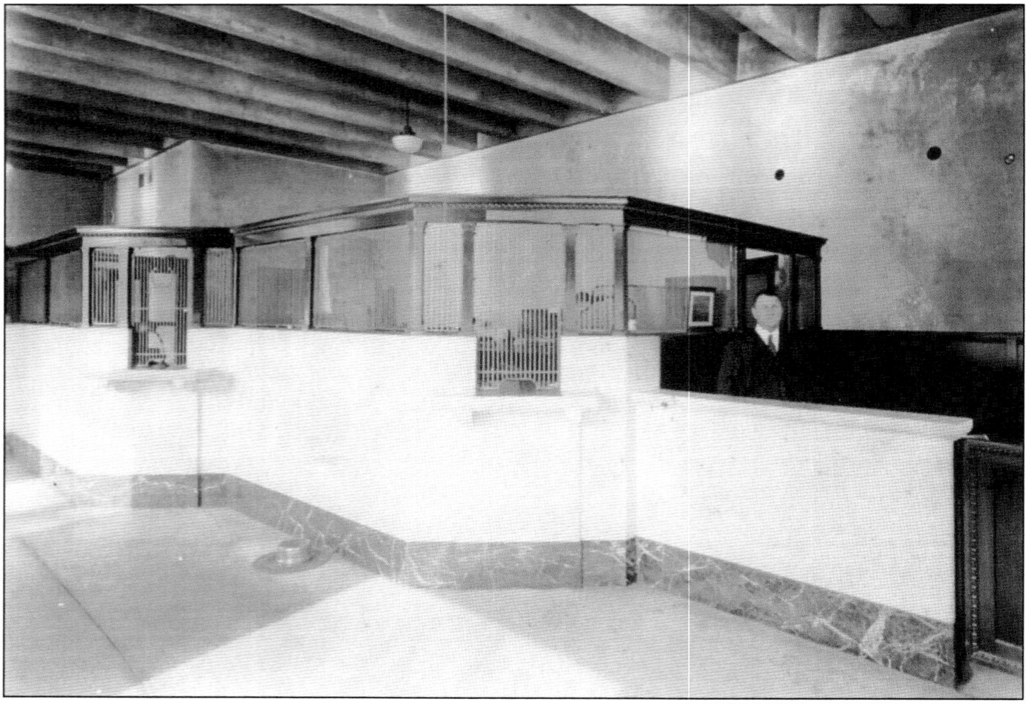

In July of 1929, Clarence Schnabel stands outside the teller windows of the new bank. The walls, ceiling, and floors are yet to be finished for the scheduled August opening. The newer bank was built on the same spot but as a one-story building. Note the fireproof concrete ceiling beams and the new spittoon on the unfinished floor. (Courtesy of J.D. Williams collection.)

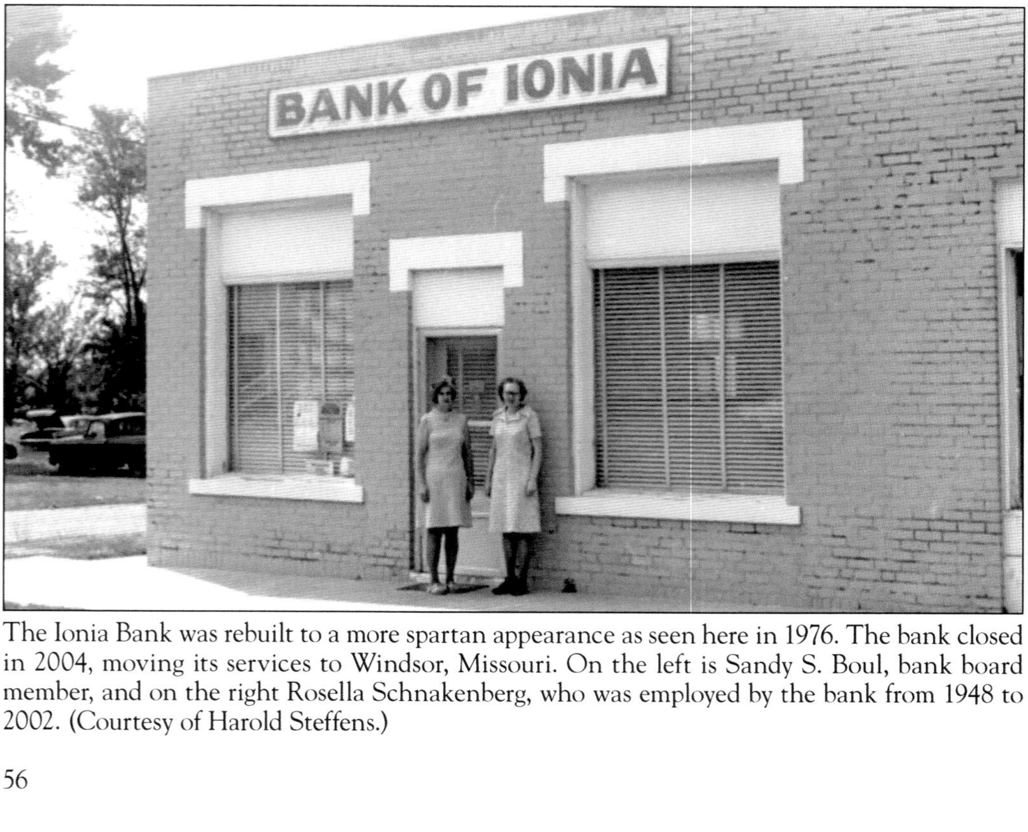

The Ionia Bank was rebuilt to a more spartan appearance as seen here in 1976. The bank closed in 2004, moving its services to Windsor, Missouri. On the left is Sandy S. Boul, bank board member, and on the right Rosella Schnakenberg, who was employed by the bank from 1948 to 2002. (Courtesy of Harold Steffens.)

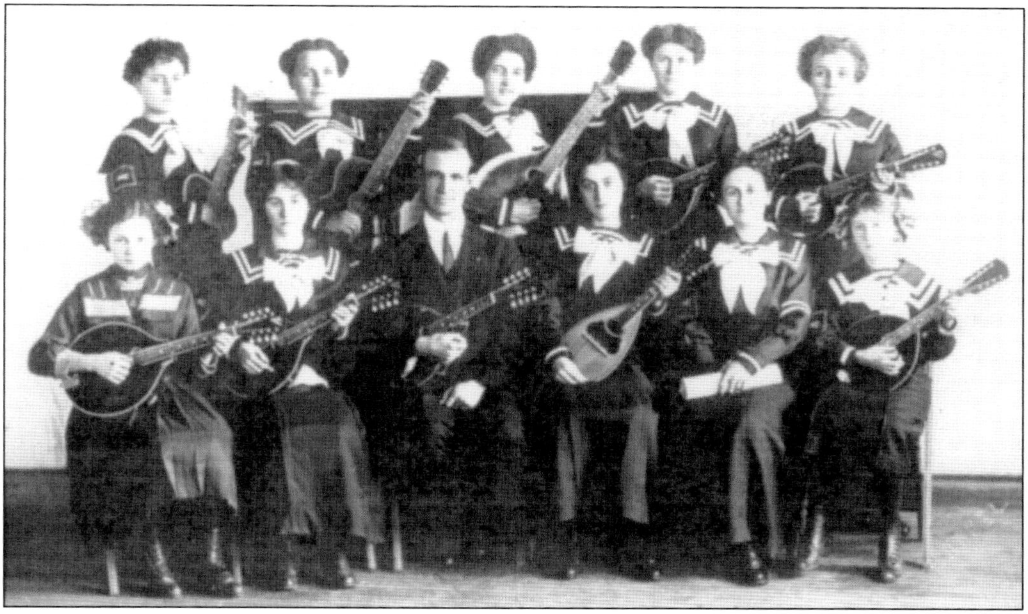

The musical culture of Ionia was enhanced by the Ionia Mandolin Girls Club. The band toured frequently, giving concerts to all the area towns. Pictured from left to right are (front row) Mildred Van Wey Wisdom, Irma Van Wey Schnabel, director Dean Sands, Blanch Windle, Marie Robinson Nicholson, and unknown; (back row) Mary Schnabel Marsh, Netty Tucker Howe, Ina Van Wey Passon, Mrs. Betty Fear, and Margaret Berry McConnell.

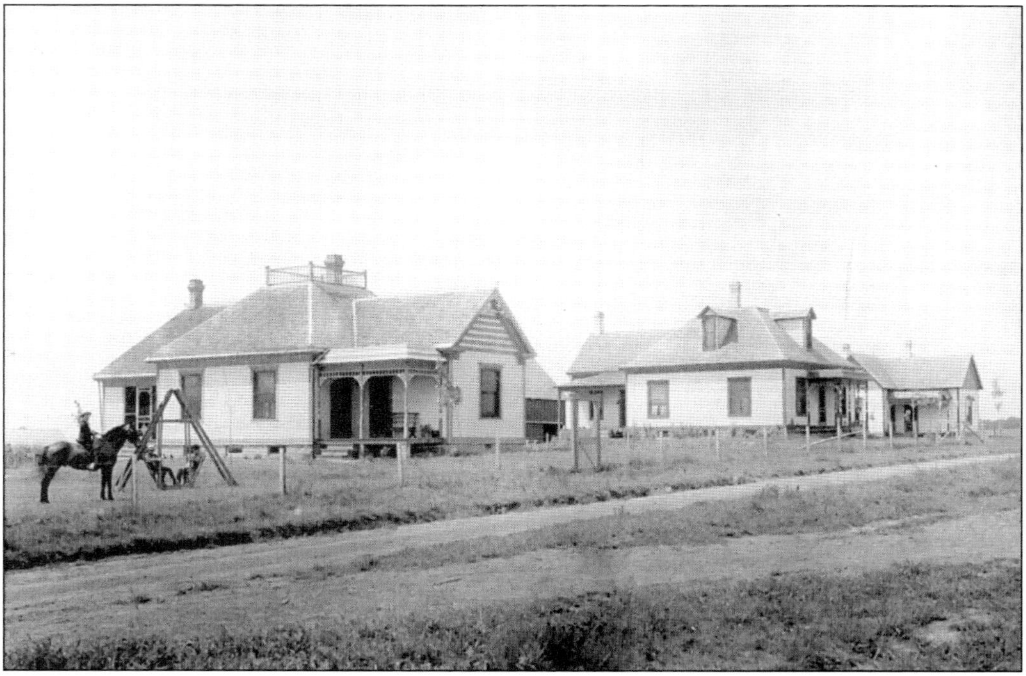

This home on North Main Street, built in the 1880s and still standing in 2010, has been owned for 51 years by Harold and Mary Ann Steffens. (Courtesy of Harold Steffens.)

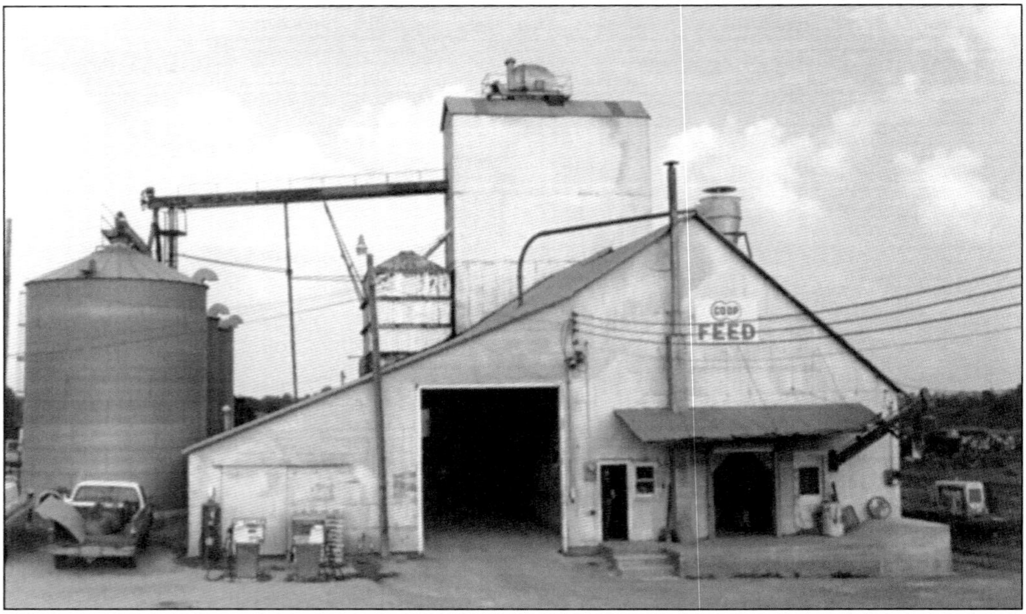

Since the 1920s, Producer Exchange Elevator has been the major industry in Ionia. Still in operation, the facility stores and ships million of bushels of grain to a worldwide market each year. This 1969 view show the original building, still served by the Rock Island Railroad. (Courtesy of Harold Steffens.)

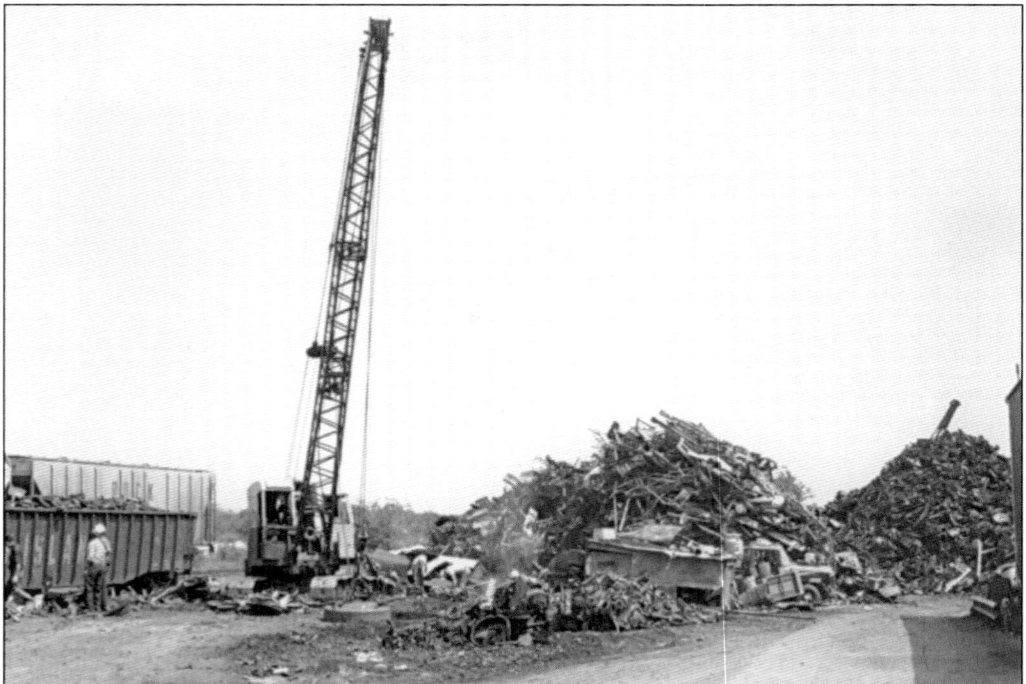

Ionia's other main industry was Fridley's Scrap Yard. It shipped out two to three carloads of metal scrap weekly via the railroad. When the Rock Island shut down in 1980, the yard was sold to another firm and then closed and moved to Sedalia, Missouri. (Courtesy of Harold Steffens.)

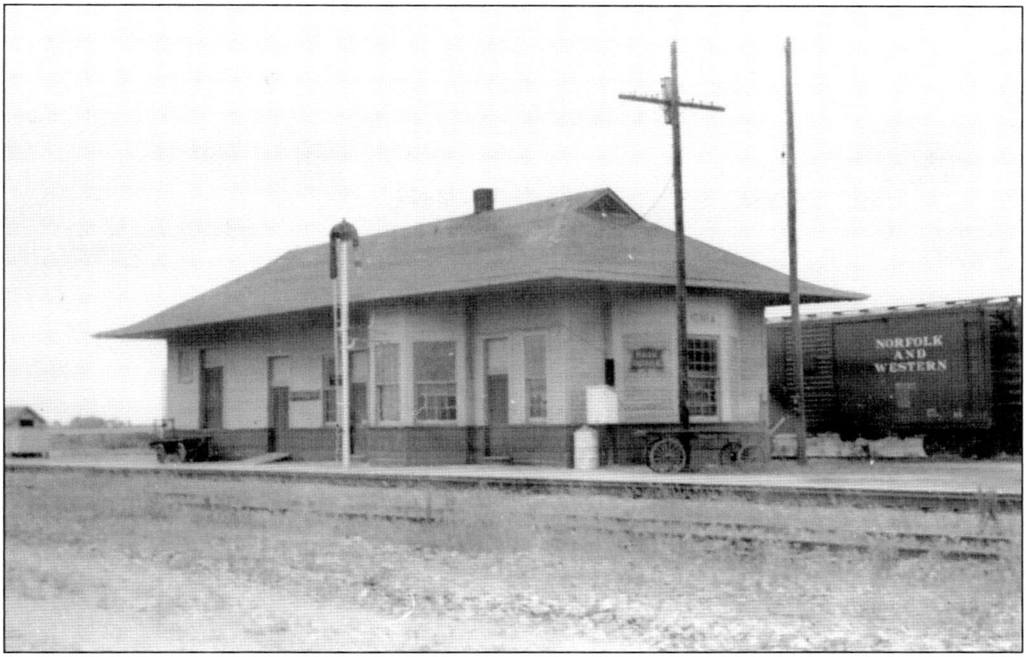

The Rock Island Depot at Ionia is pictured in 1957. The line was built in 1904, making the town a major shipping point for grain and livestock. (Courtesy of Howard Killam.)

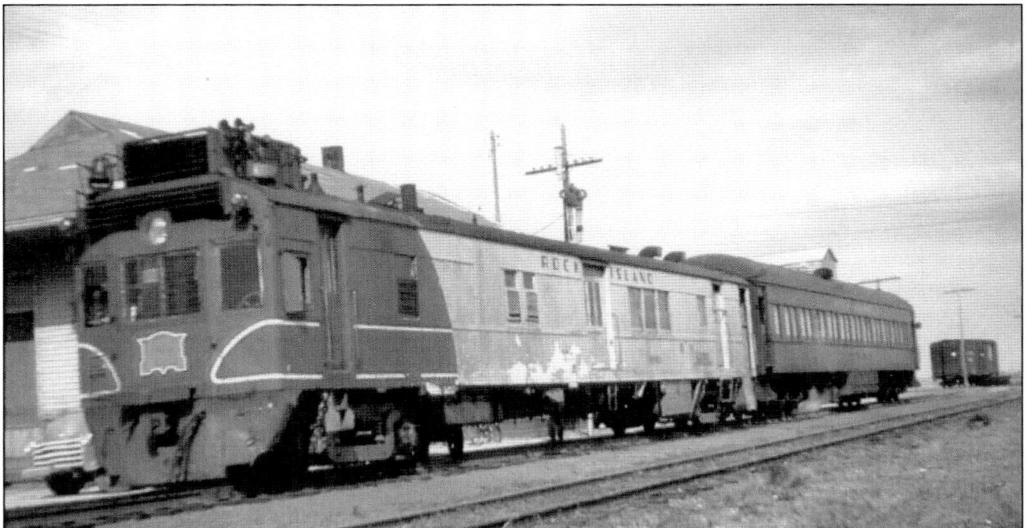

The Rock Island motor coach for Kansas City calls at Ionia in 1957. Passenger train service ended in 1959, and freight service ended with the shutdown of the railroad in 1980. (Courtesy of K.L. Bird collection.)

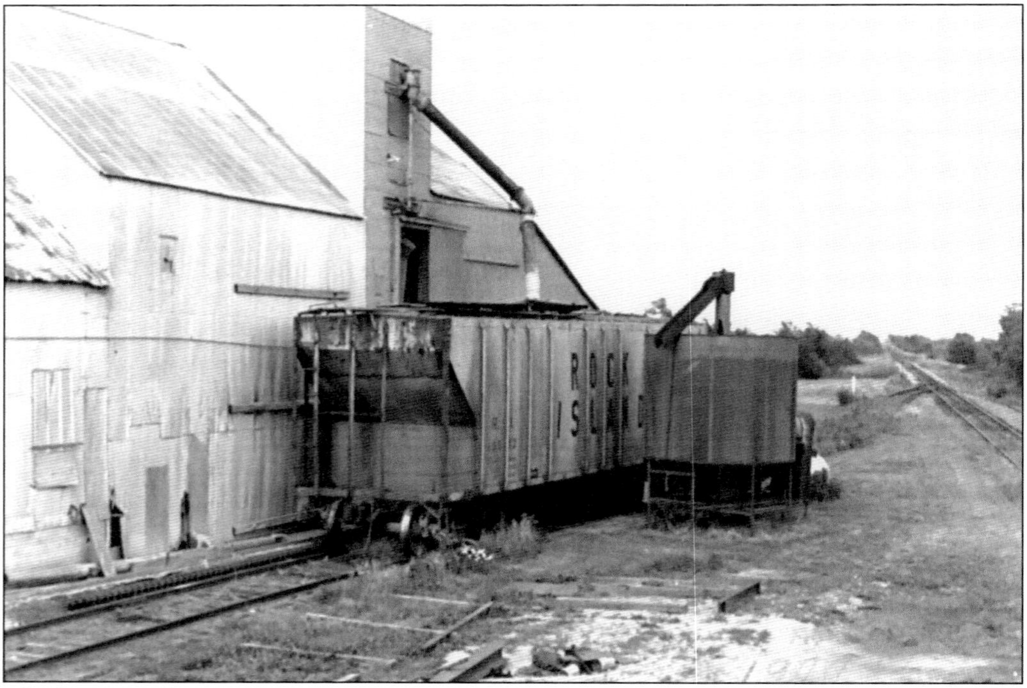

The last car of grain shipped out on the Rock Island line is seen here being loaded at the Producer Exchange Elevator in the fall of 1979. The railroad line shut down in 1980. (Courtesy of Harold Steffens.)

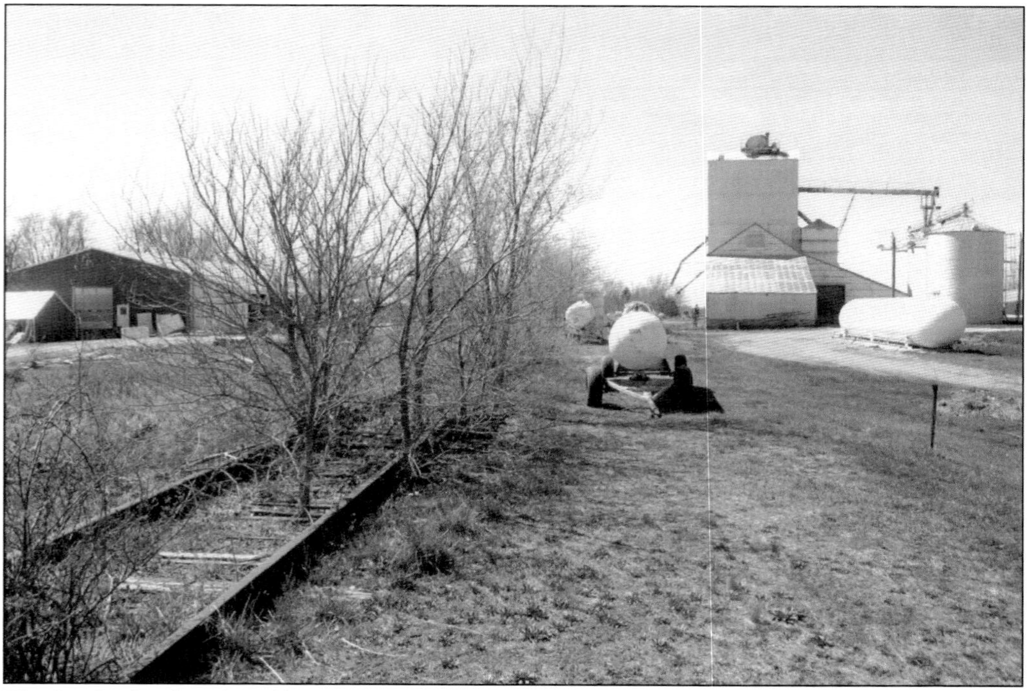

The Rock Island Railroad line is intact at Ionia, but it has not seen a train since 1980. Owned by a utility company, the 298-mile line is being saved as a potential transportation corridor of the future. Trains may once again ply the restored railroad through Ionia. (Courtesy of Ken Bird.)

Four

VILLAGE OF MORA

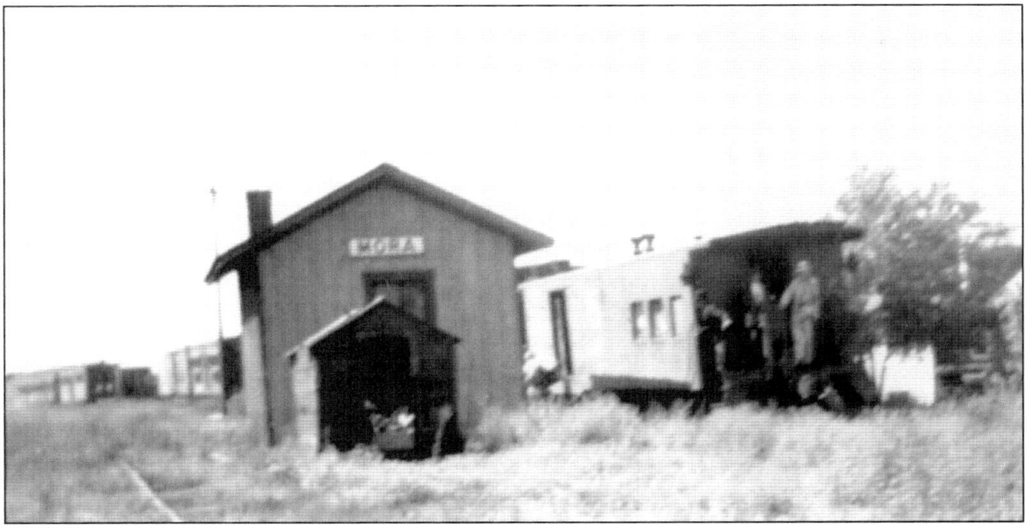

Mora is located five miles north of Cole Camp and was founded by the Sedalia, Warsaw and Southern Railroad in 1880. It once had a station, water tank, post office, stock pens, and a sawmill. Today, Mora has a post office and a busy lumberyard, but the railroad was abandoned in 1946. The southbound Missouri Pacific train is seen passing through Mora in the summer of 1944. It ran six days a week (not on Sundays). (Courtesy of Ilene Brandes collection.)

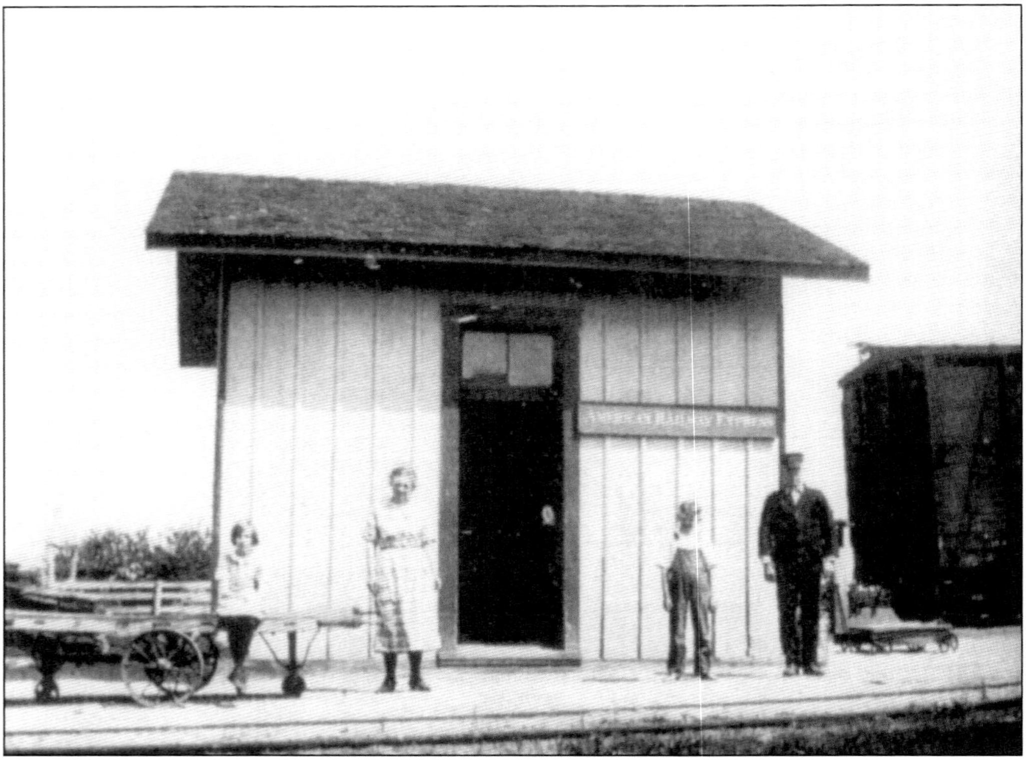

John Moss, his wife Emma, and their daughter Inez and their son Guido are pictured at the depot in Mora in 1918.

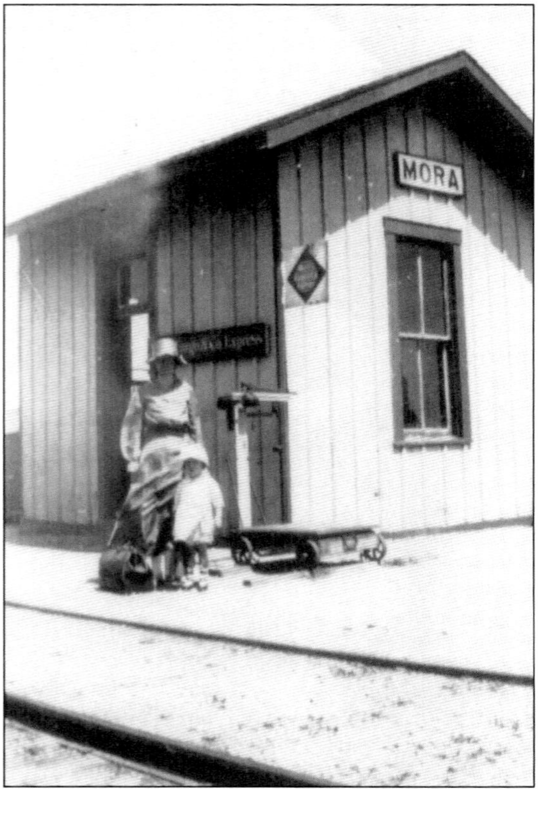

Mother and child wait for the northbound Sedalia train in this 1905 photograph.

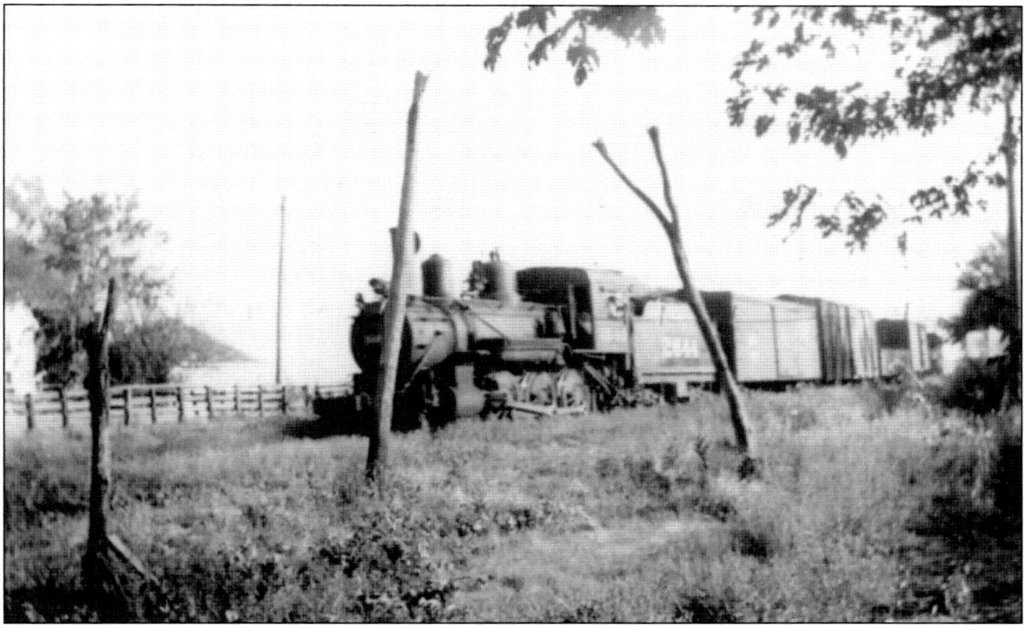

The northbound Missouri Pacific train passes through Mora in June 1944. Mora was the first station in Benton County on the 42-mile Sedalia to Warsaw branch line. (Courtesy of Eileen Brandes collection.)

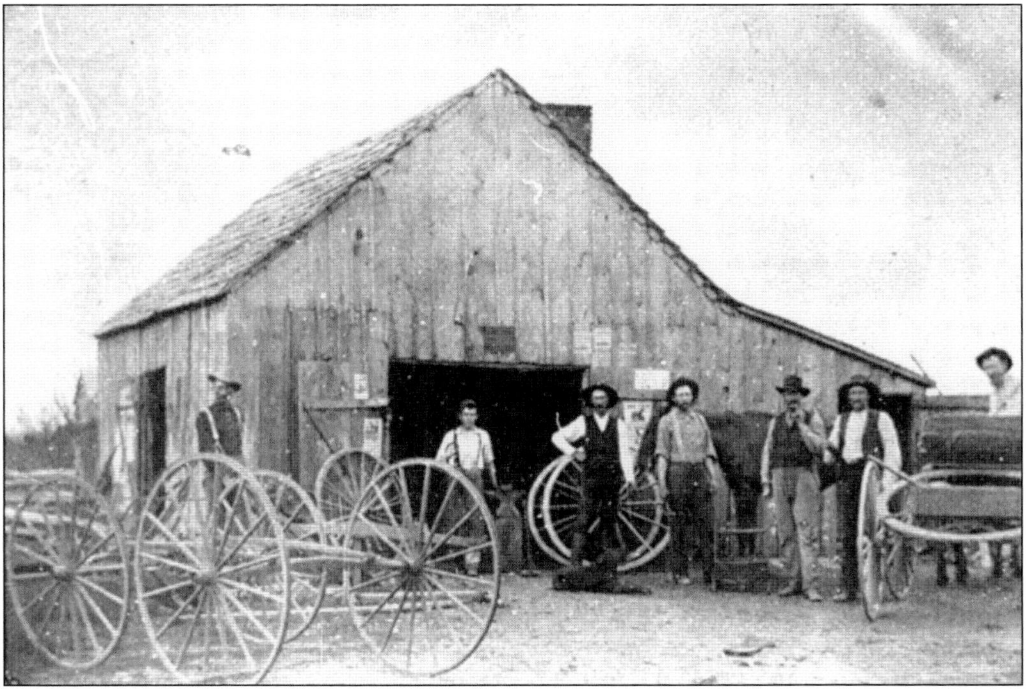

The blacksmith shop of Dietrick Kueck (fourth from the left) was established in 1886. He operated the business until his death in 1894 of typhoid fever.

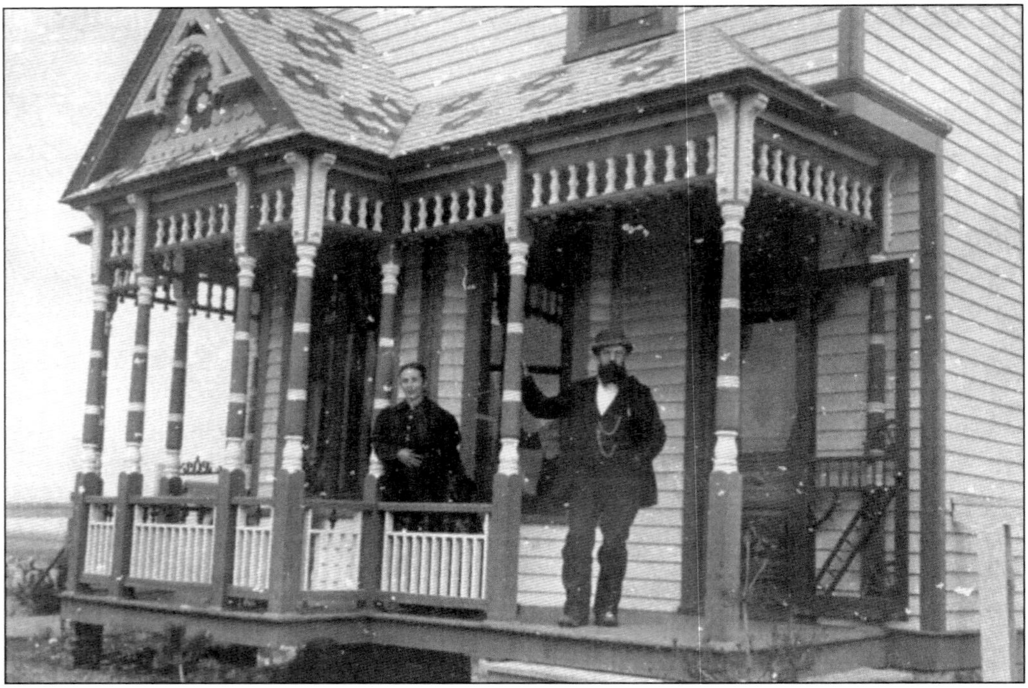

Dr. Guido Schaff and his wife stand on the porch of their home in Mora. Schaff started his Mora practice in 1897 and opened the town's first drugstore.

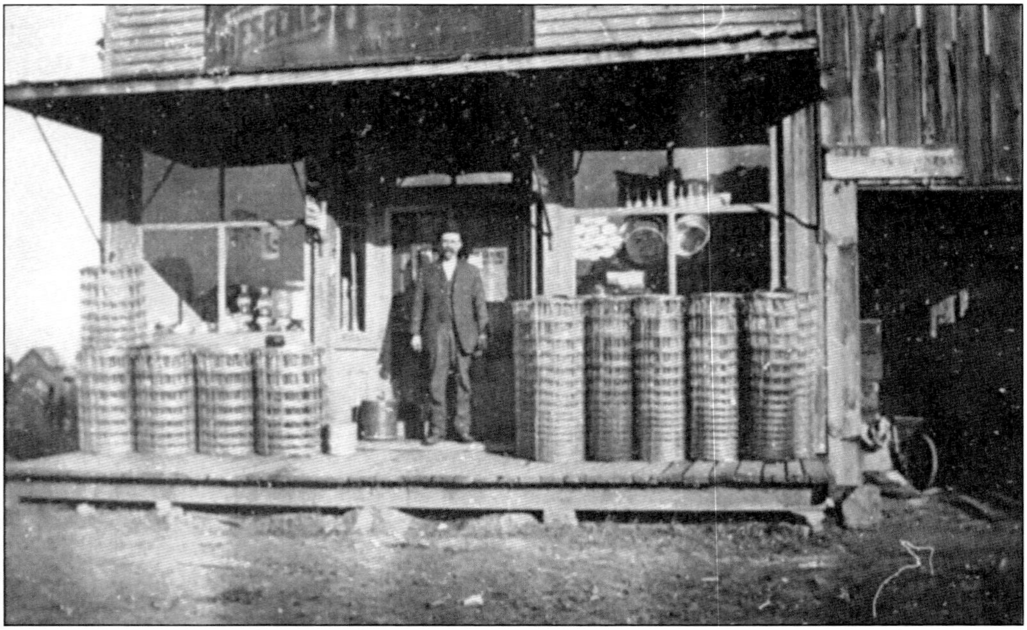

John Bluhm operated the general store in Mora and served from 1902 to 1920 as the Missouri Pacific station agent.

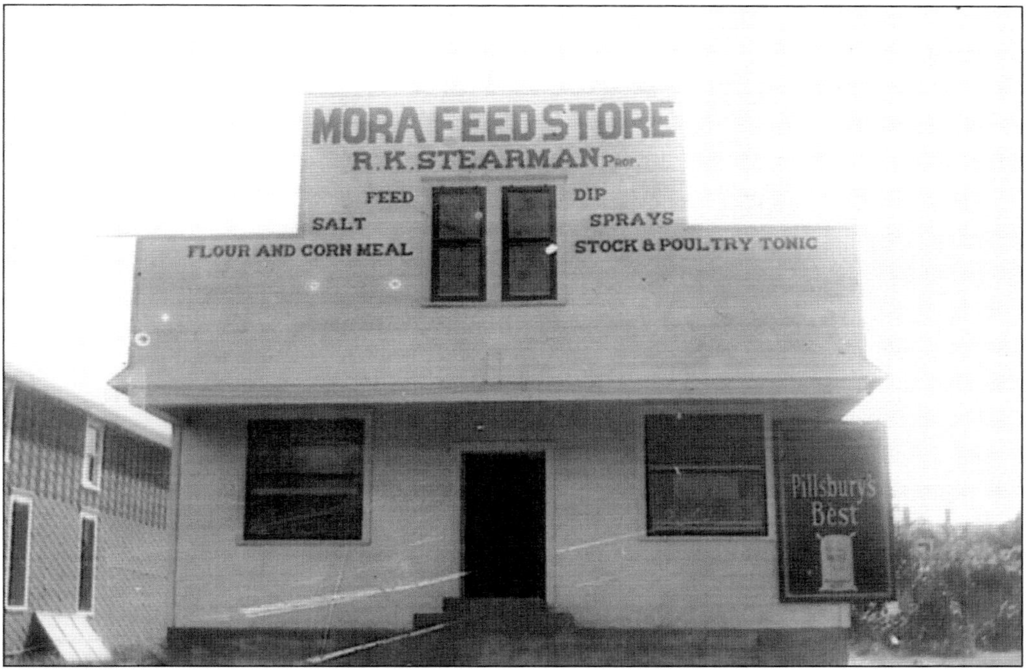

This feed store in Mora was operated by R.K. Stearman in the 1920s.

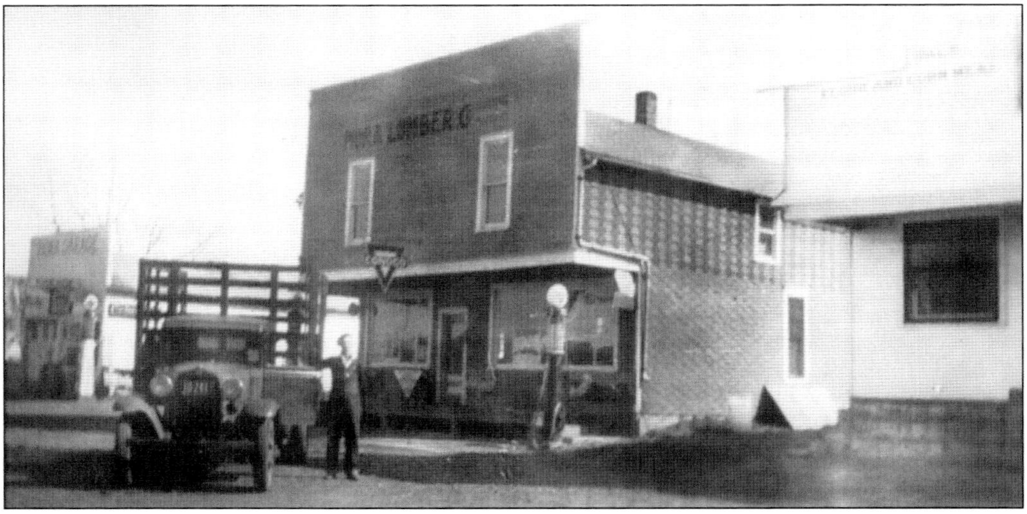

The Mora Lumber Company offered also offered gasoline, as can be seen in this c. 1917 photograph. Stationmaster John Moss also owned the lumber company at this time.

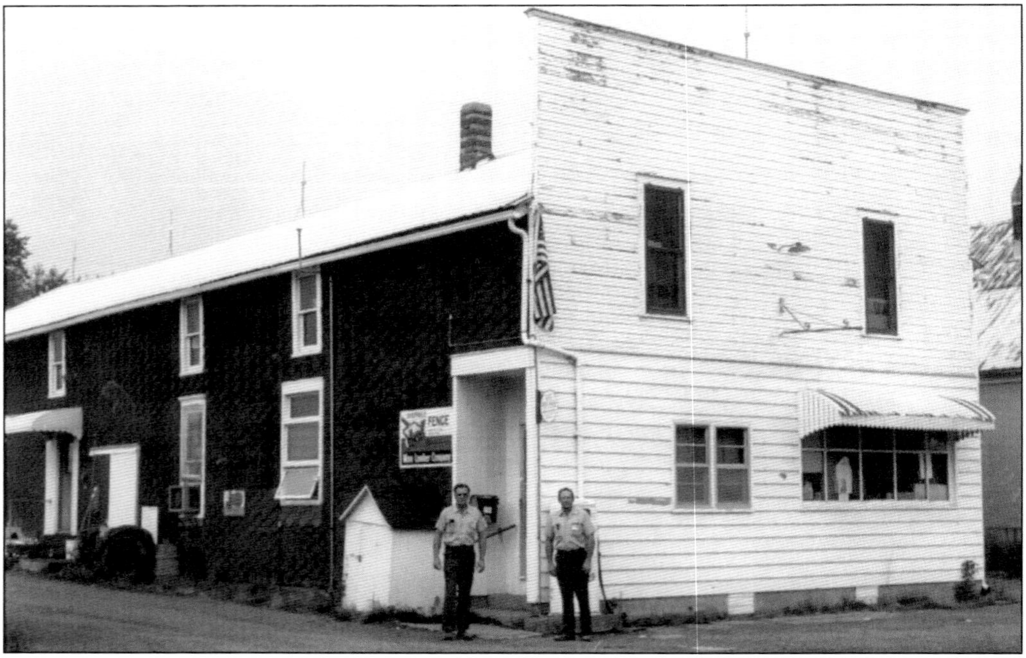

The Mora Lumber Company is pictured in 1976. The business continues to operate, offering specialty lumber to contractors and craftsmen.

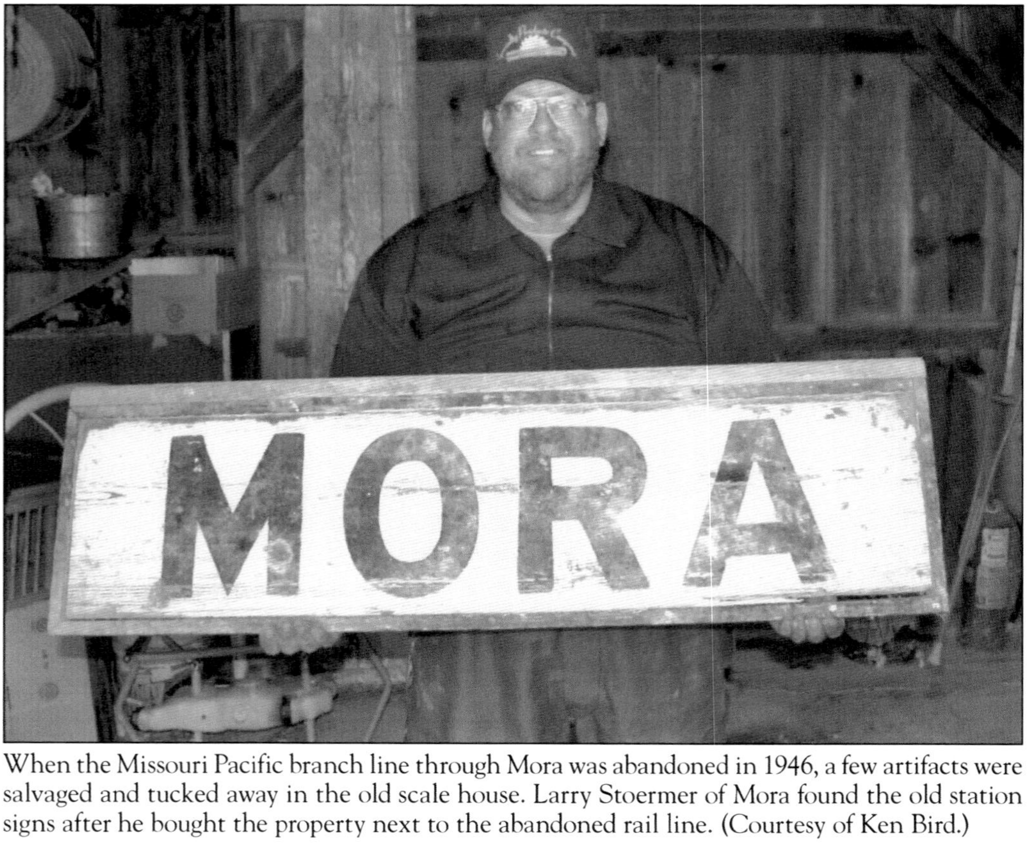

When the Missouri Pacific branch line through Mora was abandoned in 1946, a few artifacts were salvaged and tucked away in the old scale house. Larry Stoermer of Mora found the old station signs after he bought the property next to the abandoned rail line. (Courtesy of Ken Bird.)

Five

Transportation and Industry

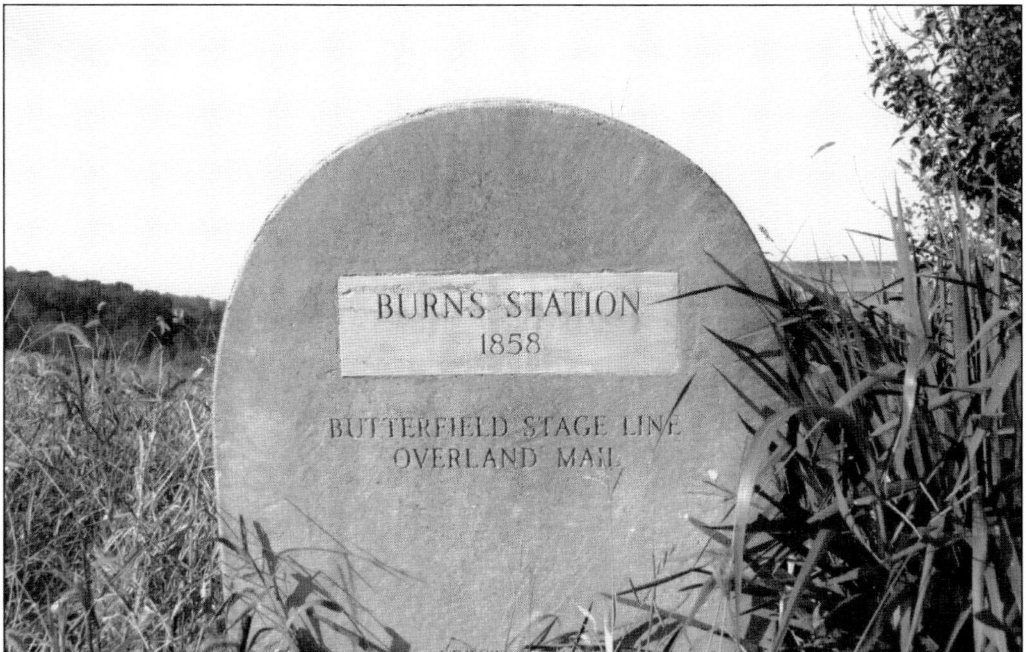

This marker for the Butterfield stage stop at Burns Station is located four miles south of Cole Camp on the Butterfield Trail route. The coach horses were exchanged at Burns Station after the journey from Tipton, Missouri.

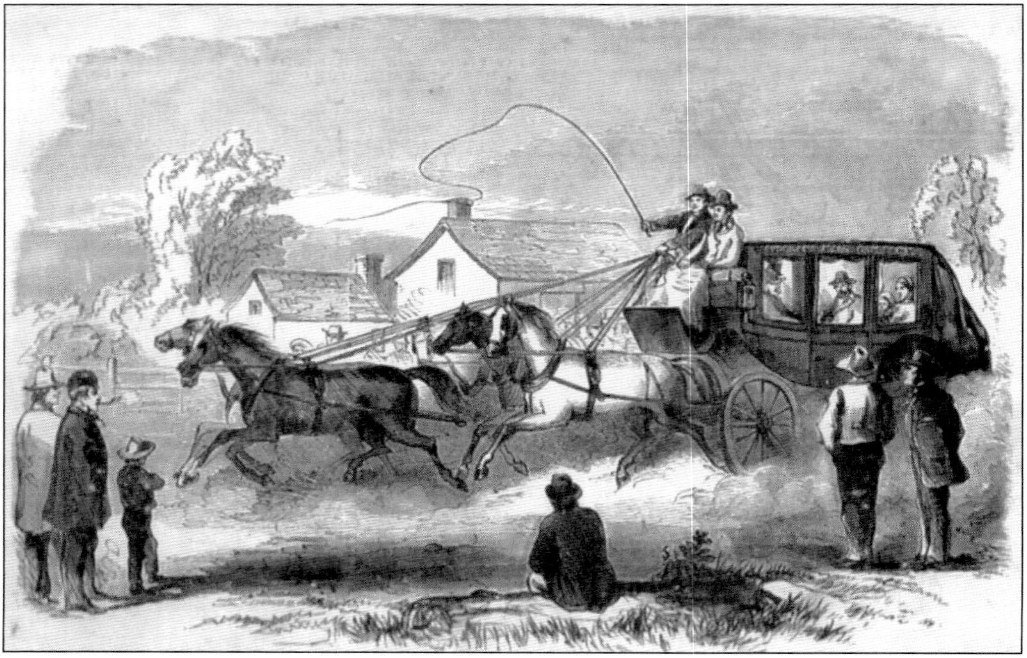

The Cole Camp area was bisected by both the old north/south Military Road between Booneville and Springfield, Missouri, and an eastward road from the capital at Jefferson City, Missouri. In 1858, John Butterfield started his stage line between the Pacific railhead at Tipton and points in California. The Military Road was then called the Butterfield Trail, even after the demise of the stage line in the war-plagued year of 1861. This drawing from Frank Leslie's illustrated newspaper shows the Butterfield Stage leaving Tipton in 1858. (Courtesy of Missouri Historical Society Collection.)

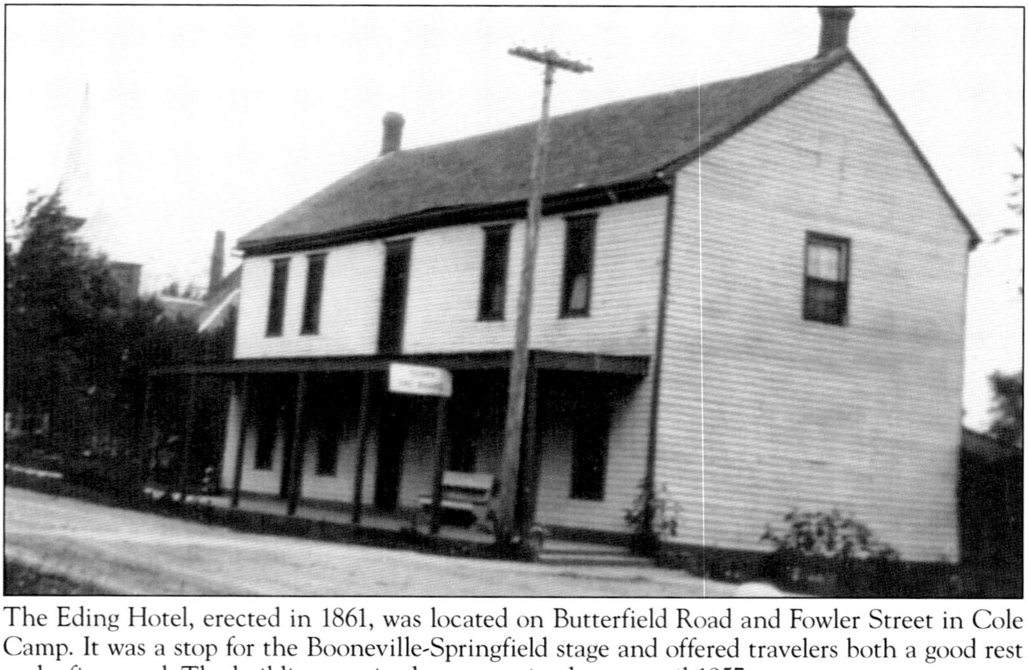

The Eding Hotel, erected in 1861, was located on Butterfield Road and Fowler Street in Cole Camp. It was a stop for the Booneville-Springfield stage and offered travelers both a good rest and a fine meal. The building survived as a rooming house until 1957.

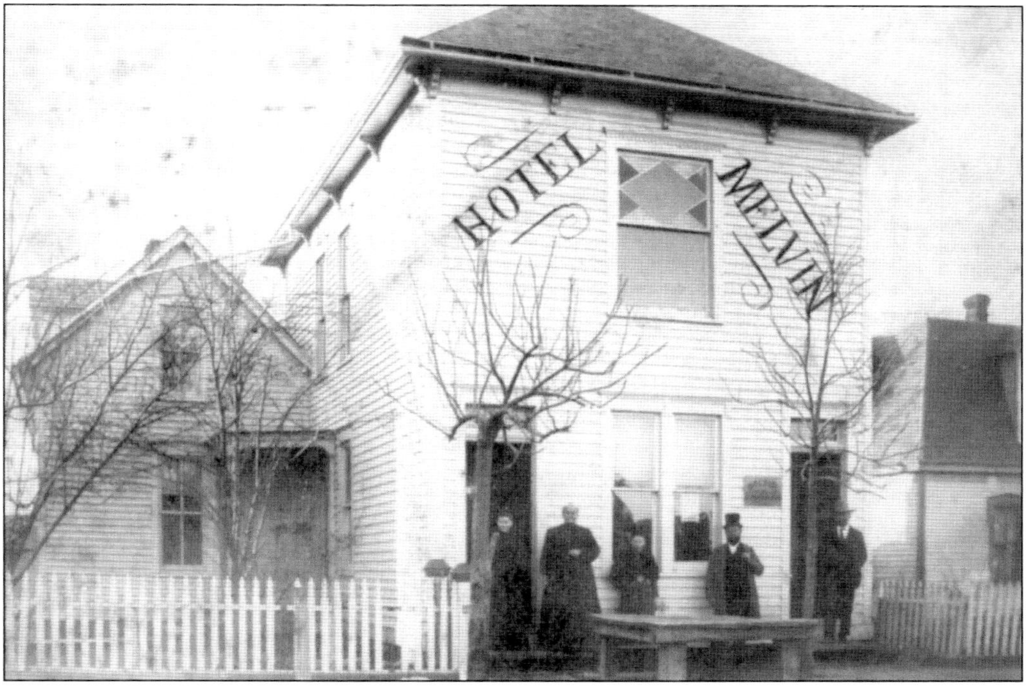

The 1880s Melvin Hotel was expanded in the early 1900s. It ceased operation as a hotel in the 1940s and is in use as a shop in the Cole Camp historic district.

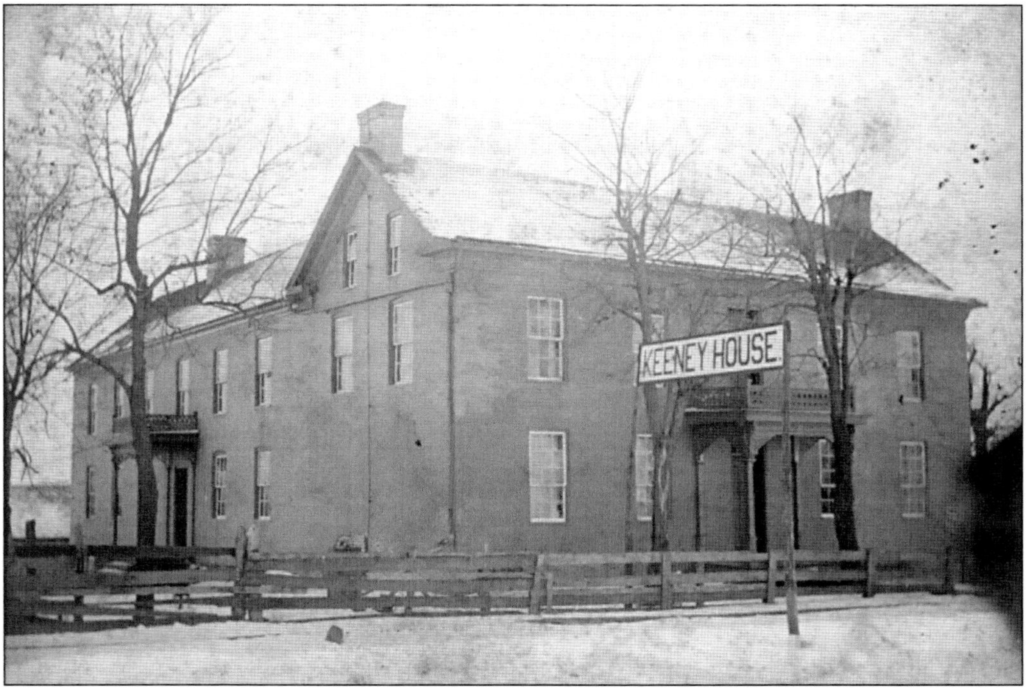

The Keeney House Hotel on south Butterfield Road was built in the 1850s and was the largest hotel in Cole Camp. It was destroyed by fire in 1901, and the bricks were used to build a home that still stands on the old hotel site.

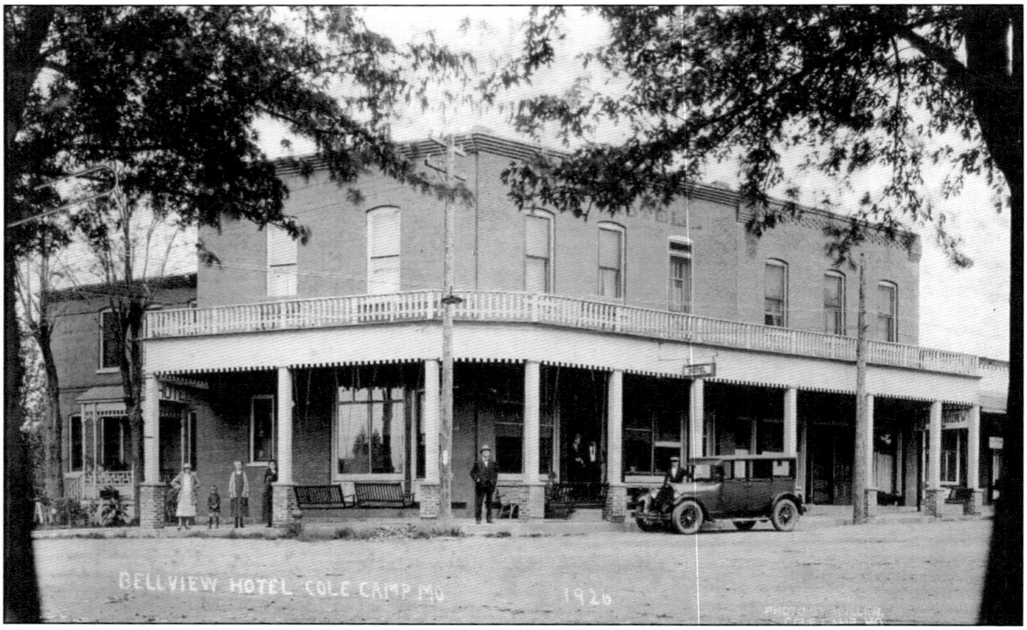

The Belleview Hotel was established by P.M. Bell in 1890 and found favor with the drummers and others who arrived by train. Later years saw the hotel benefit from the proliferation of the automobile and subsequent tourism. This image is from 1926.

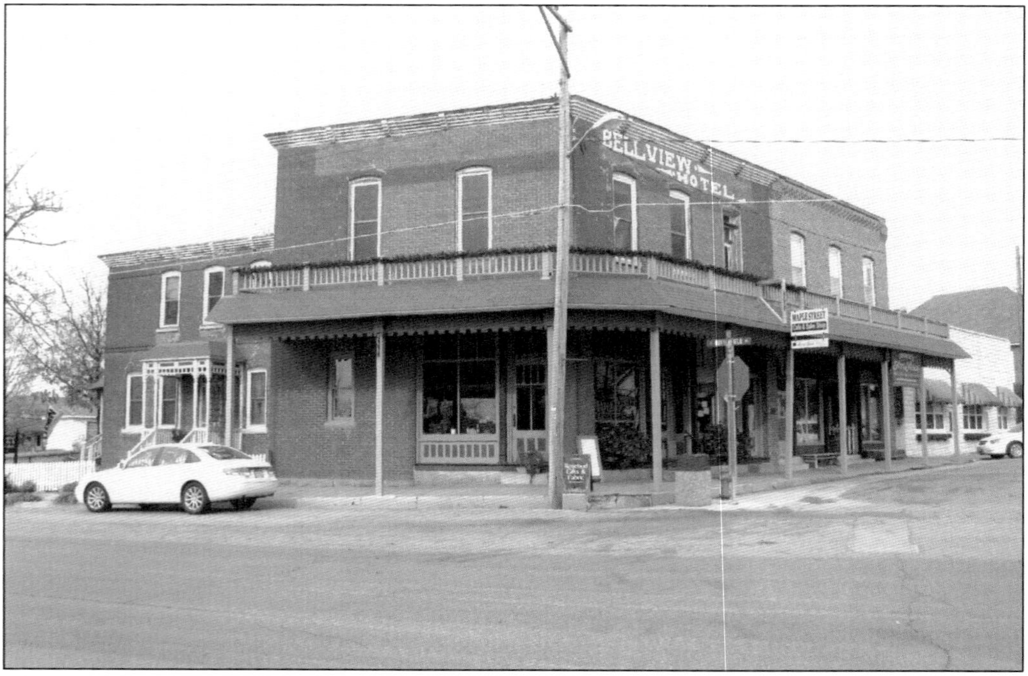

The Belleview is a major building in the Cole Camp historic district, and while it no longer offers rooms, it is a fine restaurant.

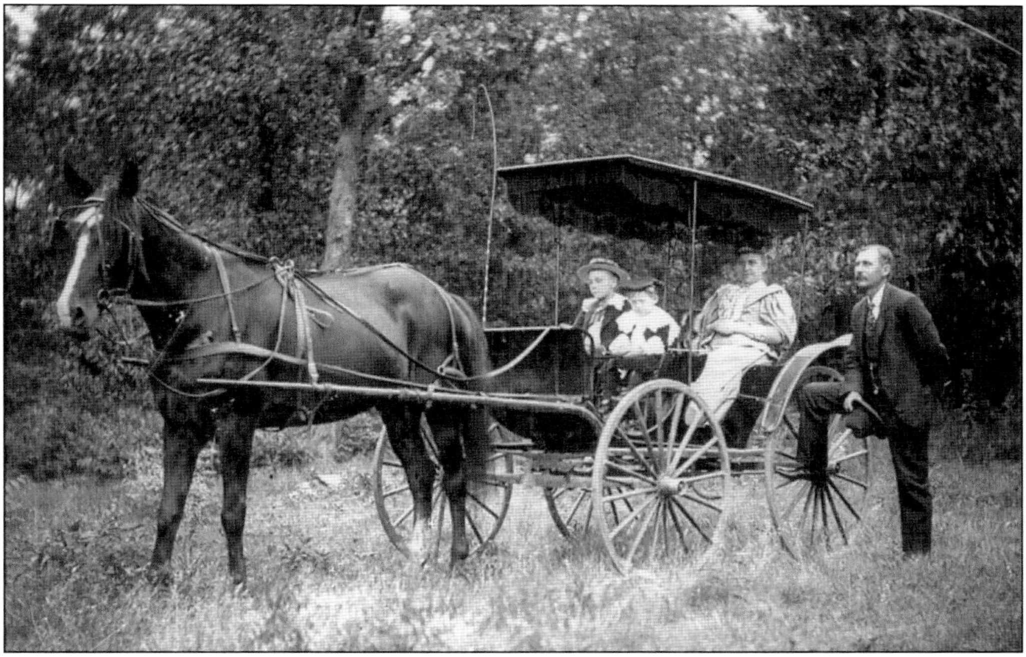

Sophia and Henry C. Boeschen, with their children Amos (right) and Lawrence, are out for a Sunday drive in 1899. Boeschen operated a store and post office at Boeschenville, three miles northeast of Cole Camp. This was family transportation at its best in the late 19th century.

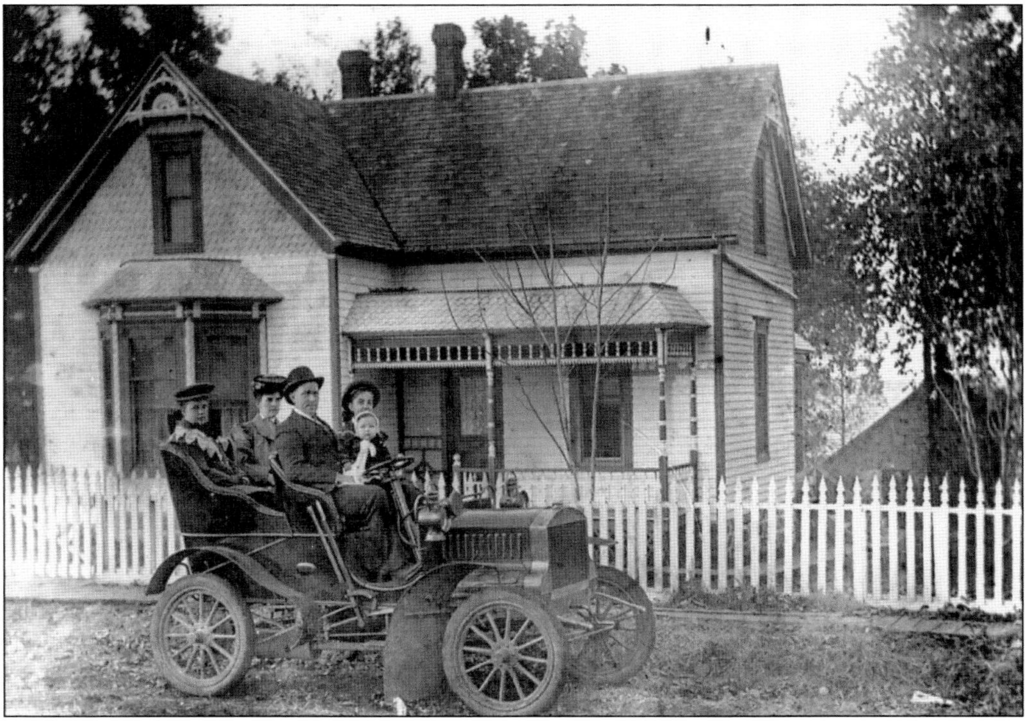

F.S. Hinefelt and friends enjoy a ride in the first automobile to be registered in Benton County. The car is a 1906 Lambert Model 4. It had a gearless friction drive transmission. The Lambert was manufactured from 1906 to 1916.

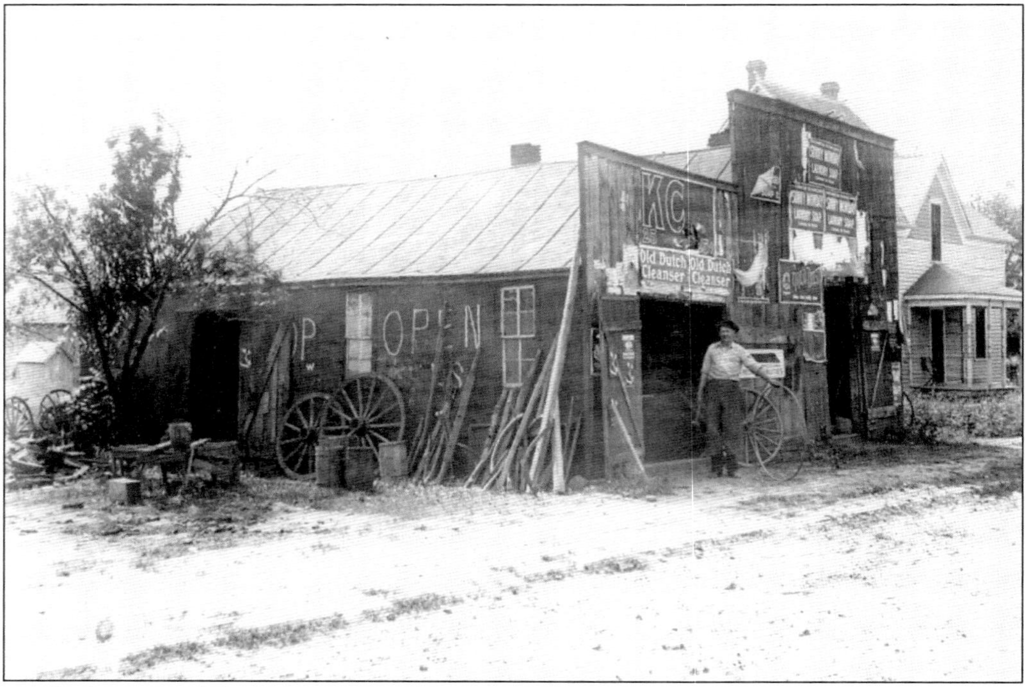

While the automobile was making inroads in Cole Camp, there was still a need for a blacksmith. Louis Meyer operated this facility on Butterfield Road until 1910, when it became the site of Trinity Lutheran Church.

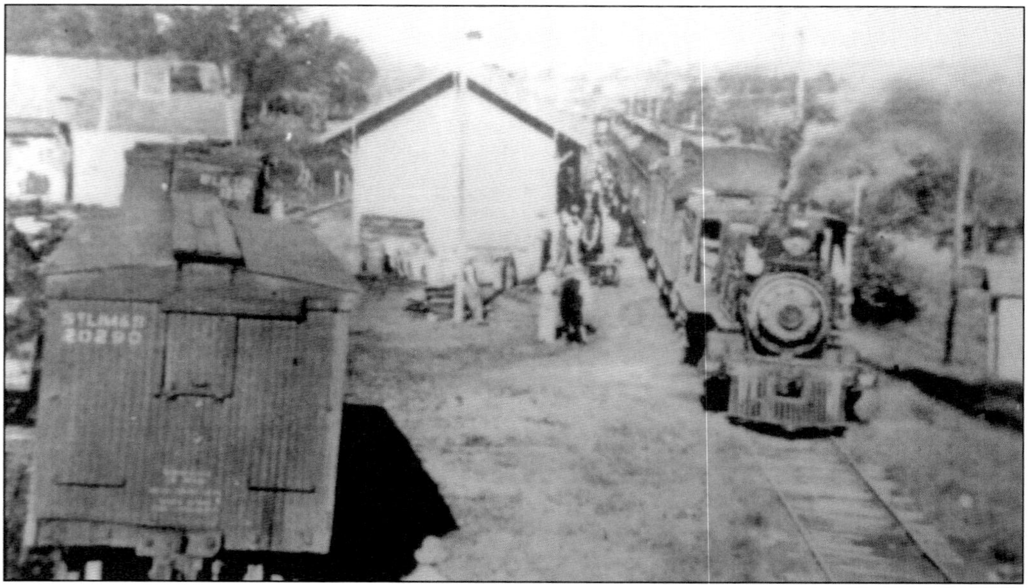

In this 1910 view, a special northbound Sedalia, Warsaw and Southern Railroad train is leaving Cole Camp for the Missouri State Fair in Sedalia.

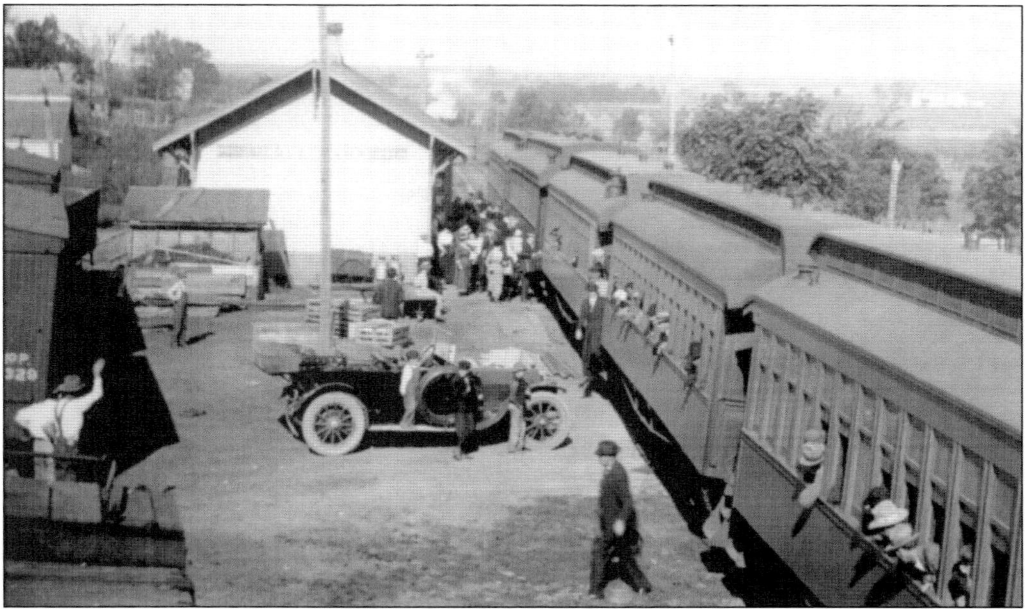

While an abundant number of passengers are visible in this 1917 view, the encroaching automobile will eventually doom the business on the Missouri Pacific branch line through Cole Camp.

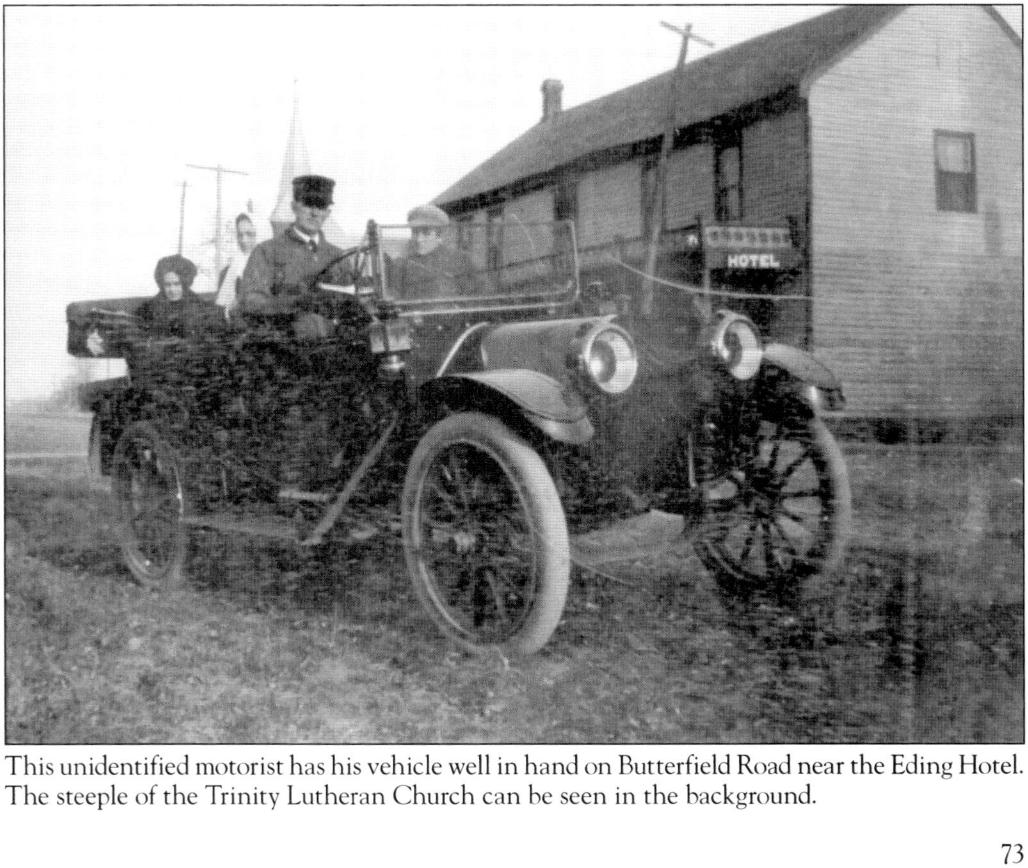

This unidentified motorist has his vehicle well in hand on Butterfield Road near the Eding Hotel. The steeple of the Trinity Lutheran Church can be seen in the background.

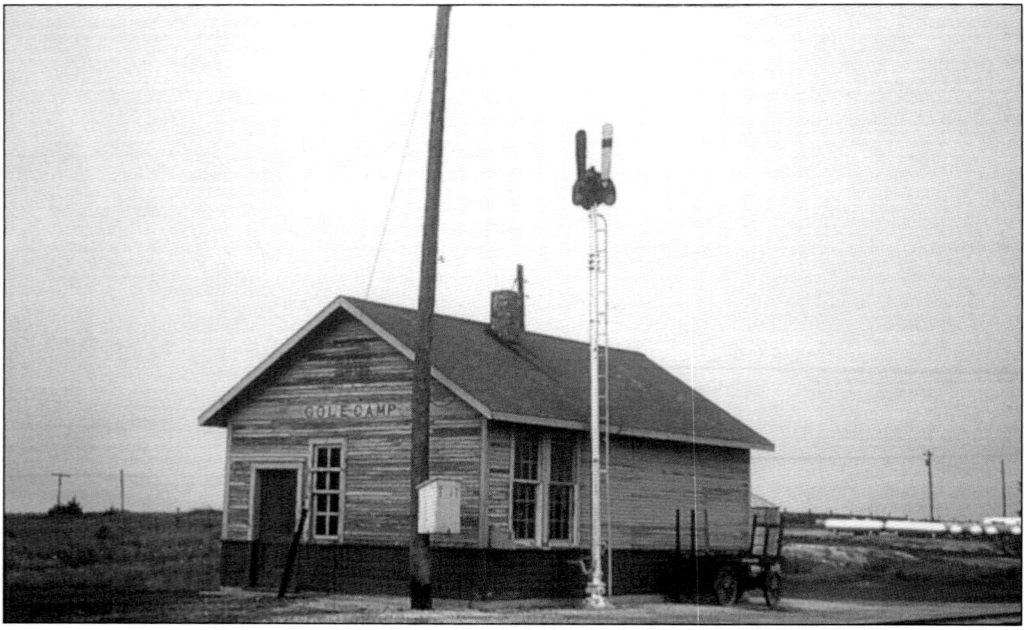

In 1904, the Rock Island Railroad completed a line between St. Louis and Kansas City, bypassing Cole Camp two miles to the north. A local story claims the station was originally named "NAY" by the railroad due to the line bypassing the town. The station name was changed to Cole Camp in the 1920s. In this 1957 view, the station baggage cart stands ready to meet the daily passenger train that served the station. (Photograph by Howard D. Killam.)

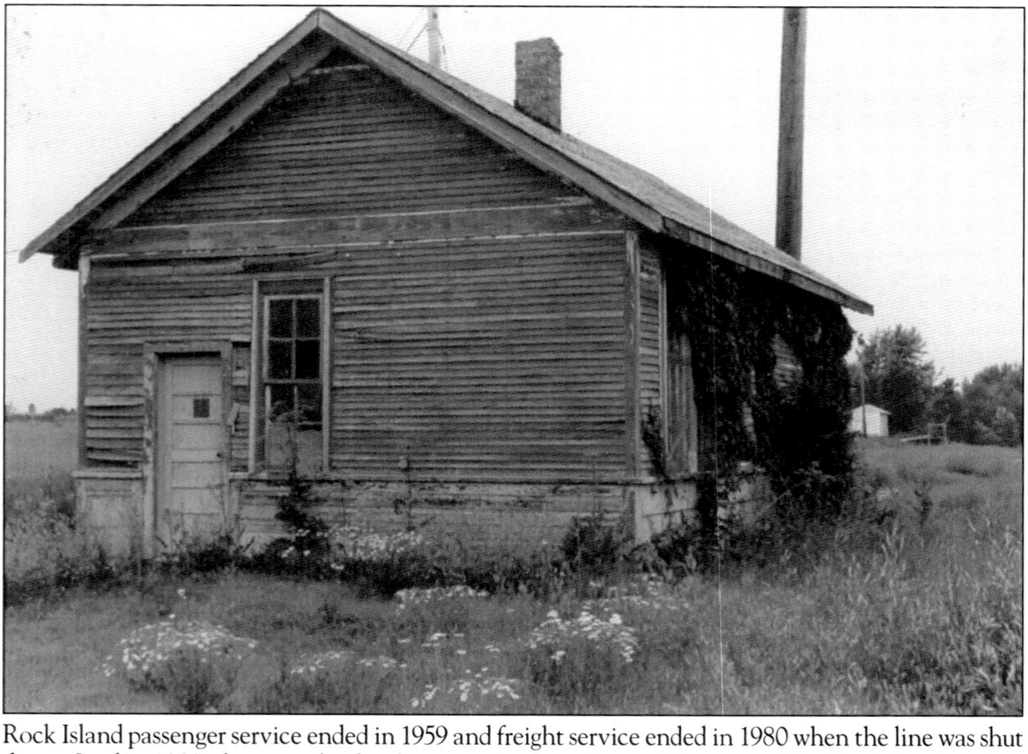

Rock Island passenger service ended in 1959 and freight service ended in 1980 when the line was shut down. In this 1982 photograph, the depot awaits demolition. (Photograph by Jim Monahan.)

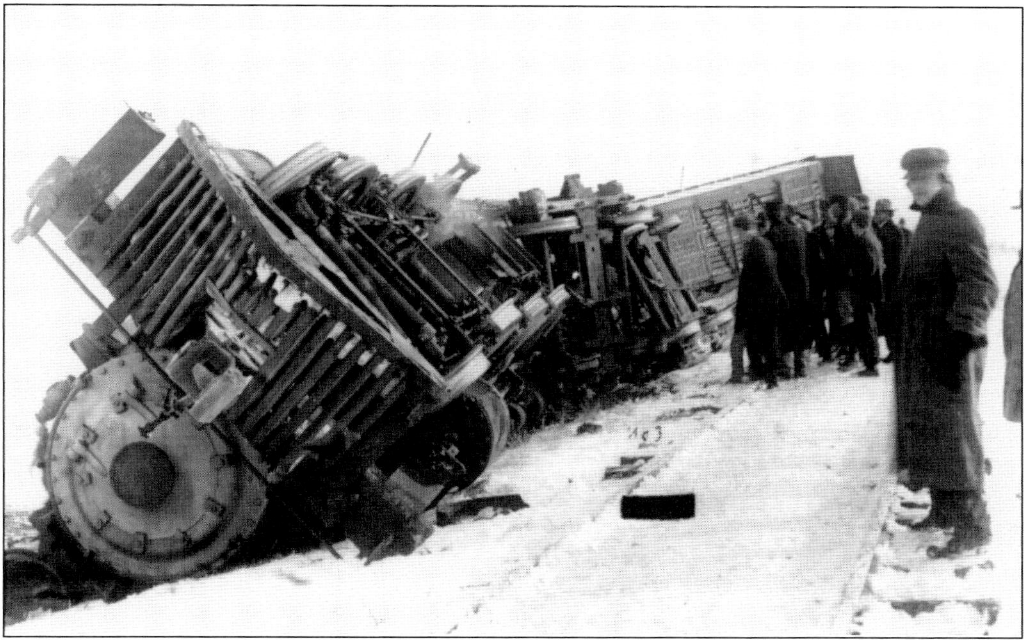

Tragedy was not uncommon on the railroads, and Cole Camp suffered a fatal wreck on a snowy February 4, 1913, day as the morning train, No. 697 from Sedalia, derailed while entering town, overturning engine no. 3630. Conductor Patrick Curran and engineer Joseph Altemiller were crushed when the wood cab of the engine was shattered.

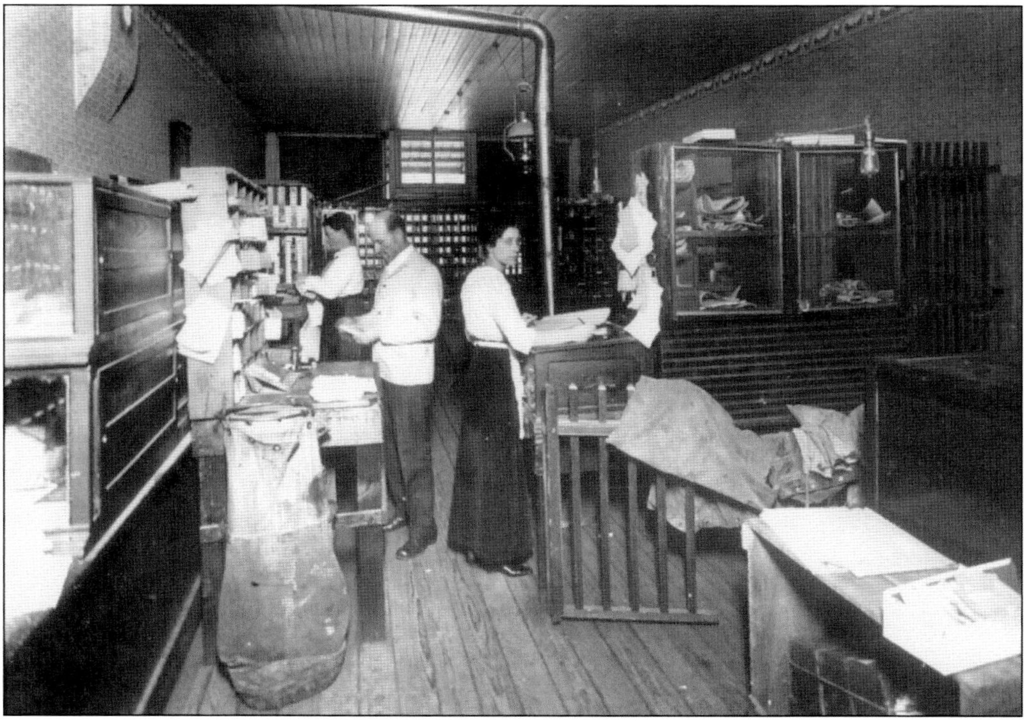

Cole Camp postmaster John S. Fowler helps sort the mail in this image from 1918. Mail arrived and was dispatched daily on both the Missouri Pacific and Rock Island Railroads.

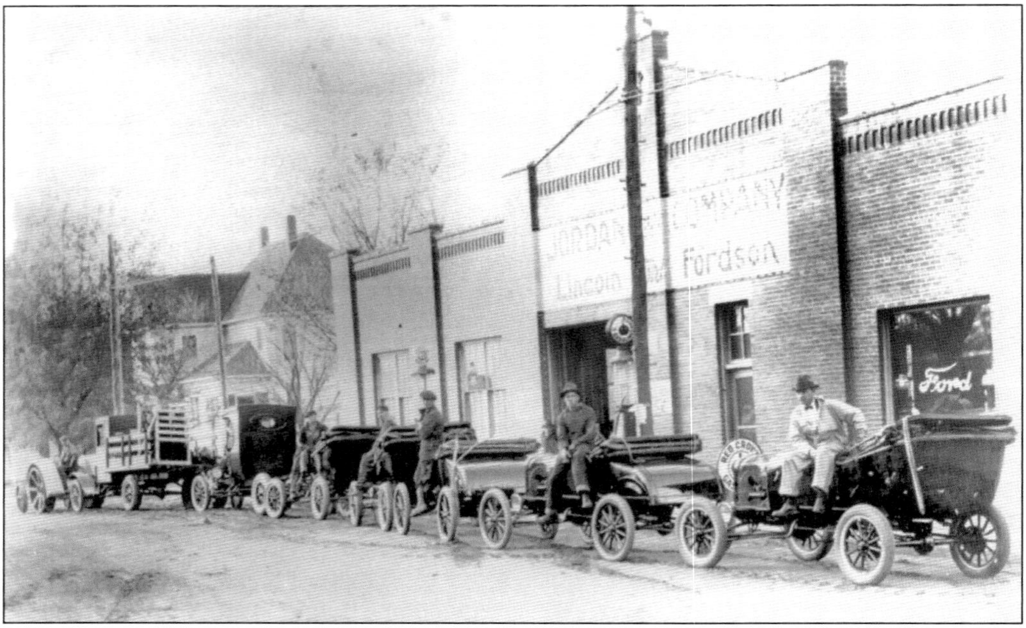

In the mid-1920s, Dorsey Jordan operated a Ford agency in a new brick building on east Second Street. It was purchased by Walter C. Weymuth and Joseph Kreisel in 1932, and they operated the W-K Garage there until 1949, when they were granted a Chevrolet dealership. In 2009, W-K Chevrolet was forced by General Motors' bankruptcy to close its Cole Camp location, but the Weymuth family continues to operate a larger Chevrolet dealership in Sedalia, Missouri. An auto-parts store now occupies the building in 2011.

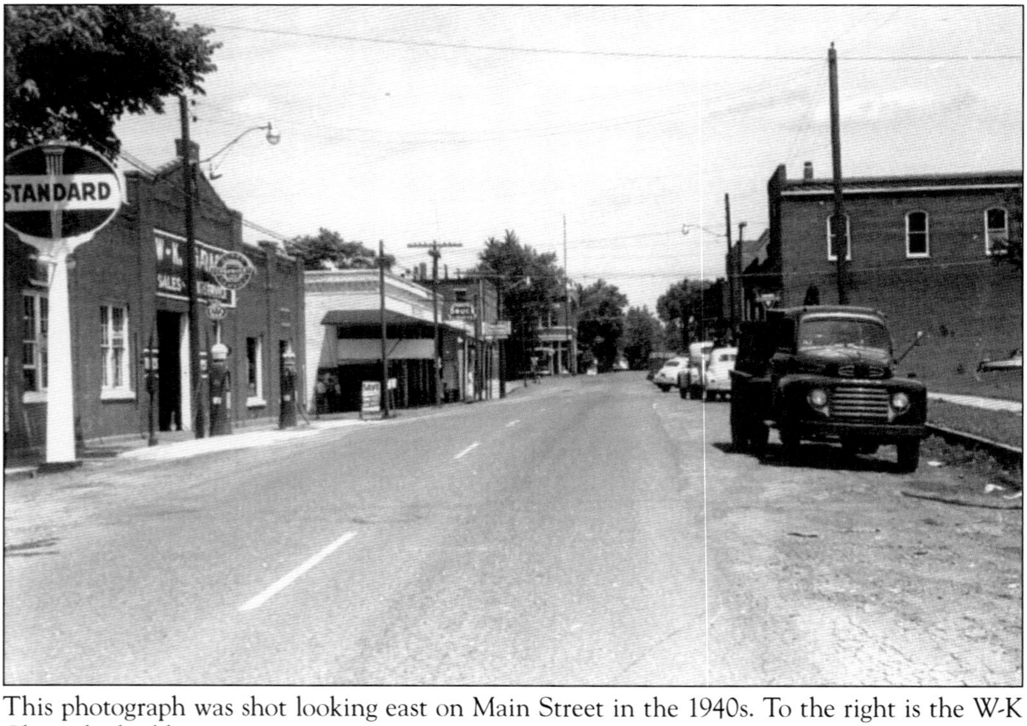

This photograph was shot looking east on Main Street in the 1940s. To the right is the W-K Chevrolet building.

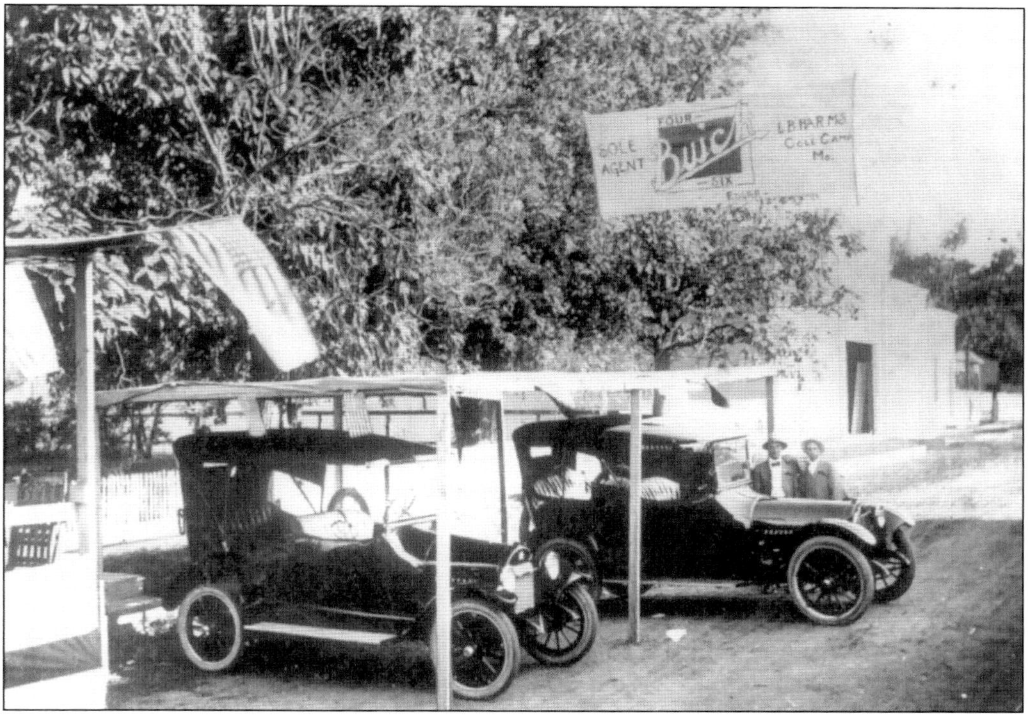

Louis Harms and John Swind display new 1910 six-cylinder Buicks for sale at their dealership. Louis Harms also operated a feed store in Cole Camp.

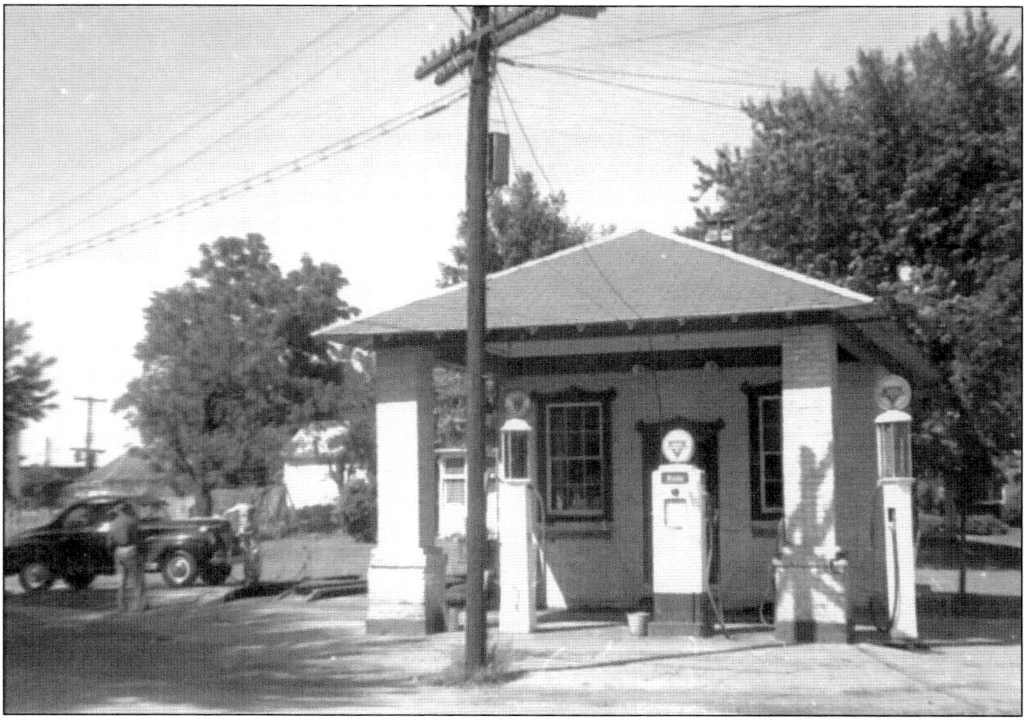

This is a typical 1940s service station in Cole Camp. The outdoor lift on the left provided little comfort when making repairs in winter.

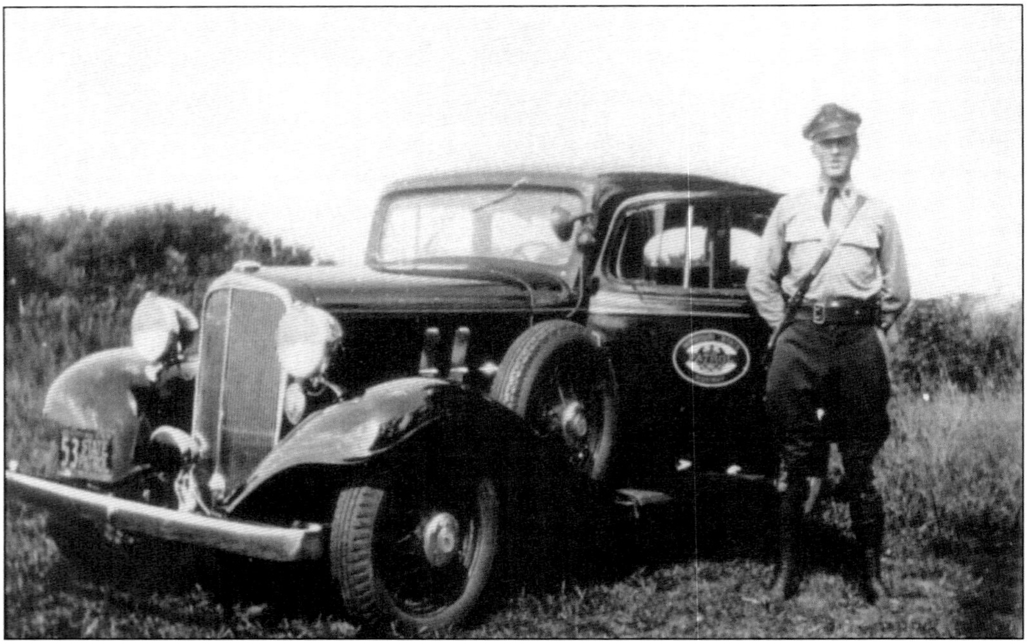

The proliferation of the automobile offered would-be criminals a faster getaway, and in 1931 the State of Missouri established its highway patrol with 55 men enlisted. The first Missouri highway patrolman assigned to the Cole Camp area was Chester Oliver, pictured here on duty in 1935.

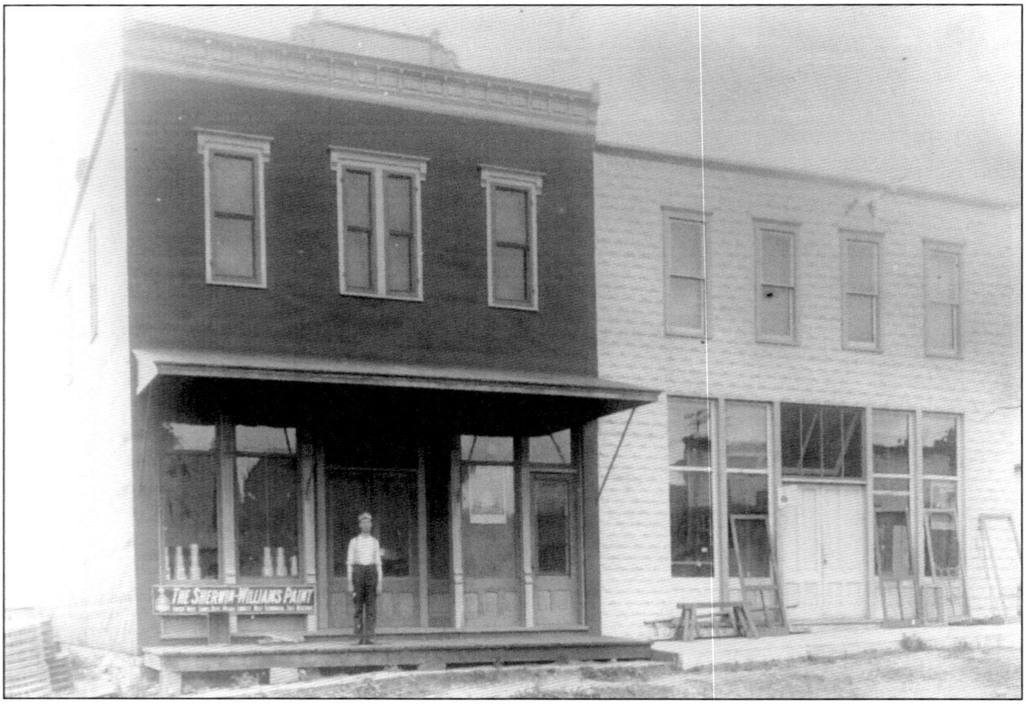

The shop of E.L. Eickhoff on North Maple Street turned out delicate finished woodwork for the interior and exterior trimming of homes. It was in this building that the first gun stocks were manufactured in Benton County, a business that still operates, now located in the town of Lincoln.

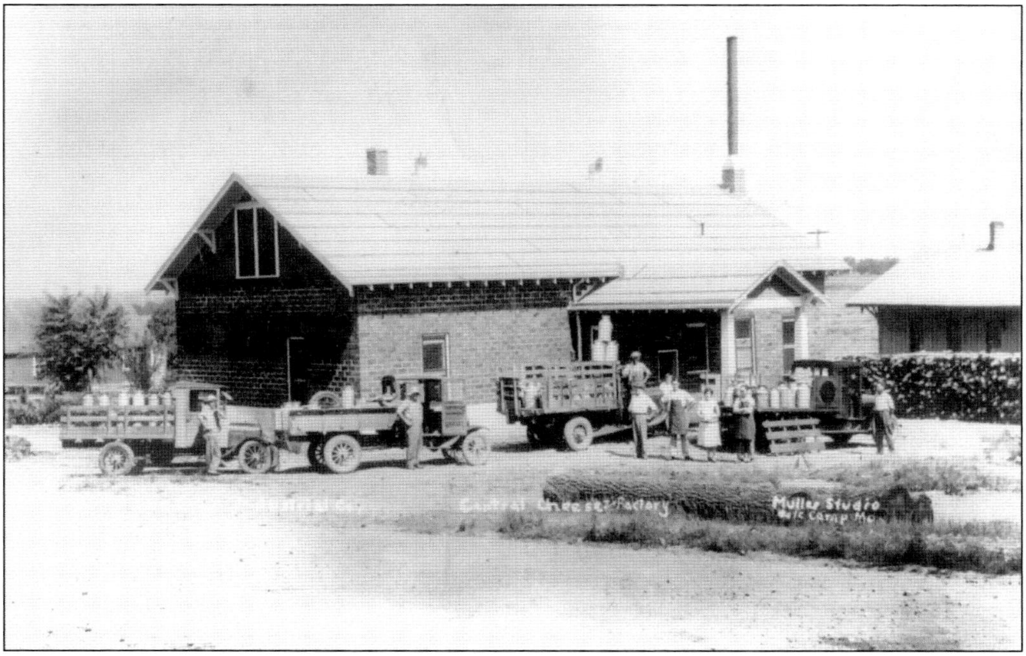

In 1928, Cole Camp businesspeople formed the Cole Camp Industrial Company, and one of the first businesses established was the Central Cheese Company. The idea was to use the milk products from area farmers to make cheese. The Depression was hard on the cheese factory, and profits were illusive. The ill-fated factory closed in 1940.

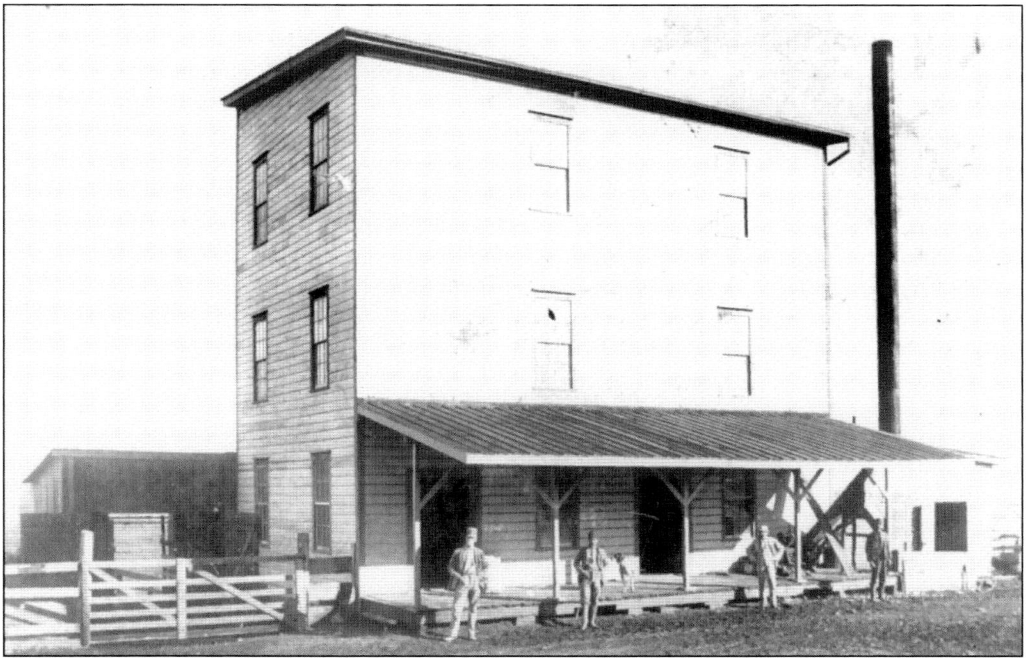

In 1895, Edgar Schwald constructed the Daisy Roller Mill and a building next to the mill that housed the Cole Camp Electric Company generating plant. Originally powered by a steam engine, the lights were on from dark to 11:00 p.m. When a gas engine replaced the steam engine, power was on 24 hours a day.

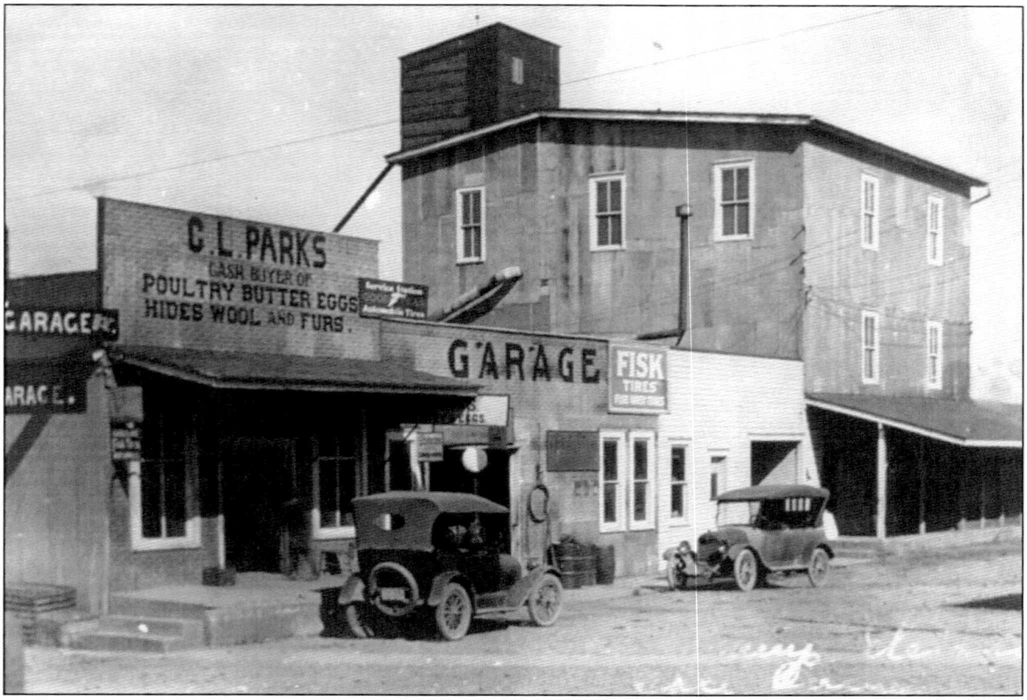

The expanded mill building is pictured in 1926. The mill and attached buildings still exist, grinding and mixing feed for area farmers.

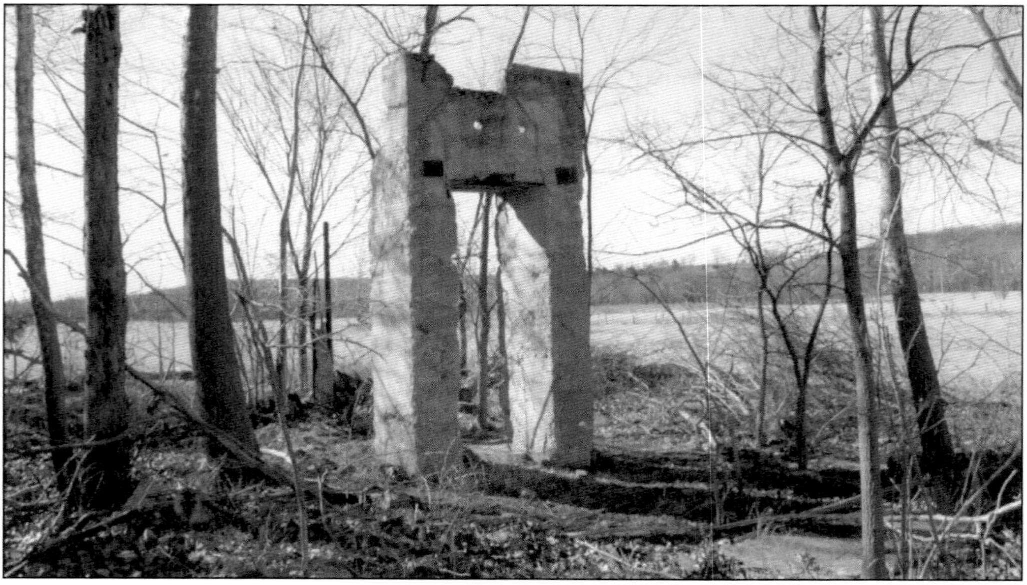

Three miles southwest of Cole Camp was the mining community of Tahoma. Originally known as Blaine, the name was changed to Melton in the 1880s after Maj. Richard Melton, a local railroad and mining developer. Melton would be changed to Raymond when the mine was sold to George Raymond in 1900; it was renamed as Tahoma in 1909. Employing over 80 men, the town once had eight mines that were worked for lead and barites. It boasted a hotel, general store, post office, and 40 families. The mines closed in 1916 when the ore veins gave out. Today, the only thing remaining of the mines at Tahoma is an ore crusher.

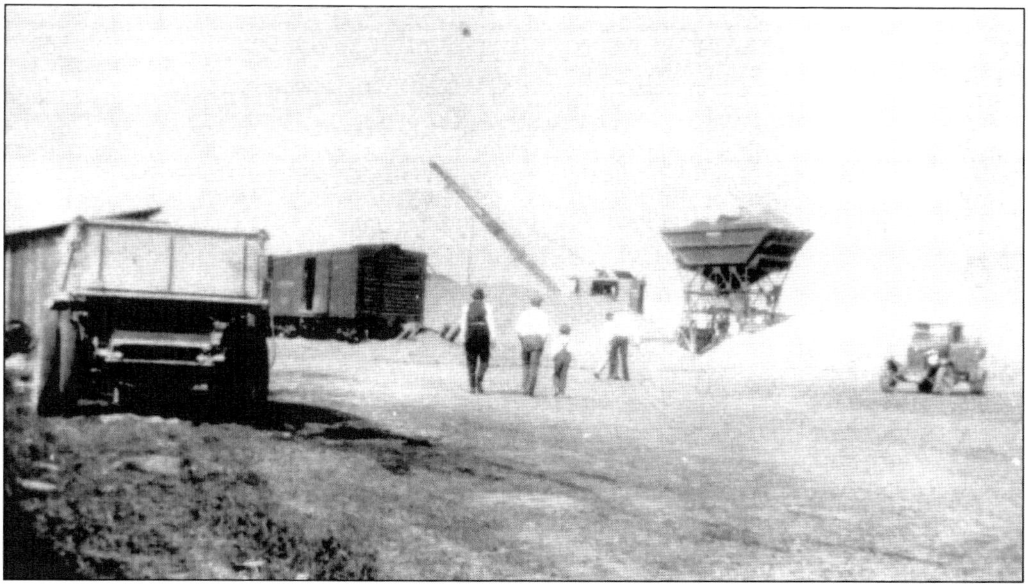

The building of US Highway 65 in the 1930s required crushed rock, and much of it was brought over the Missouri Pacific Railroad Warsaw branch line with materials staged on land near the Herman Schnakenberg farm north of Cole Camp. In 2010, the Missouri Department of Transportation began the final phase of a dual lane for Highway 65 between Lincoln and the junction of Highway 52 west of Cole Camp.

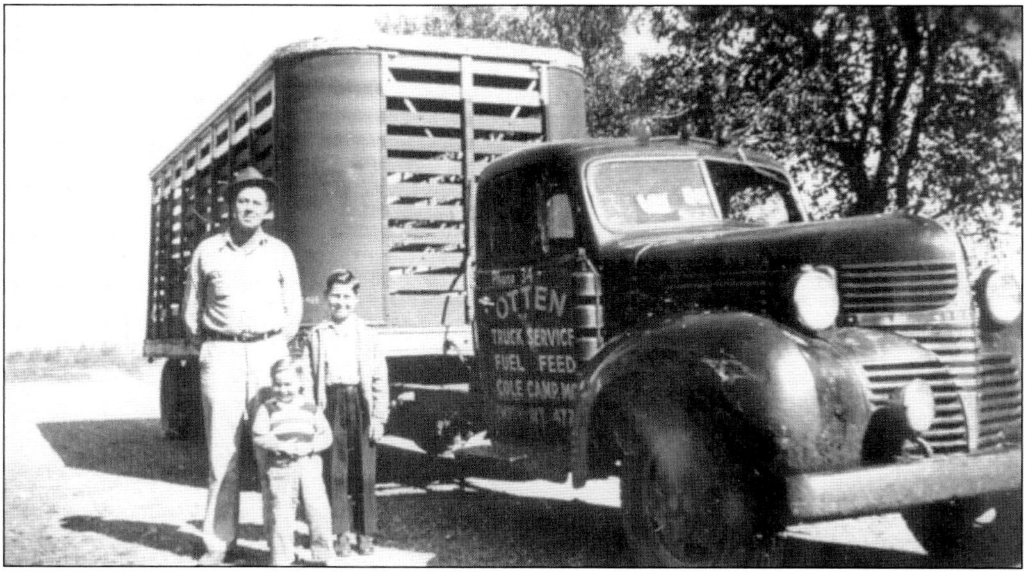

Pete Otten and his sons Jim (left) and John pose with one of Otten's trucks in the 1930s. The paving of both Highway 52 and Highway 65 increased the trucking of goods to the area.

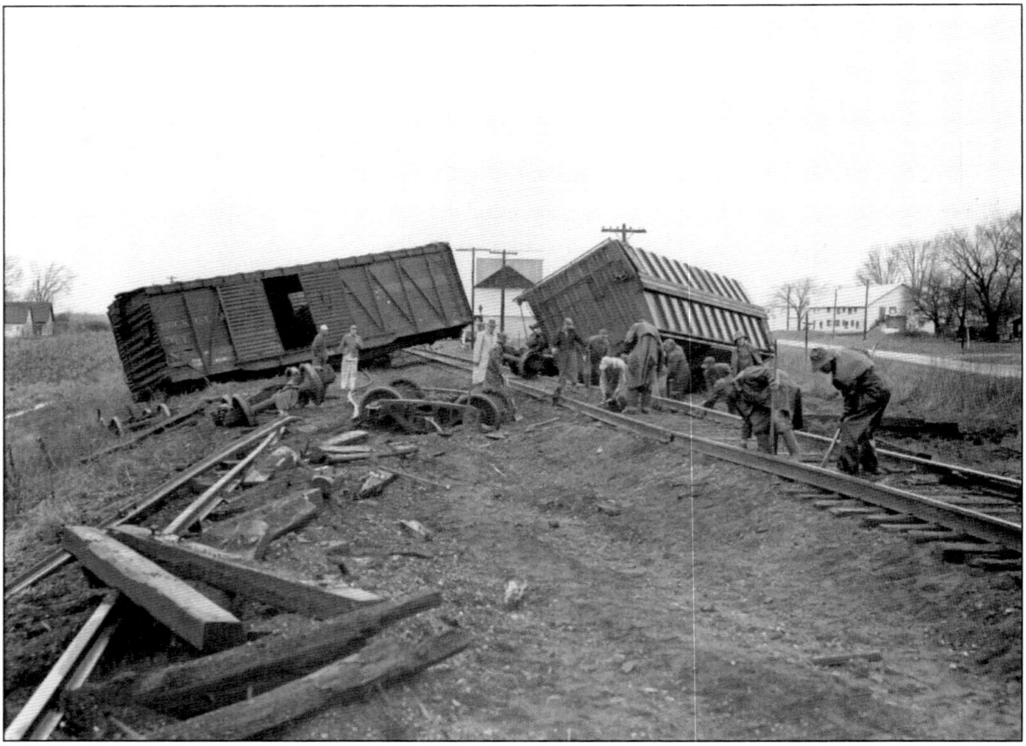

This 1959 derailment west of the Cole Camp Depot on the Rock Island Railroad was caused by a broken rail.

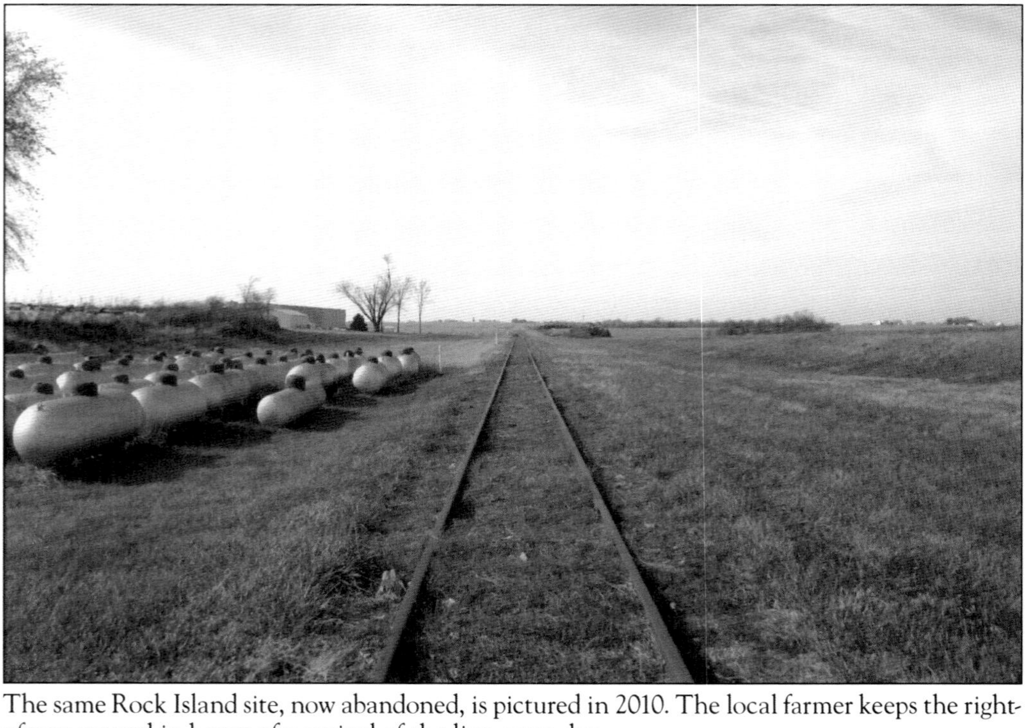

The same Rock Island site, now abandoned, is pictured in 2010. The local farmer keeps the right-of-way mowed in hopes of a revival of the line some day.

Six

Churches and Schools

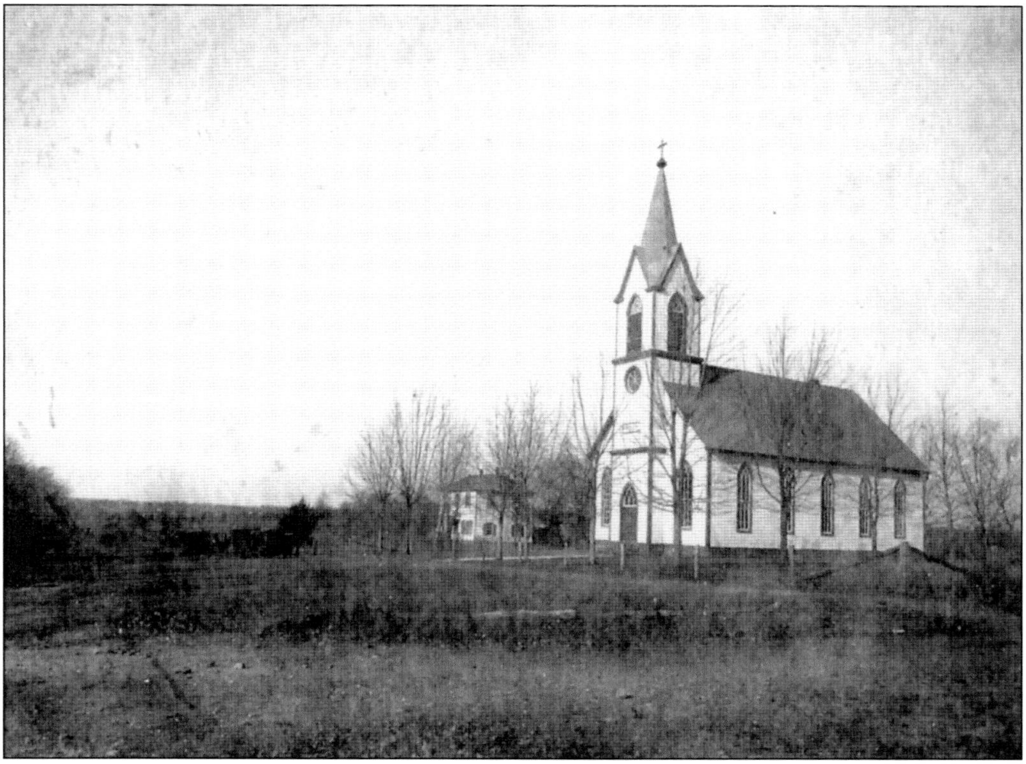

At the turn of the 20th century, there were 24 churches within a 10-mile radius of Cole Camp. Of them, 16 were Lutheran, two were Catholic, five were Methodist, and one was Evangelical. Typical of the rural churches is Holy Cross Lutheran, established in 1842 at Lake Creek north of Cole Camp. Holy Cross was the mother church of most of the Lutheran congregations in the area. In this 1890 image, it is Sunday and the buggy park of the worshipers is on the left. The church burned in 1936, but it was rebuilt and remains an active congregation.

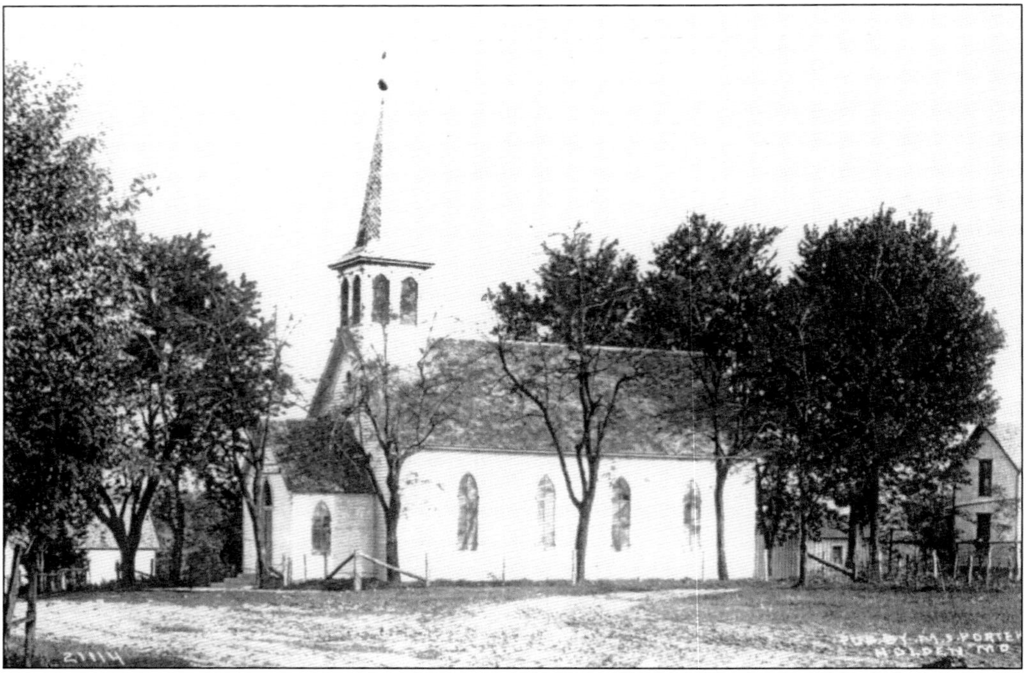

This 1895 photograph is of the original St. Paul's Lutheran of Cole Camp, which was organized in 1882.

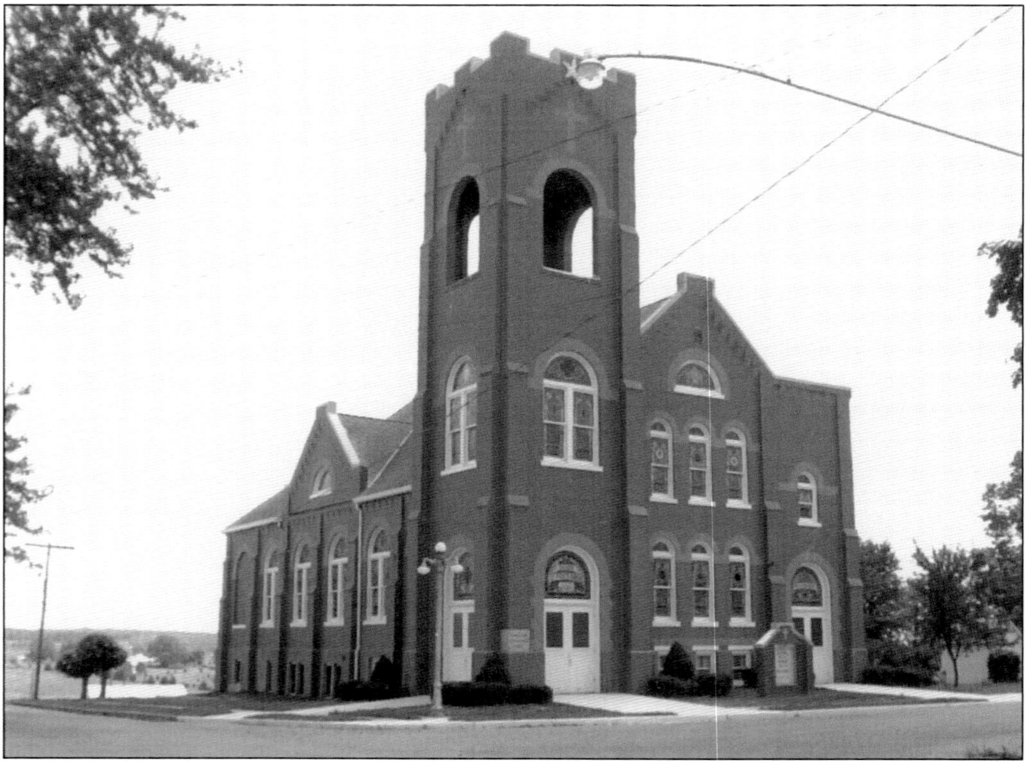

This handsome brick structure replaced the 1882 St. Paul's Church in 1918. Area contractor Peter Eickhoff built the church, which still stands on the old public square in Cole Camp.

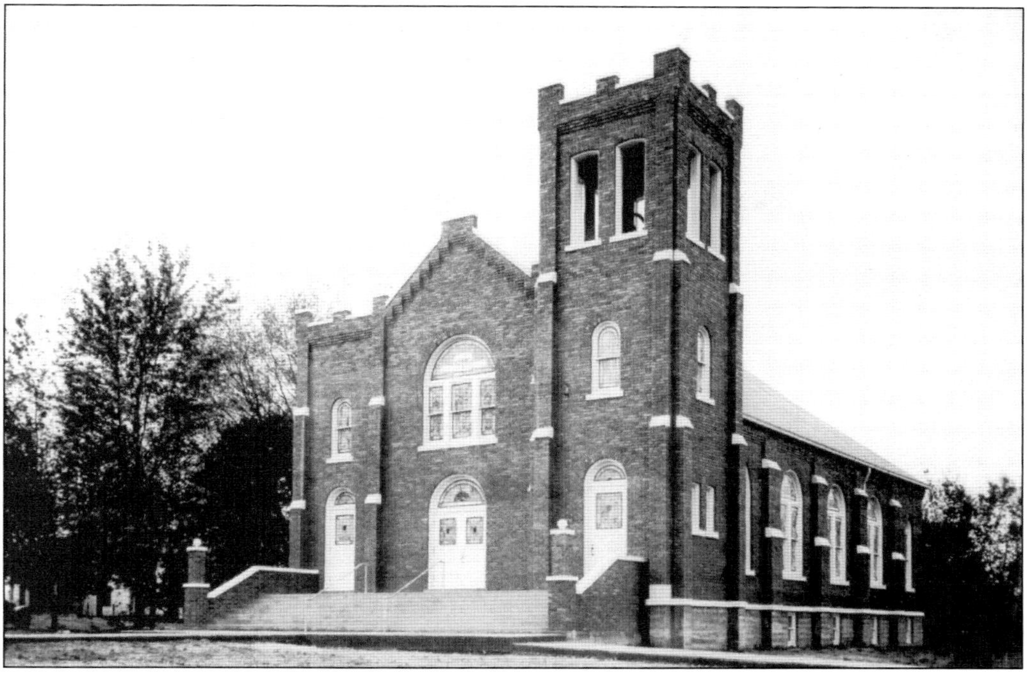

Peter Eickhoff built Zion Lutheran of Lincoln in 1925. The building replaced the old church, which was constructed in 1878 on the same location. Zion celebrated its 150th anniversary in 2009.

Sts. Peter and Paul Catholic Church of Cole Camp was organized in 1877. This building, erected in May 1913, was another product of Peter Eickhoff. It was replaced with a new church, east of Cole Camp on Highway 52, in 1988. The old structure was demolished.

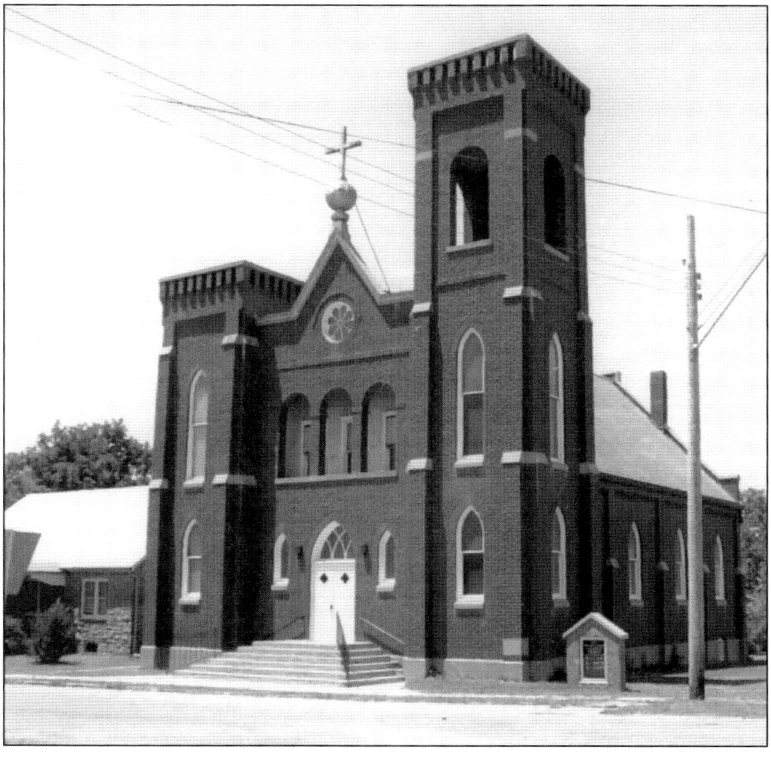

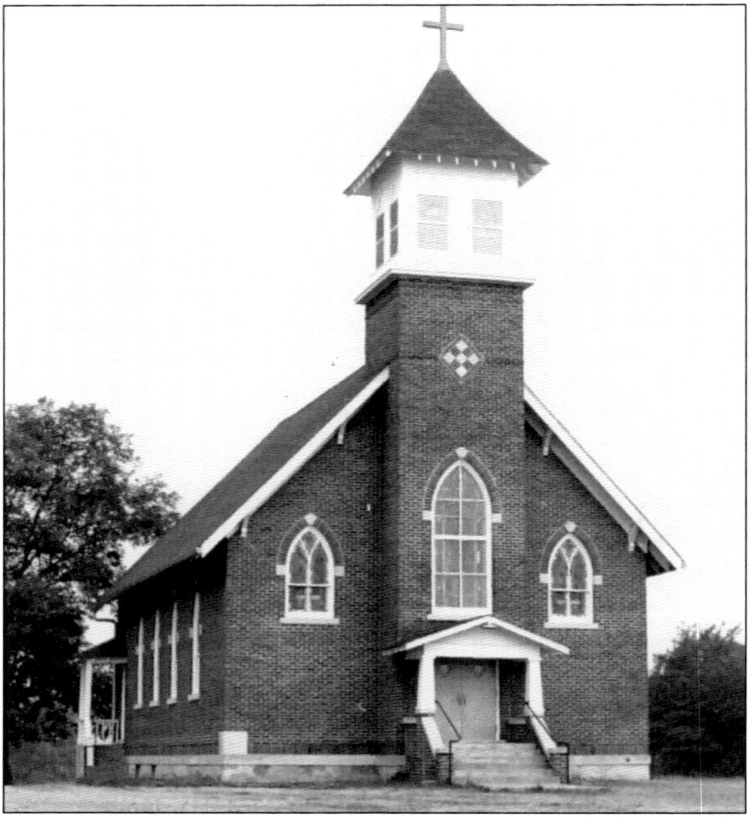

St. Patrick's Catholic Church is located near Springfork in southern Pettis County. It was established by area Irish Catholic families in 1876. The present building was constructed in 1919.

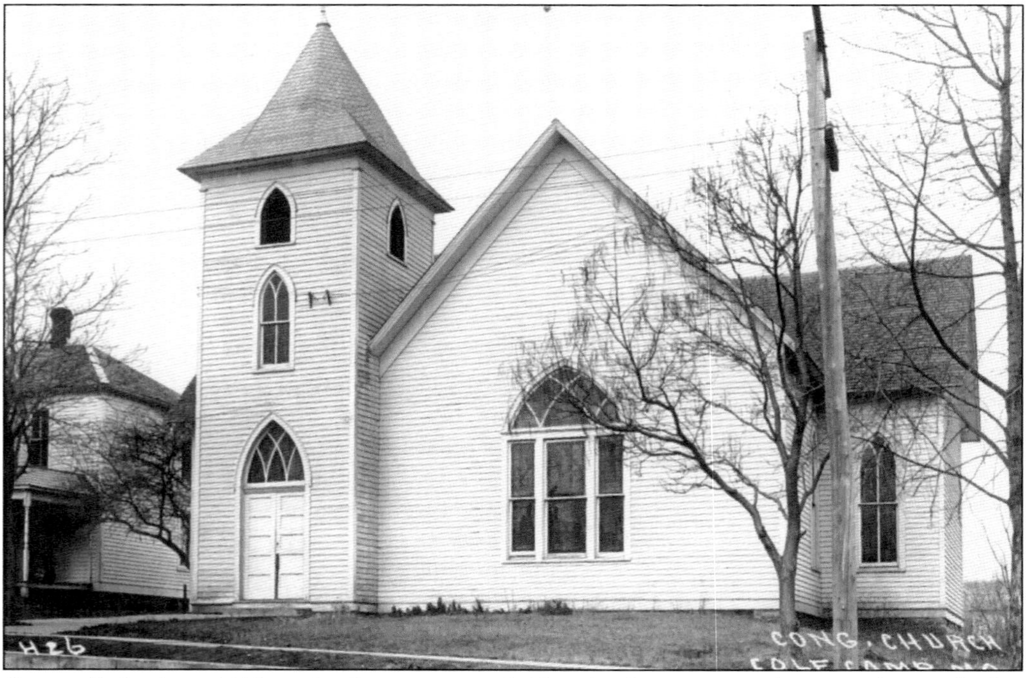

Originally built in 1913 as the Congregational Church, this structure became the Methodist Church of Cole Camp in 1946 and remains so today.

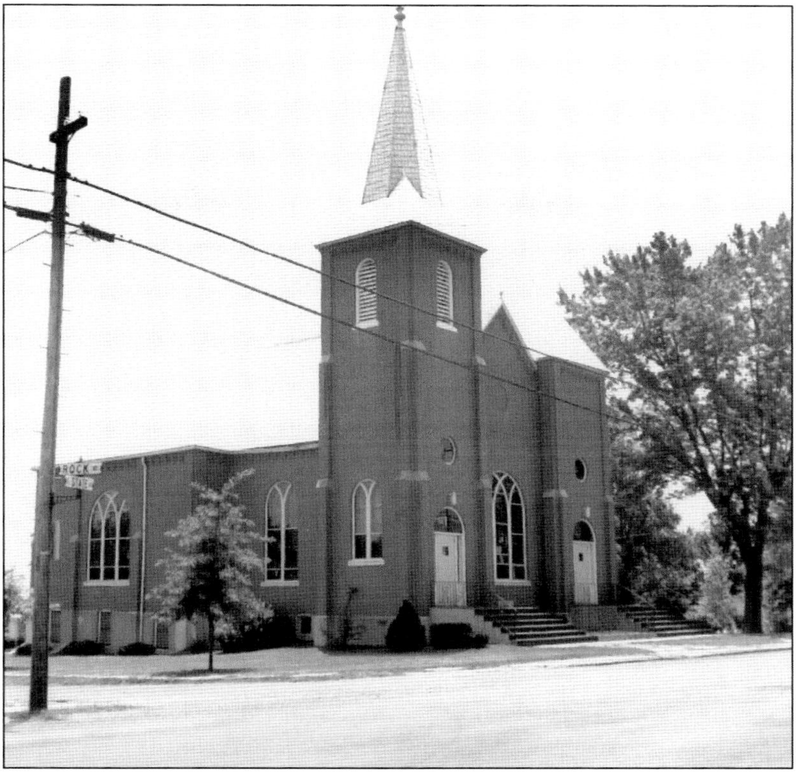

Trinity Lutheran Church of Cole Camp was established in 1896 and built this structure in 1911. Structural difficulties with the tower forced the replacement of the building in 2002. Trinity also operates a Lutheran school in Cole Camp.

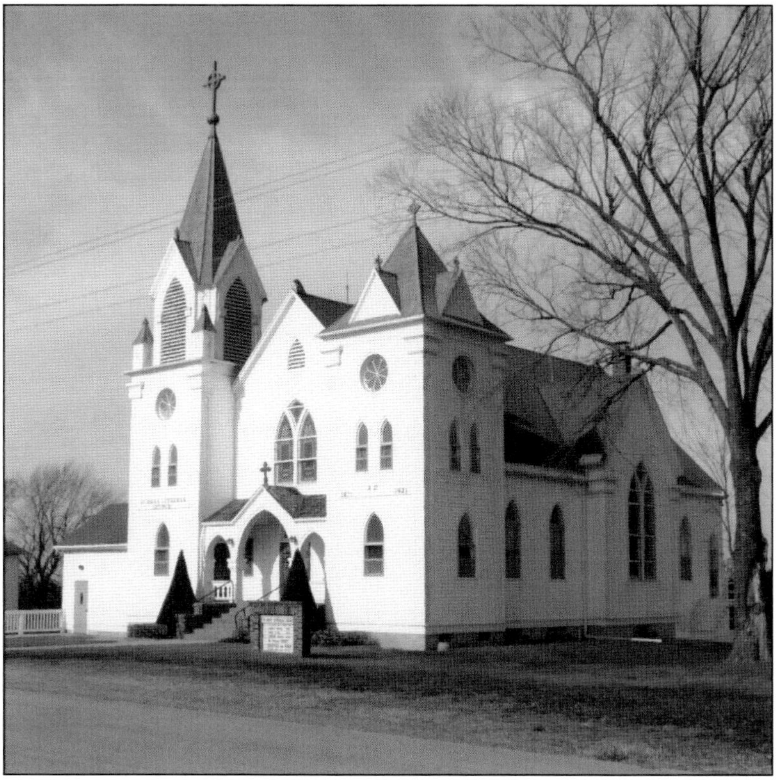

St. Johns Lutheran Church, located five miles northwest of Cole Camp, was founded in 1876. The building is a fine example of American Gothic architecture, with its twin towers and multi-arched porch.

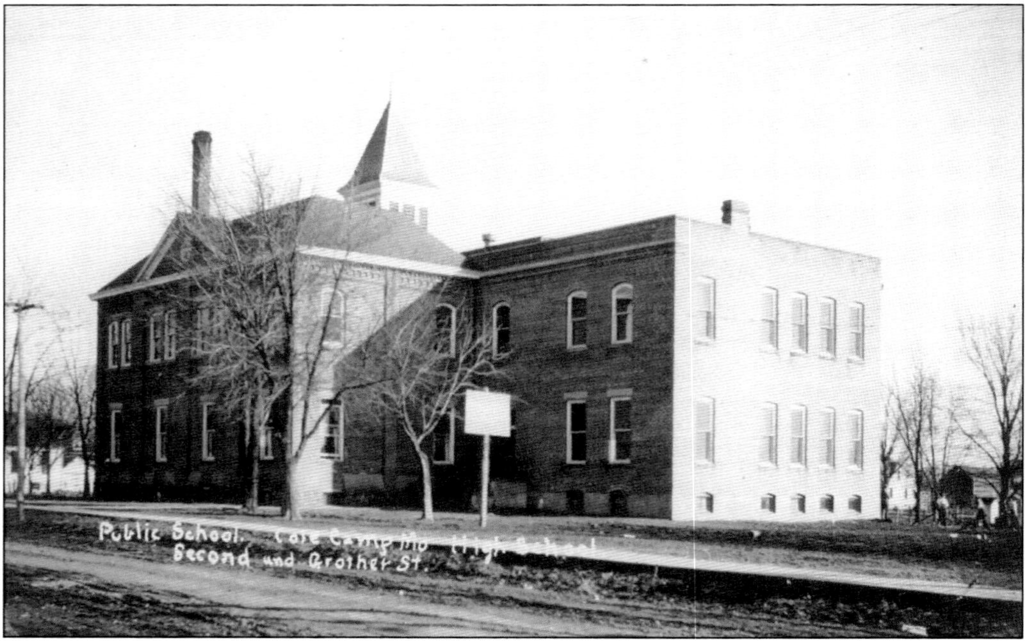

Cole Camp High School was built in 1894 and expanded over the years. It was partly demolished in 1960 when a new high school was constructed. The gymnasium portion of the building now serves as the Cole Camp Municipal Building.

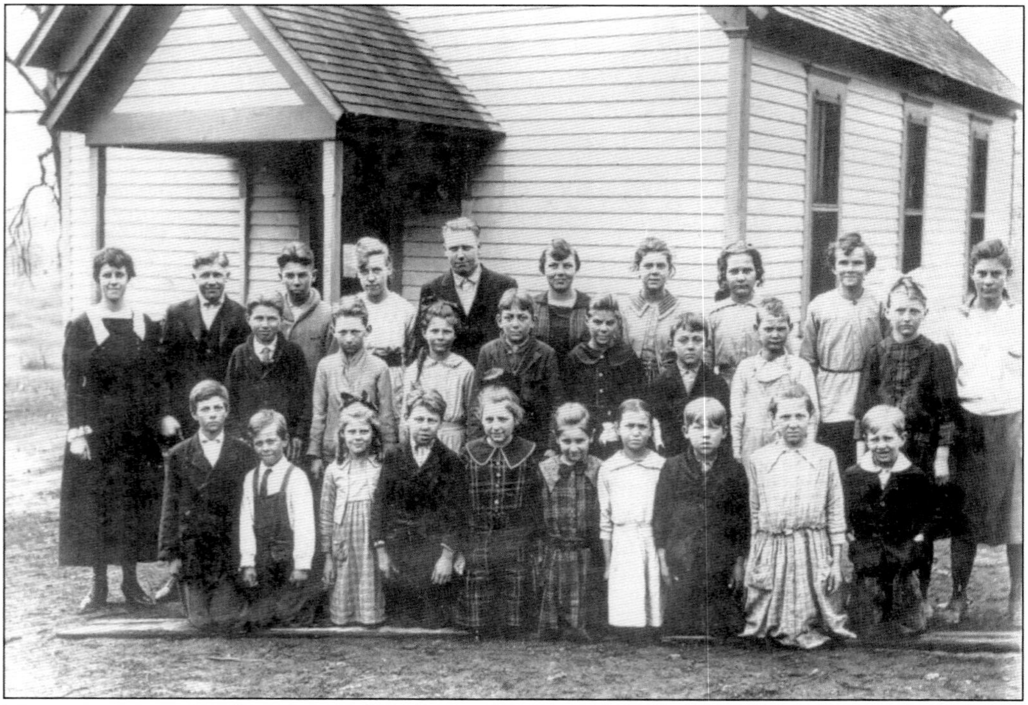

The one-room schoolhouse was the center of learning in most Cole Camp area communities. This 1920 photograph of the Barenburg School is typical of the 15 rural schools in the area at the time. Mable Kreisel (far left, third row) was the teacher of the multi-grade student body.

Seven

RECREATION

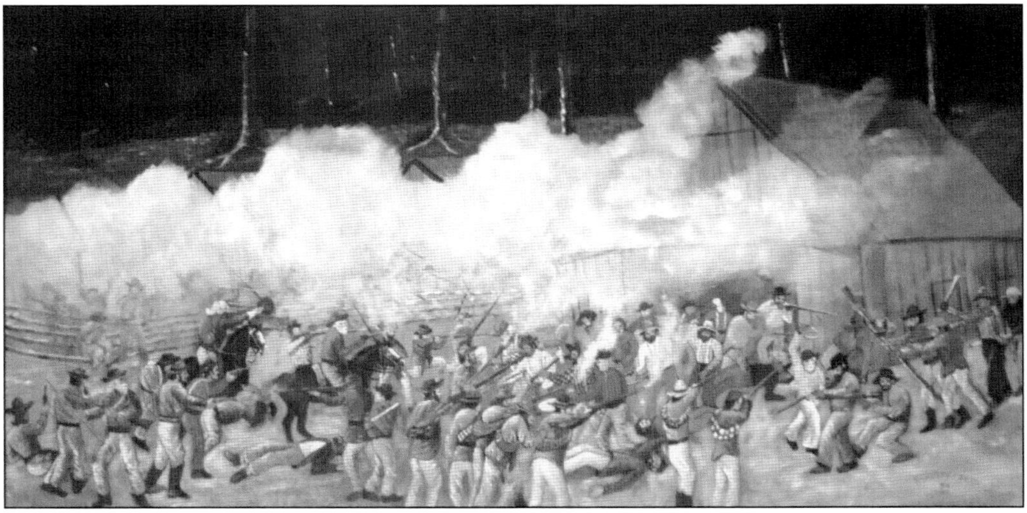

On June 19, 1861, Cole Camp was the scene of an early Civil War battle. A Union home guard, made up mostly of Cole Camp men, was surprised by a Confederate force from the Warsaw area. The home guard was defeated, with 80 men killed and 120 wounded. In 1994, Emil Hesterberg painted this scene of the battle, which took place east of Cole Camp. The painting now hangs in the Cole Camp Municipal Building.

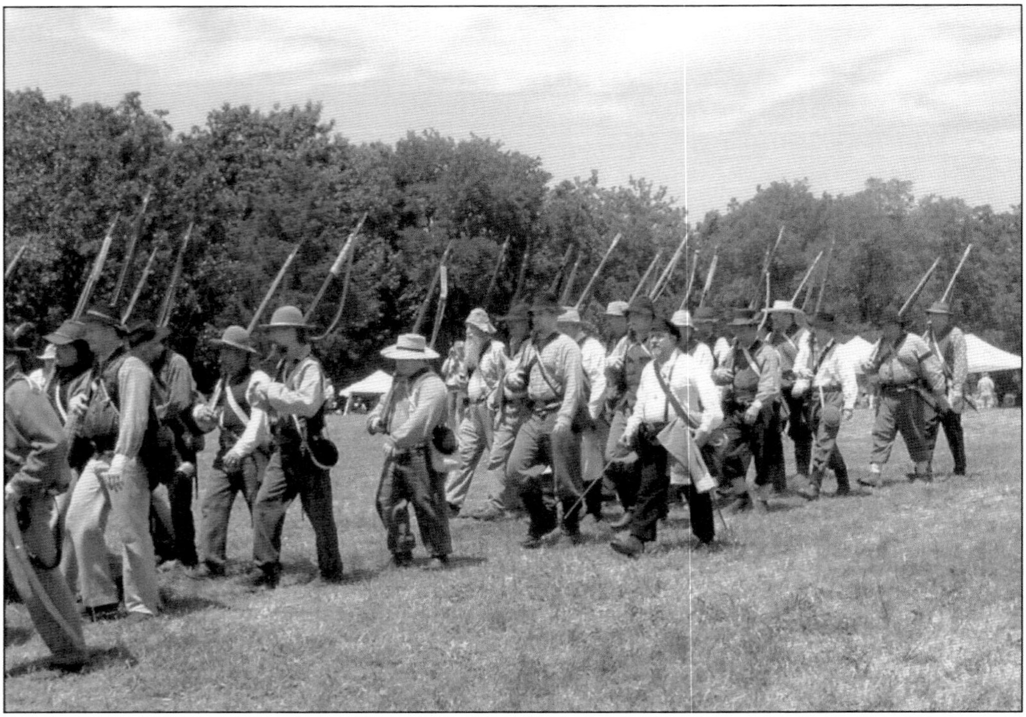

Cole Camp sponsors a reenactment of the battle every few years, and in this scene from 2006 Confederates from Warsaw march upon the unwary Cole Camp home guard.

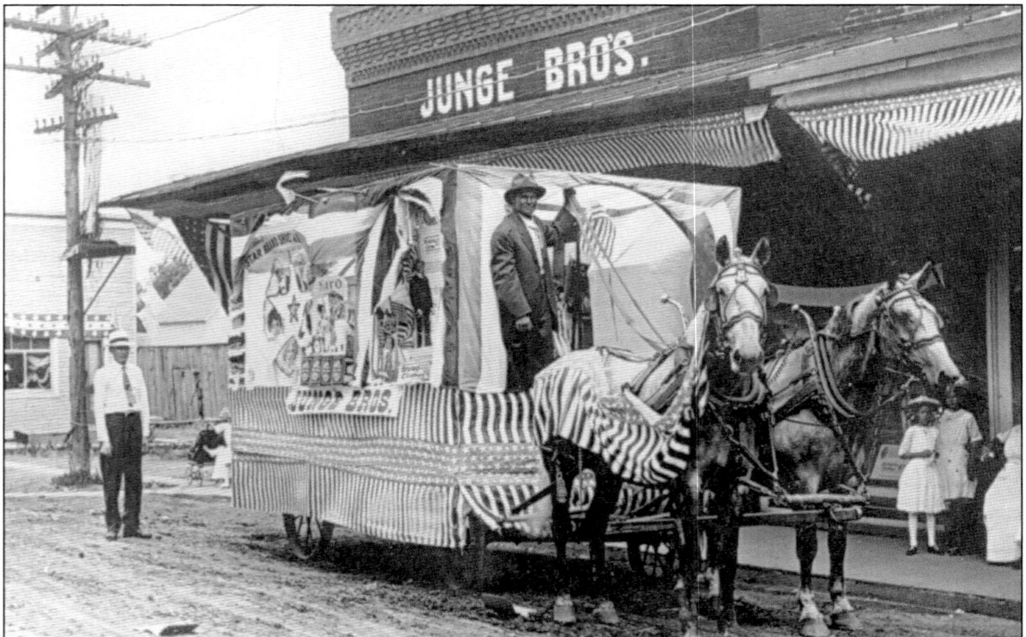

Parades have been part of the Cole Camp summer scene since the town was founded. The 1910 Fourth of July parade featured this Jung Brothers float, pictured in front of the store on East Second Street.

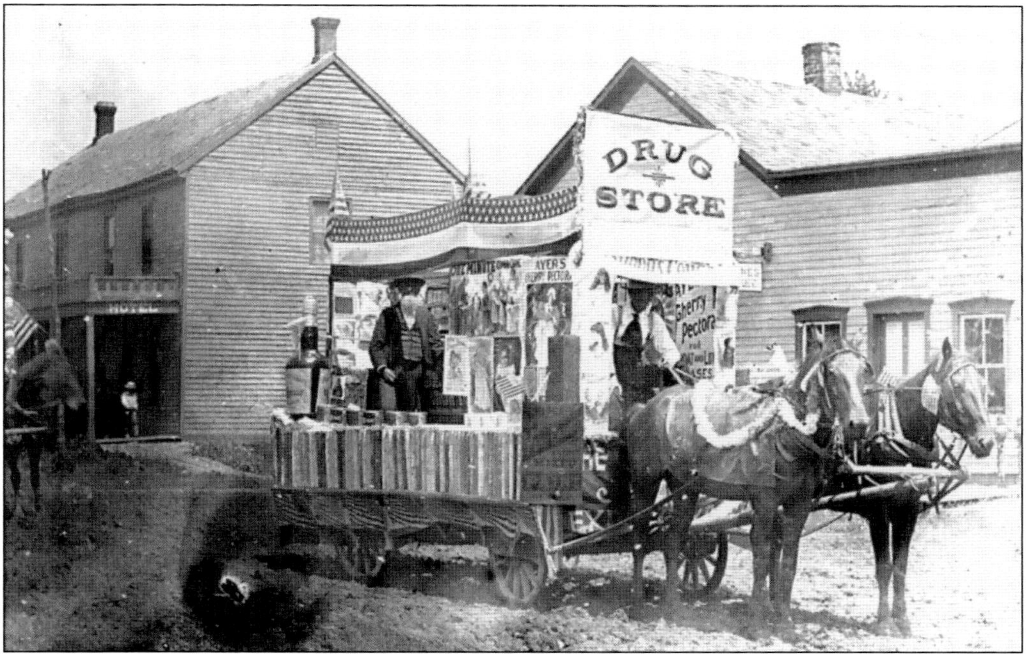

The Grother Drugstore float is pictured on Butterfield Road in the 1910 Fourth of July parade. In the background is the old Eding Hotel, once a stagecoach stop on the Butterfield Trail.

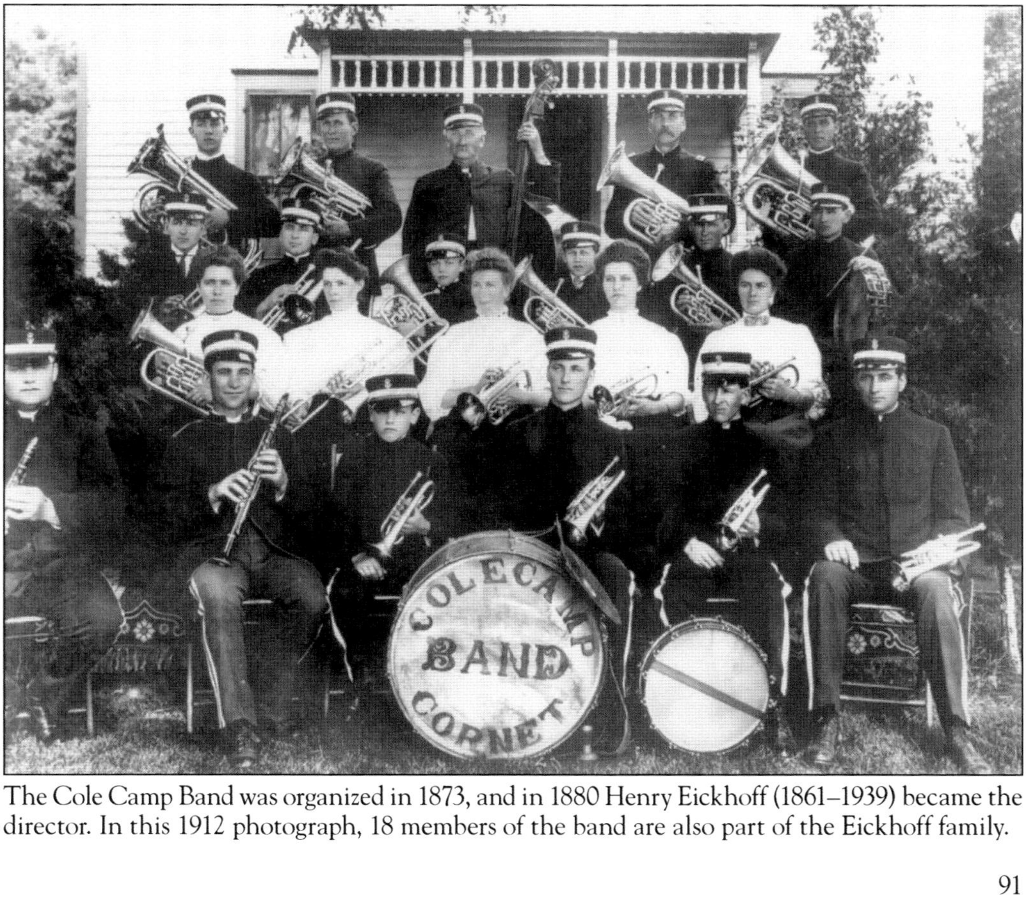

The Cole Camp Band was organized in 1873, and in 1880 Henry Eickhoff (1861–1939) became the director. In this 1912 photograph, 18 members of the band are also part of the Eickhoff family.

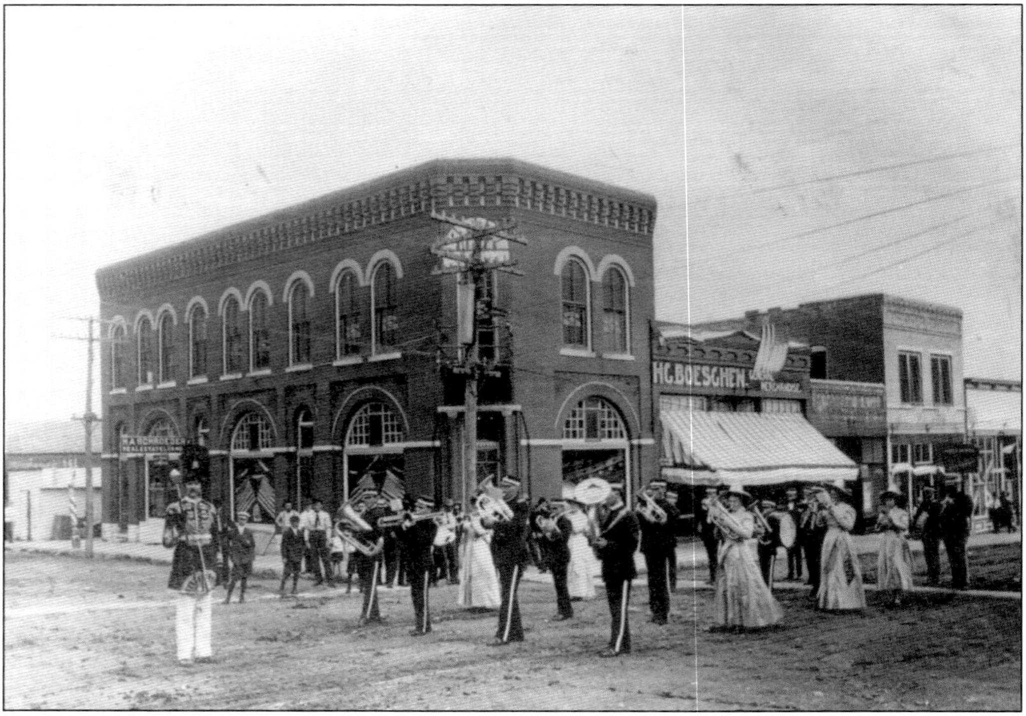

The Cole Camp Band, organized by Henry Eickhoff, parades past the Citizens Bank building in July 1899; Eickhoff leads the group in a bearskin hat. The band was once made up of 18 members of the Eickhoff family.

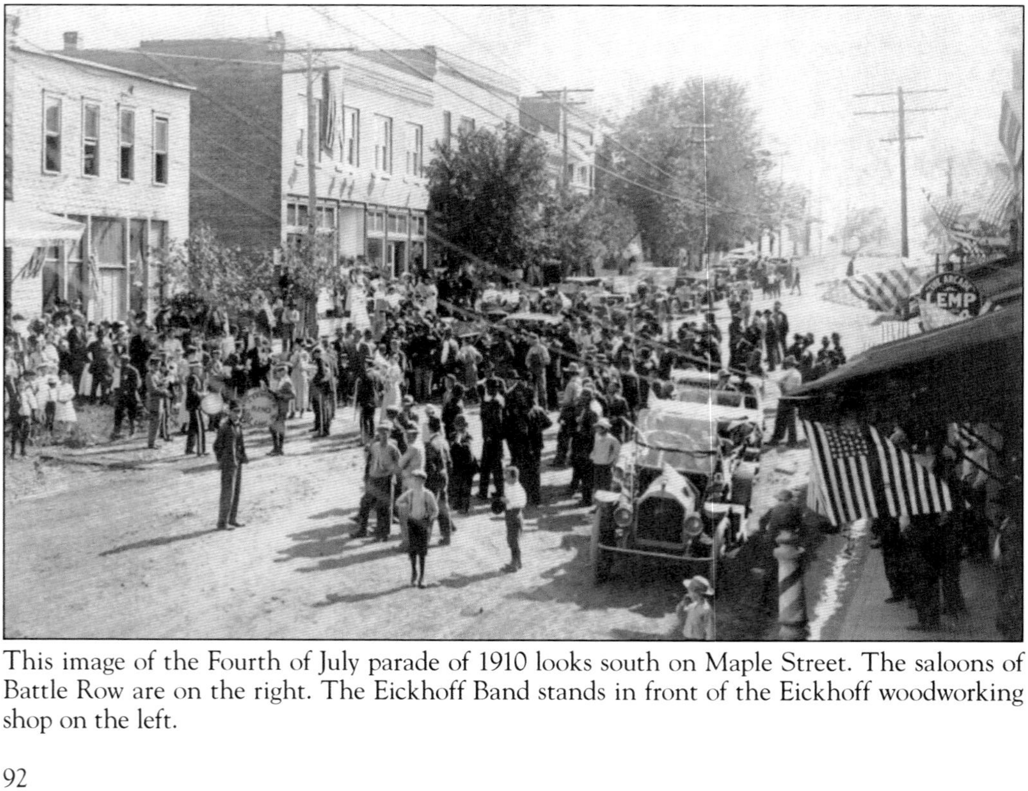

This image of the Fourth of July parade of 1910 looks south on Maple Street. The saloons of Battle Row are on the right. The Eickhoff Band stands in front of the Eickhoff woodworking shop on the left.

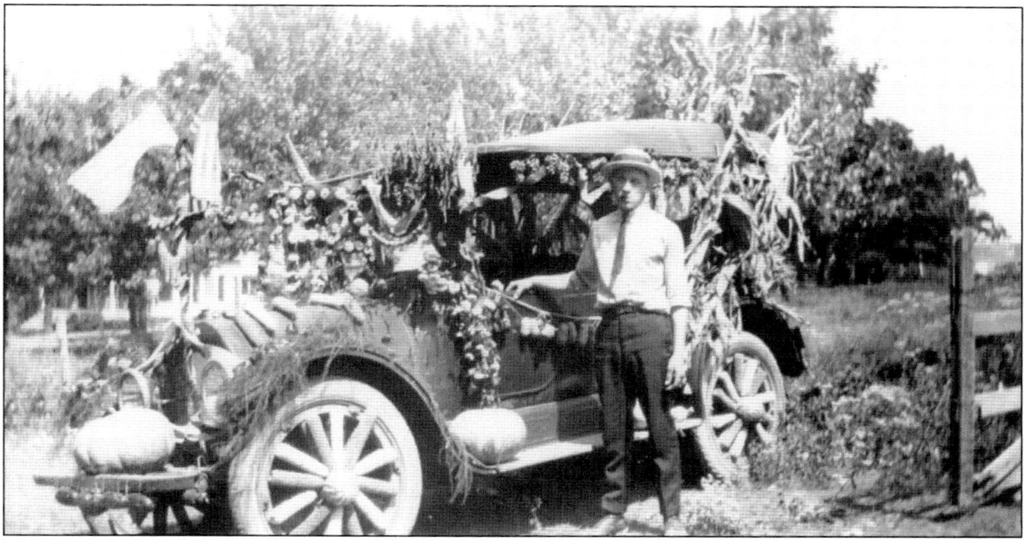

Since 1916, Cole Camp has held a fair in September with parades, agricultural displays, and lots of good food. Seen here in 1916, the fair's first year, Judge Behrens has his vehicle decorated with a harvest theme.

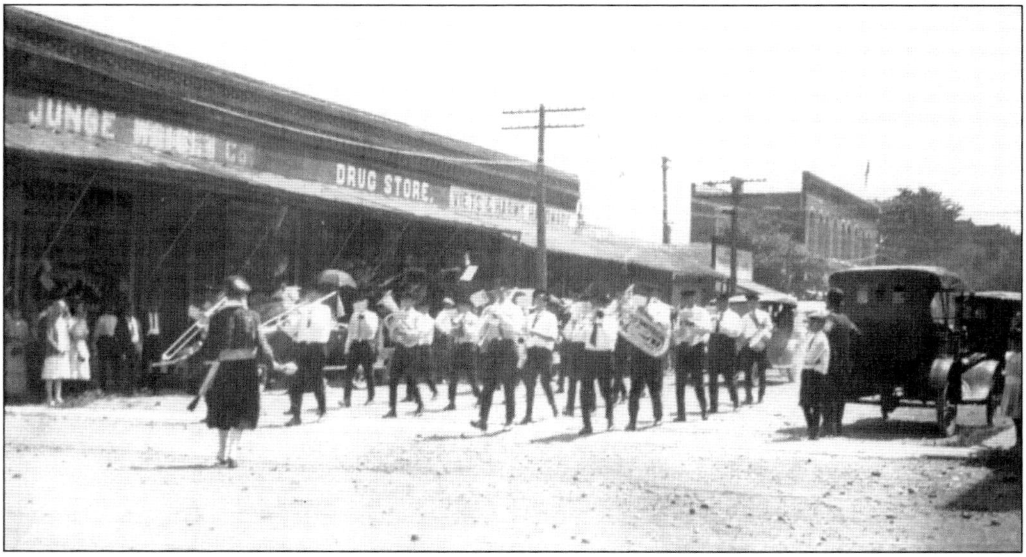

The Cole Camp Band is shown on East Second Street during the 1916 Cole Camp Fair parade.

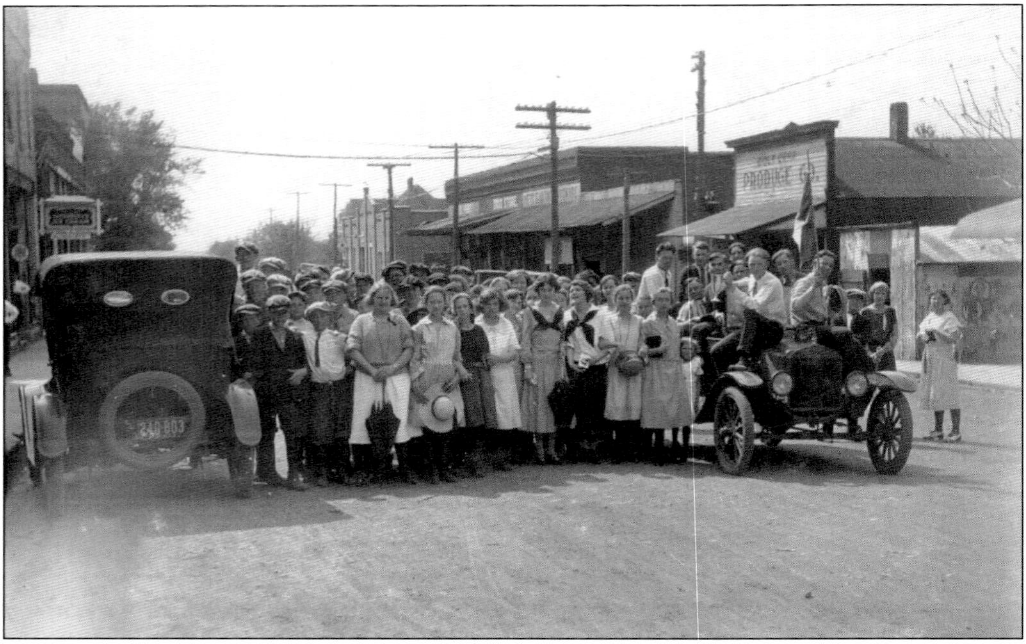

The license plates on this old Ford are from the Depression year of 1933. These young people are preparing for another parade on East Second Street.

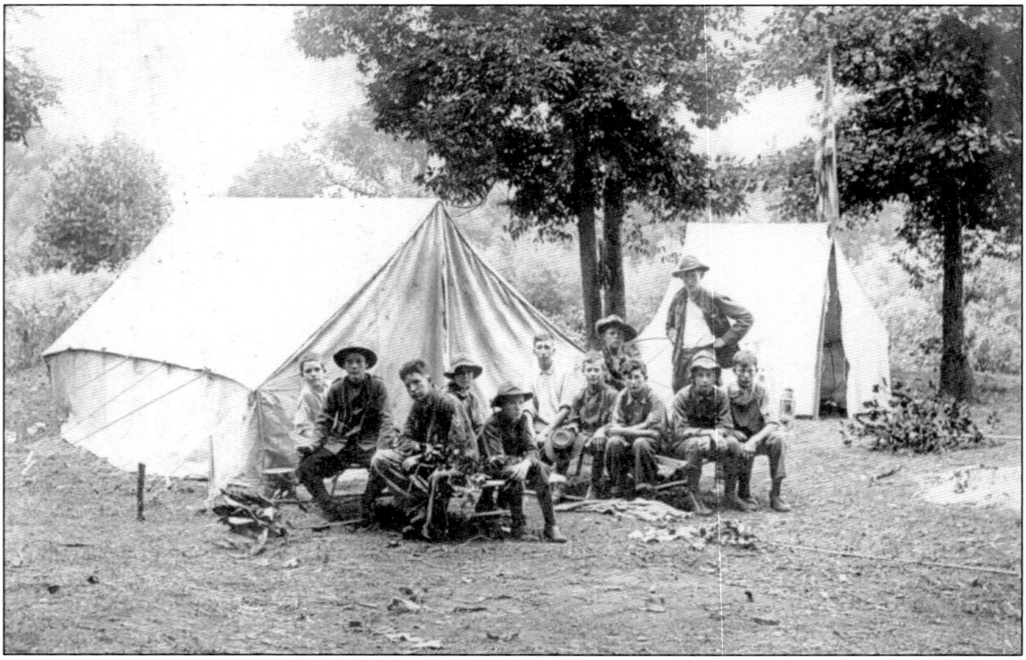

Three years after the formation of the Boy Scouts of America, Cole Camp had formed a troop of boys, pictured here camping out on Cole Camp Creek in 1913.

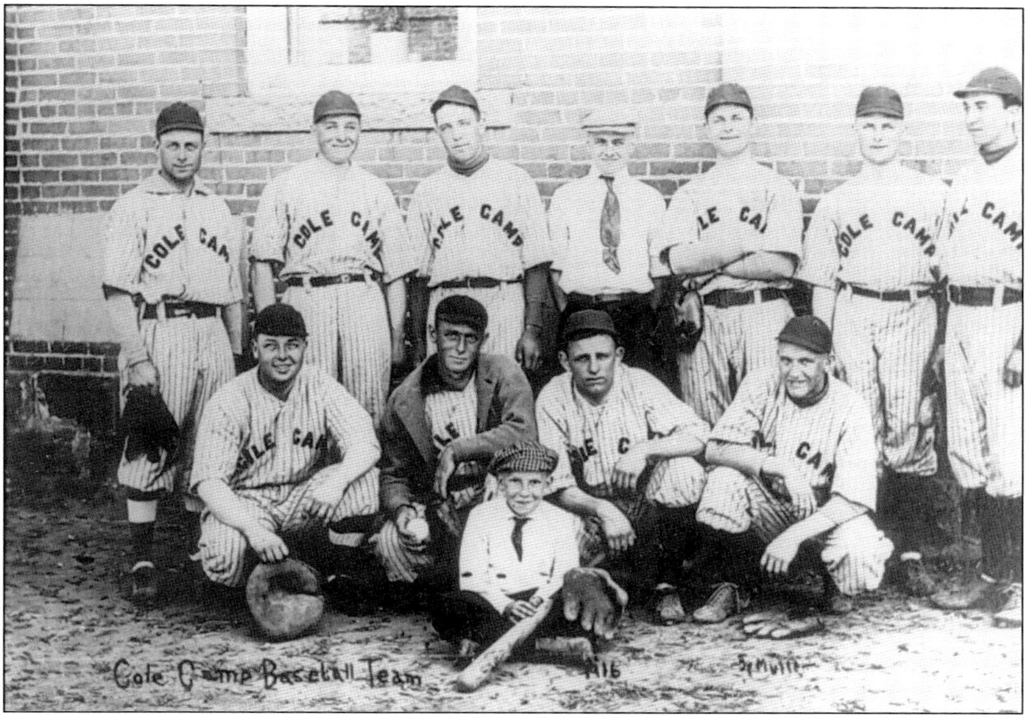

The 1916 Cole Camp baseball team provided entertainment for, and pride to, the city.

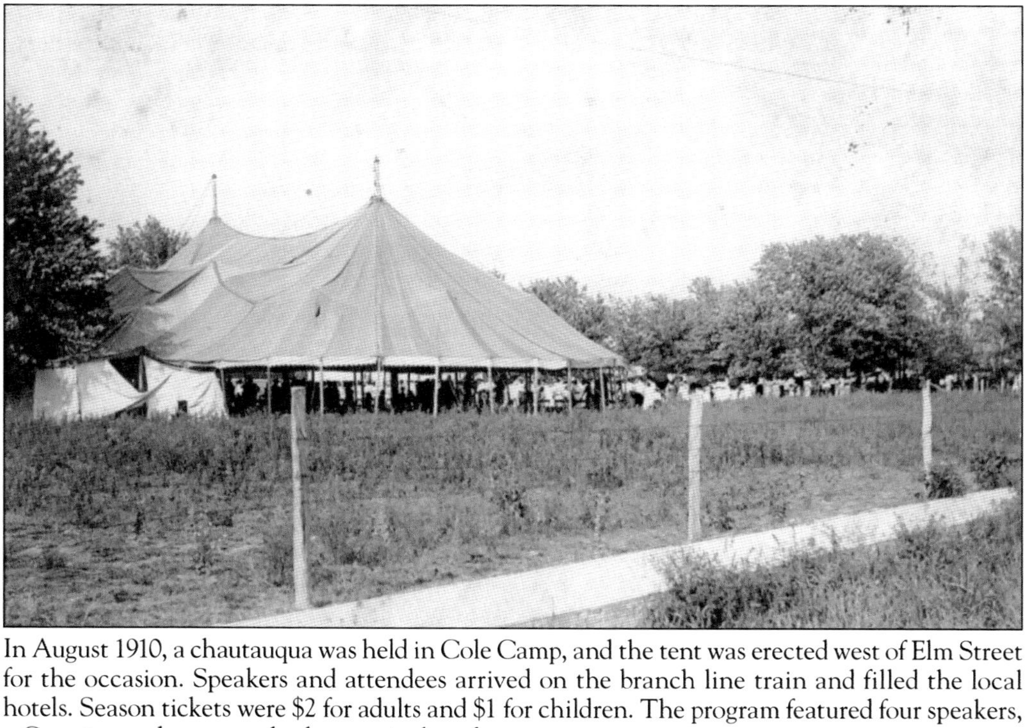

In August 1910, a chautauqua was held in Cole Camp, and the tent was erected west of Elm Street for the occasion. Speakers and attendees arrived on the branch line train and filled the local hotels. Season tickets were $2 for adults and $1 for children. The program featured four speakers, a Croatian orchestra, and other musical performers.

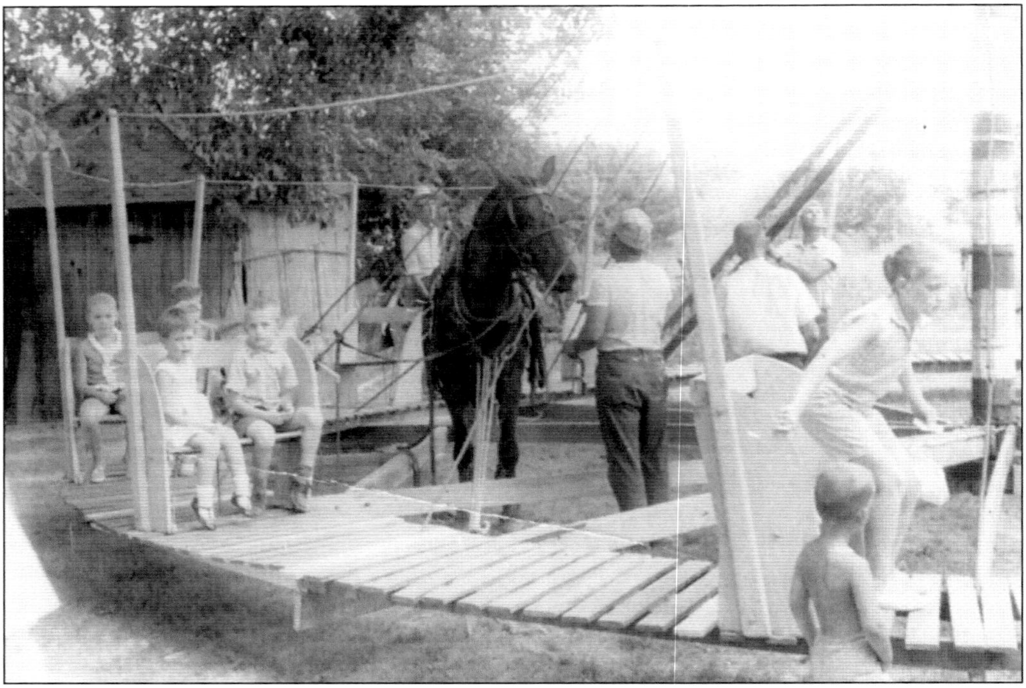

Ionia also once held a fair in the fall, and seen here is a one horsepower merry-go-round entertaining youths in the 1960s. The ride was built in 1889 by Bill Kreheier of Reistatt, Missouri. Kreheier attended the 1889 Worlds Fair in Paris, France, and was impressed with a large horsepower merry-go-round. When he returned to his hometown, he built a smaller version. After years of use, it was sold at public auction and eventually acquired by the Ionia Chamber of Commerce for $400 in 1961. It was in use until 1970, when it was sold to a town in northern Missouri. (Photograph by Harold Steffens.)

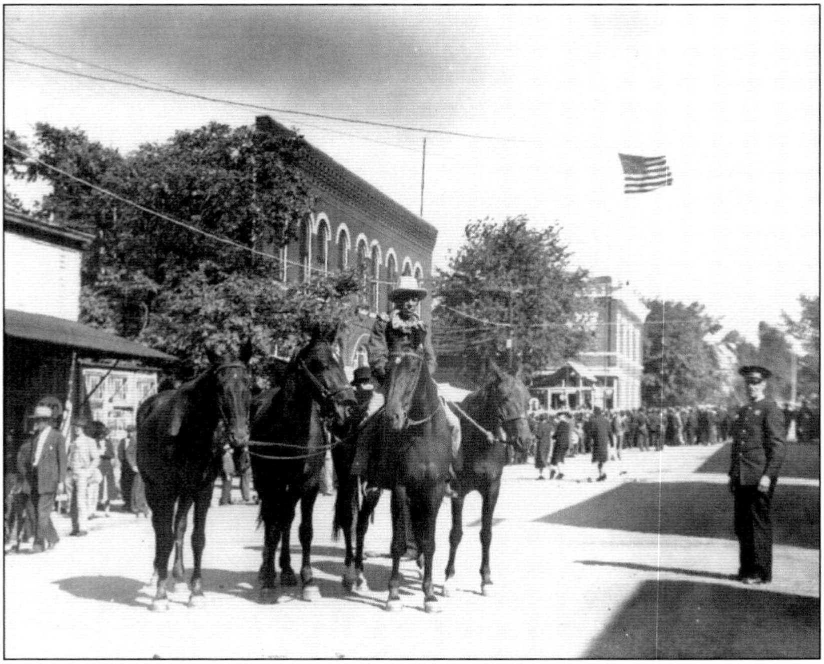

In the Cole Camp centennial year of 1939, one of the events was a reenactment of the pony express relay. A.D. Intelmann readies his horses for the route between Cole Camp and Lincoln.

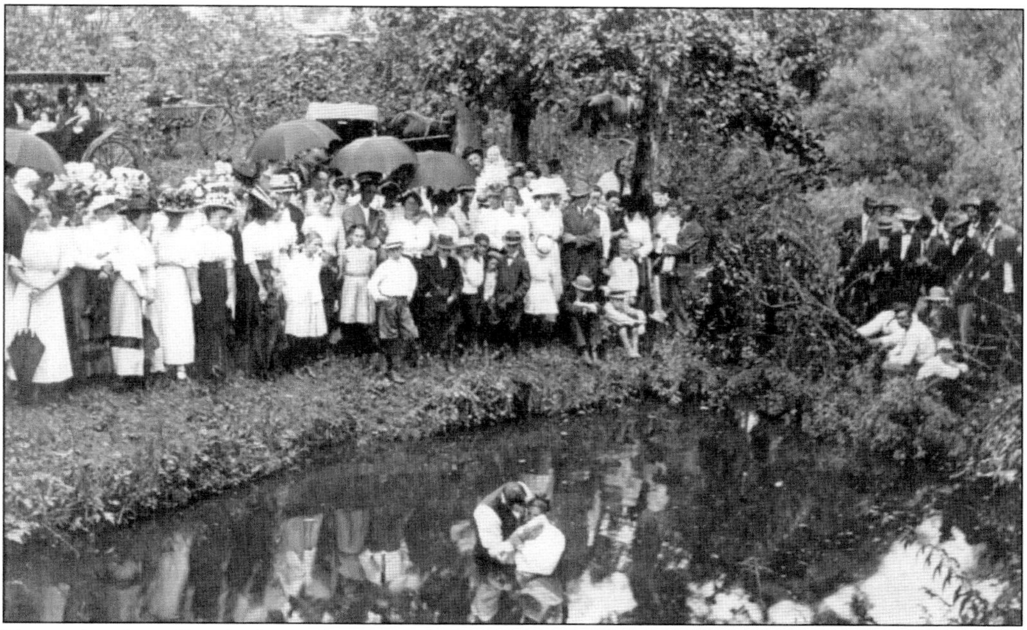

Dressed in their Sunday best, these members of the Seventh Day Adventist Church of Cole Camp are witnessing a baptism on the banks of Williams Creek in 1909.

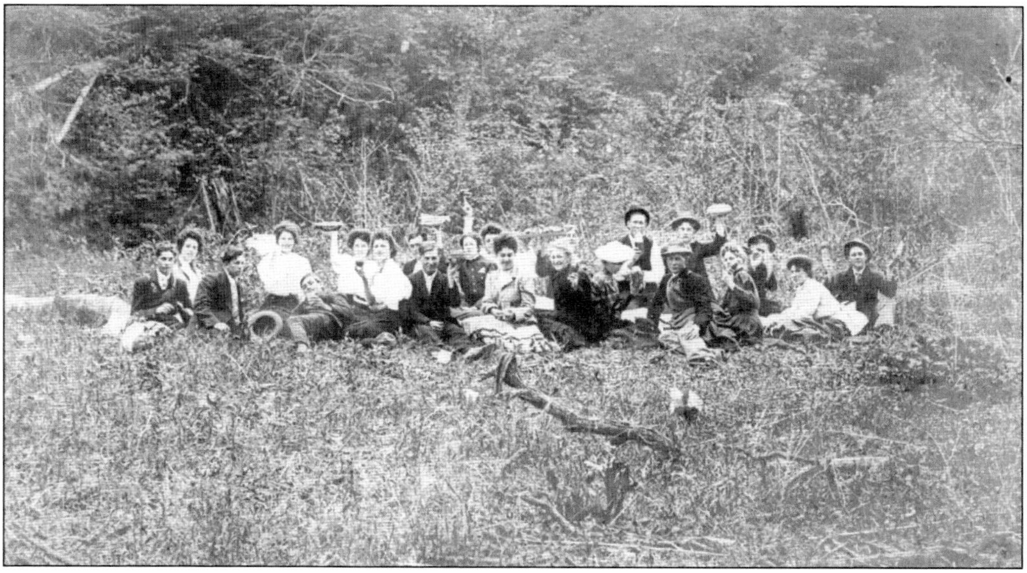

This group of young people is on a picnic along Cole Camp Creek in 1915. Homemade pies are being lifted for the benefit of the photographer.

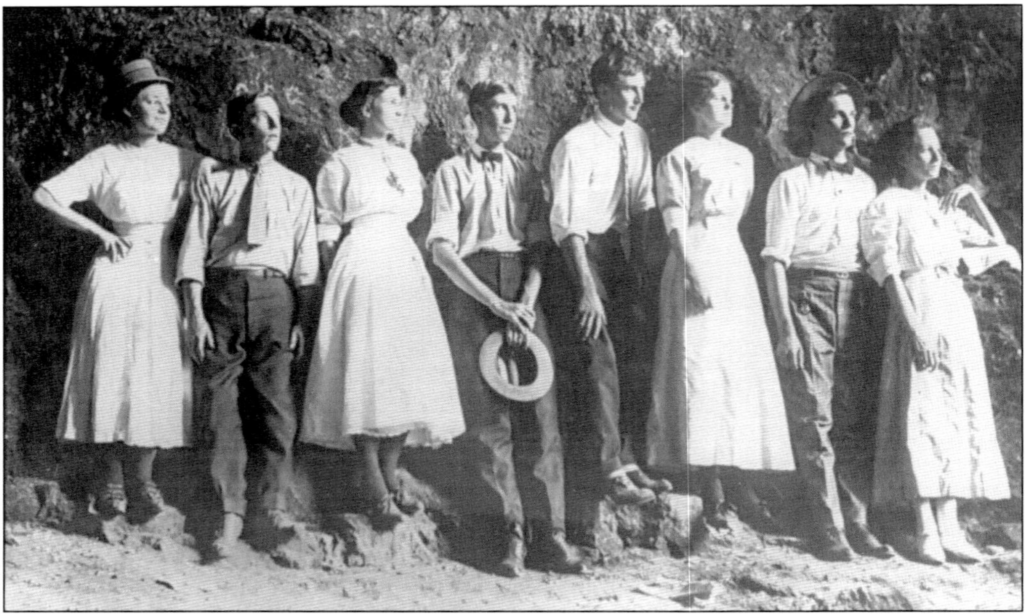

Another favorite picnic spot was the Cole Camp Cave on the namesake creek. This photograph was taken of a group of explorers inside the cave in 1915.

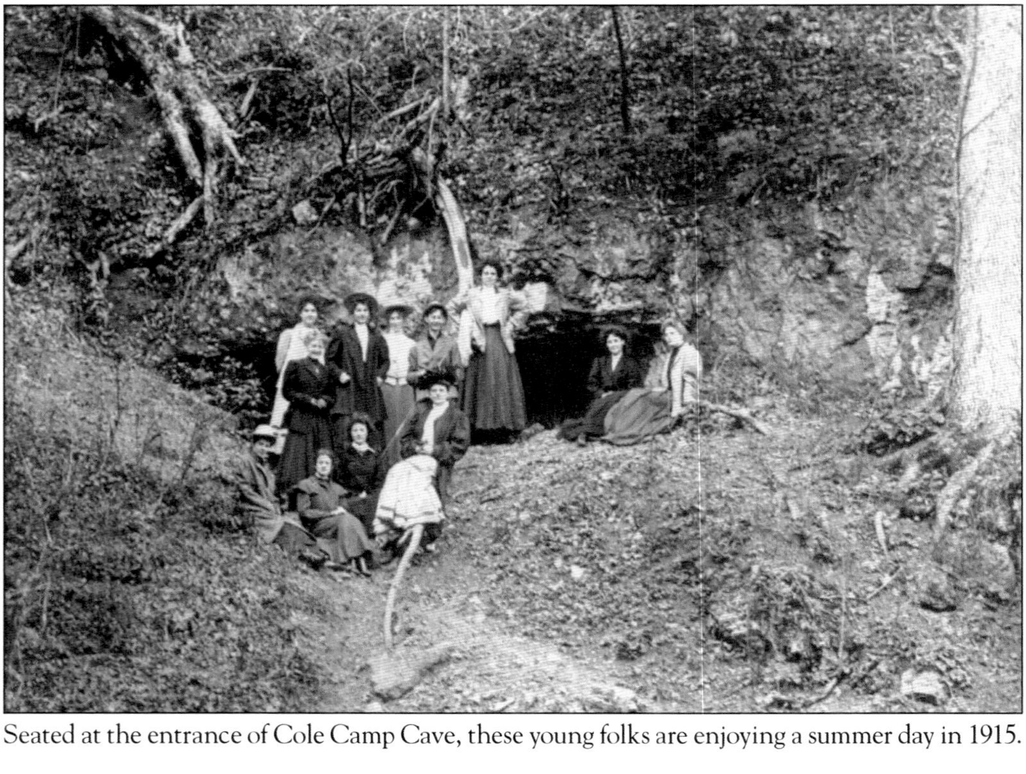

Seated at the entrance of Cole Camp Cave, these young folks are enjoying a summer day in 1915.

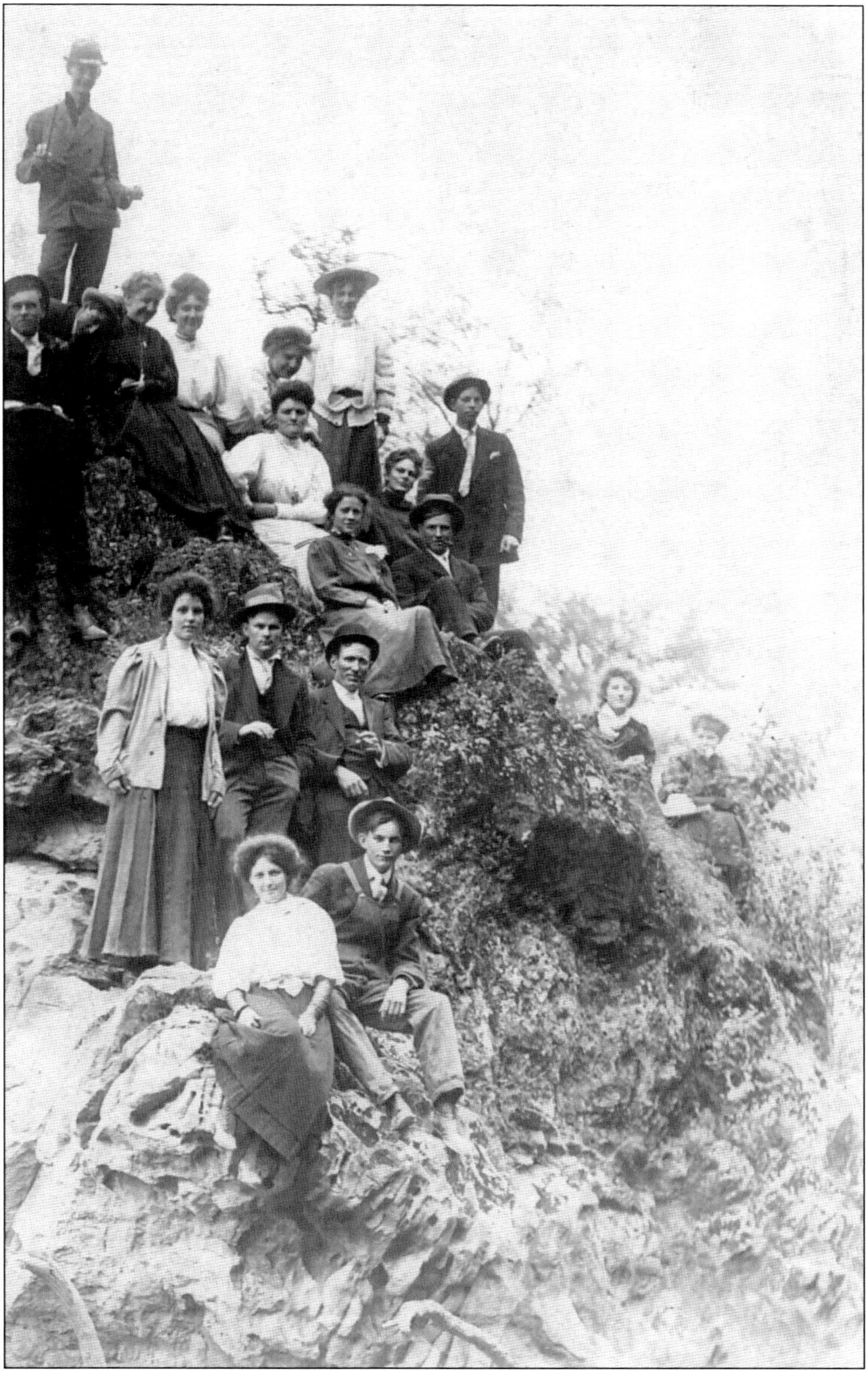

This unusual rock formation, named Haystack Rock, is near Cole Camp Cave and has always been a source of curiosity to visitors, as these young people demonstrate in 1915.

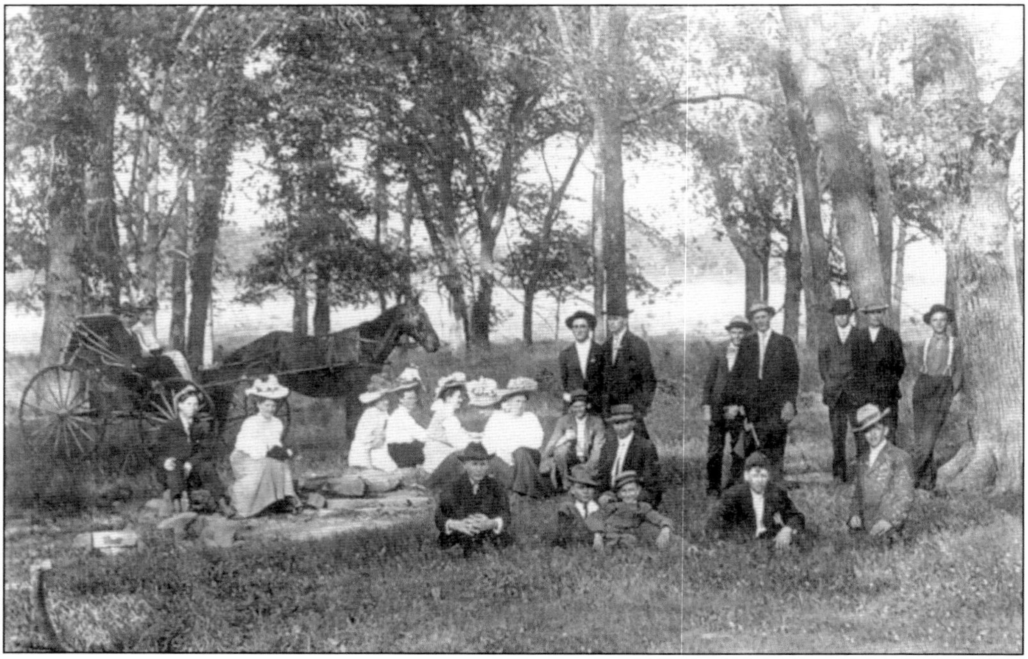

On a Sunday afternoon in 1910, a picnic is enjoyed at Walnut Grove, east of Cole Camp.

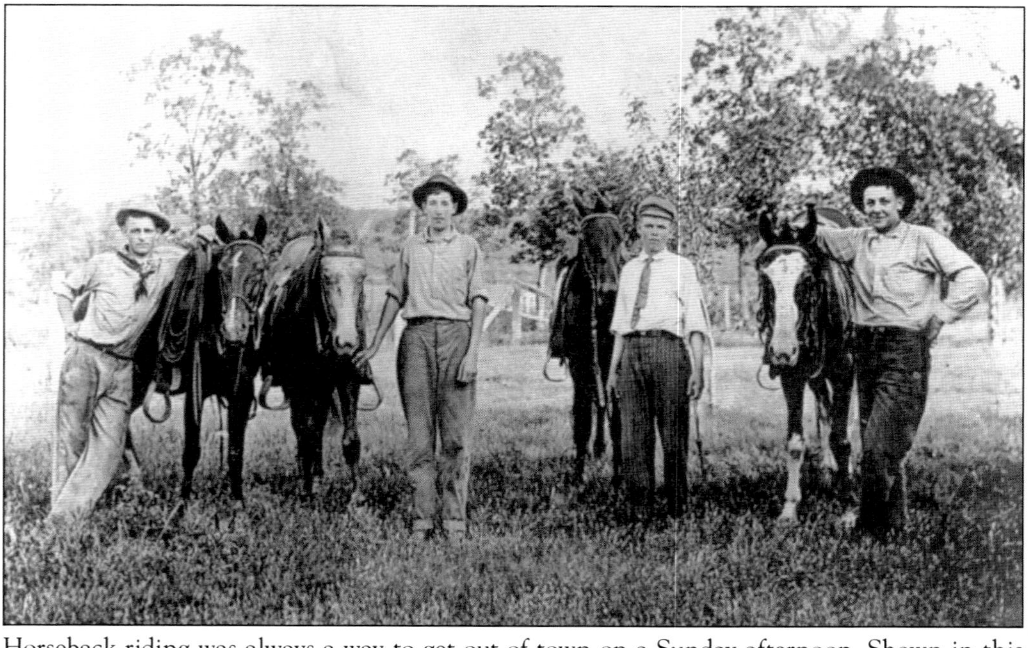

Horseback riding was always a way to get out of town on a Sunday afternoon. Shown in this 1920s photograph are, from left to right, Walter Weymuth, Ralph Schwald, Truman Shaw, and Bish Eickhoff and his horse Orphan. All the boys were from Cole Camp.

James Garrison (left) and Jake Weymuth display the results of a 1917 Sunday fishing expedition on the Osage River south of the Cole Camp area. The area derives much of it economic activity from the sports of fishing, boating, and hunting in and along the Osage River portion of Missouri's Lake-of-the Ozarks.

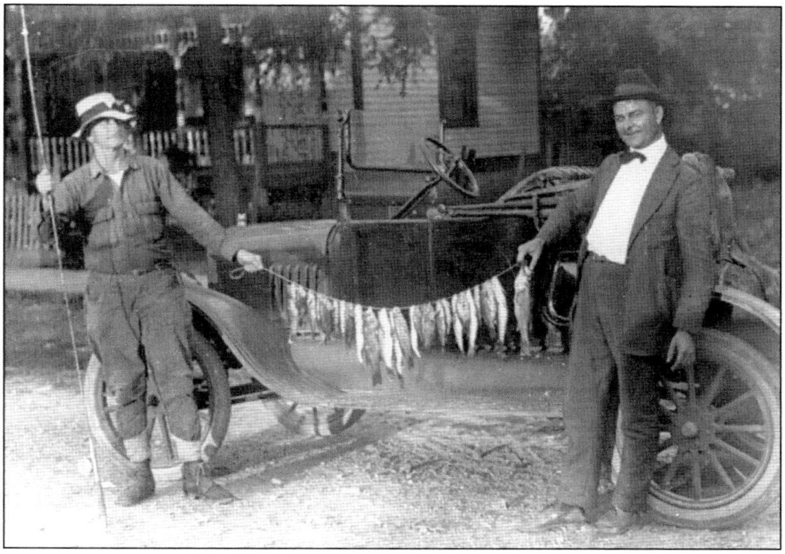

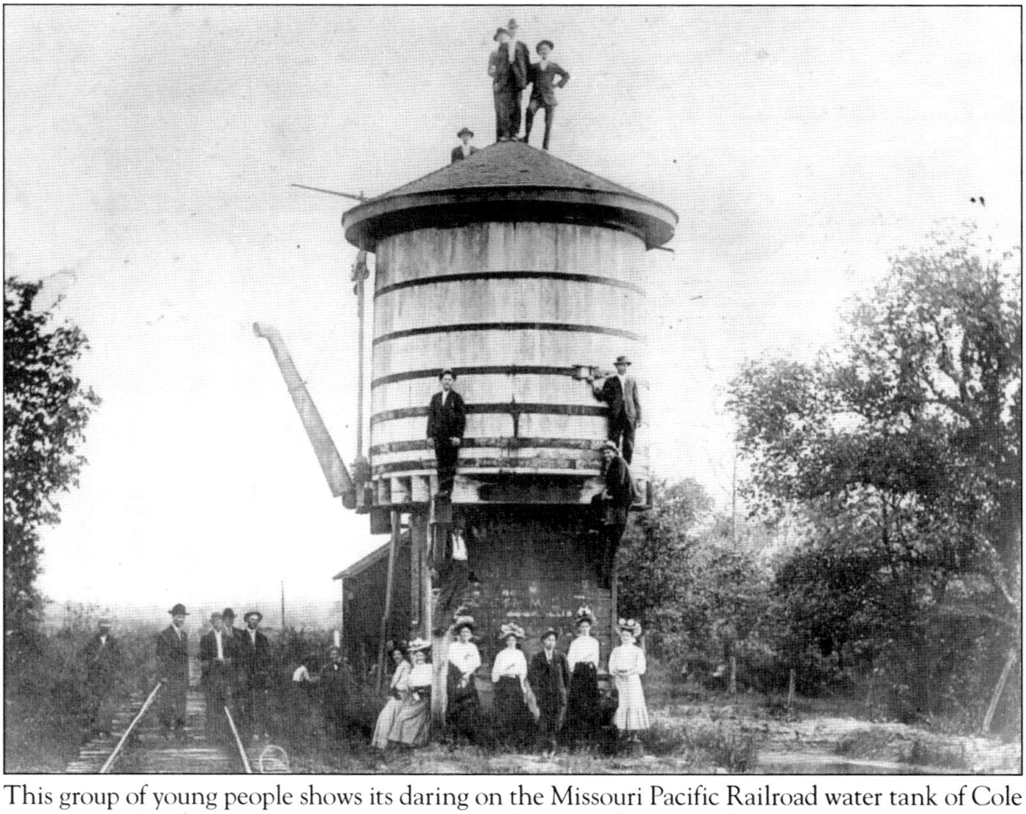

This group of young people shows its daring on the Missouri Pacific Railroad water tank of Cole Camp in 1917. The image was shot looking south, one mile west of Cole Camp.

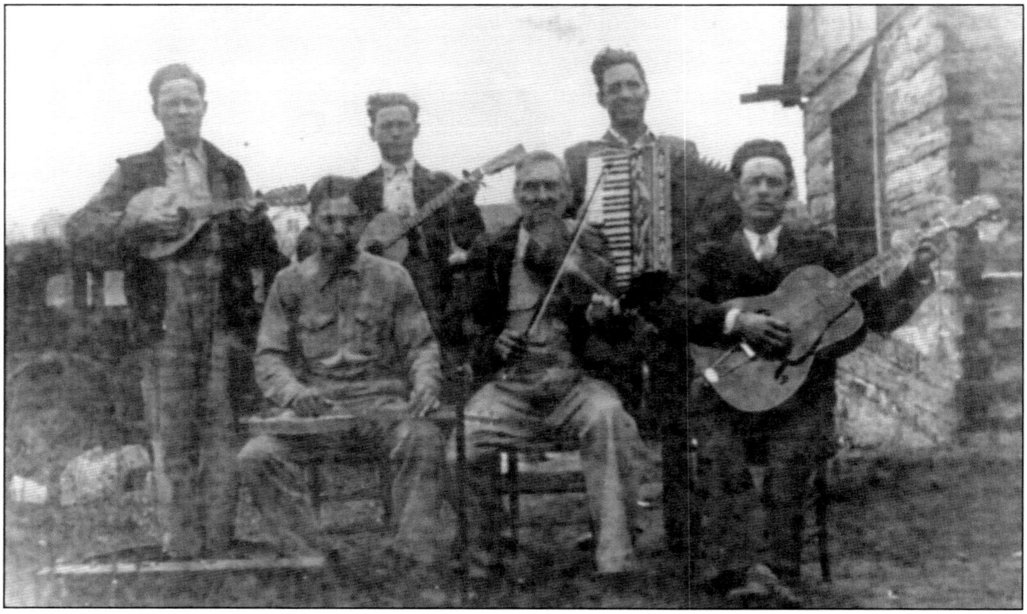

These unidentified musicians from the Cole Camp area were typical of the local musicians who provided entertainment for family gatherings, church meetings, and other events. Judging from the instruments employed, this was a well-rounded group. The photograph is from 1900.

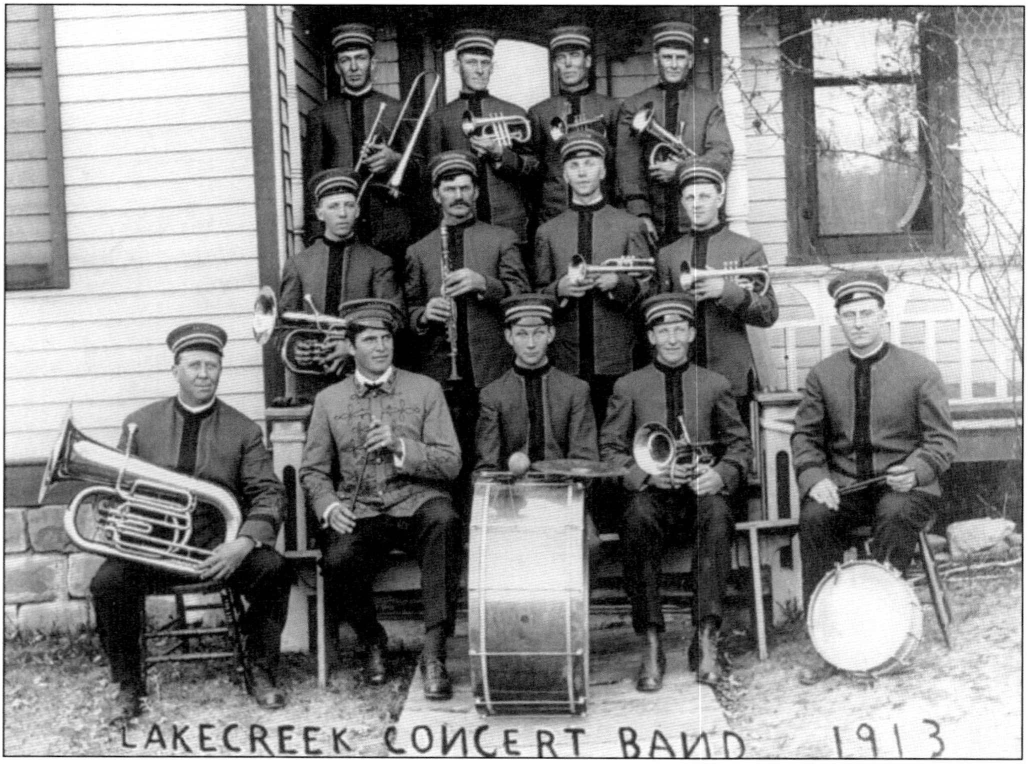

Lake Creek was a small community four miles northeast of Cole Camp and anchored by Holy Cross Lutheran Church. This band formed in 1912 and performed until 1922, when many of the musicians joined the Cole Camp Band or others in the area.

Eight

FARM LIFE

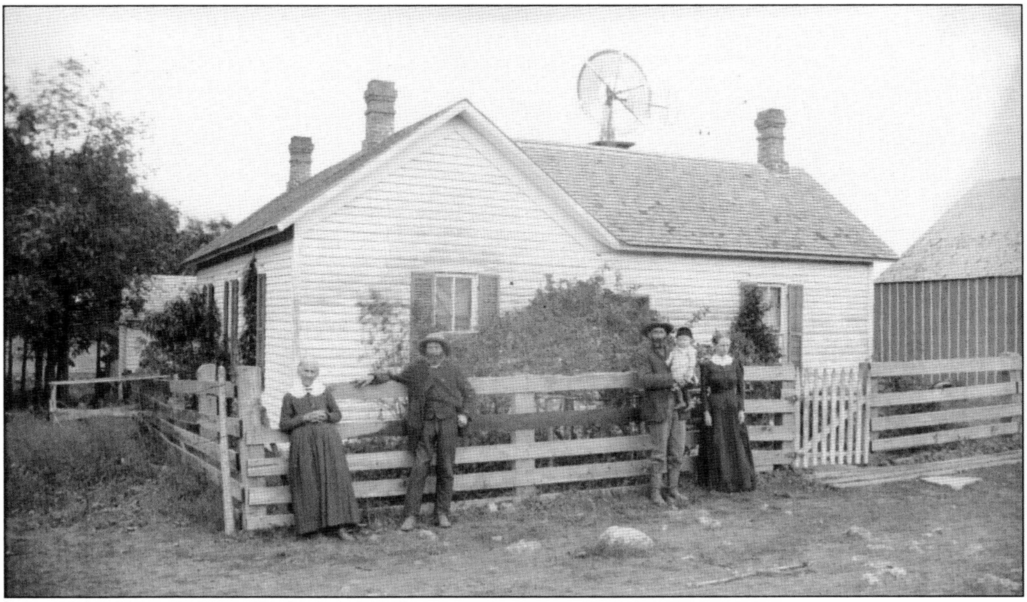

While shopkeepers were abundant in the Cole Camp area, those who pursued agriculture were the backbone of the local economy. Early German pioneers were quick to break the rich soil of the northern Benton and Southern Pettis County prairies, and the legacy of their efforts remains on the many area farms that still bear the original family names. The Merkel family stands for the photographer in the early 1900s. The camera has caught the whirling blades of the hardworking windmill.

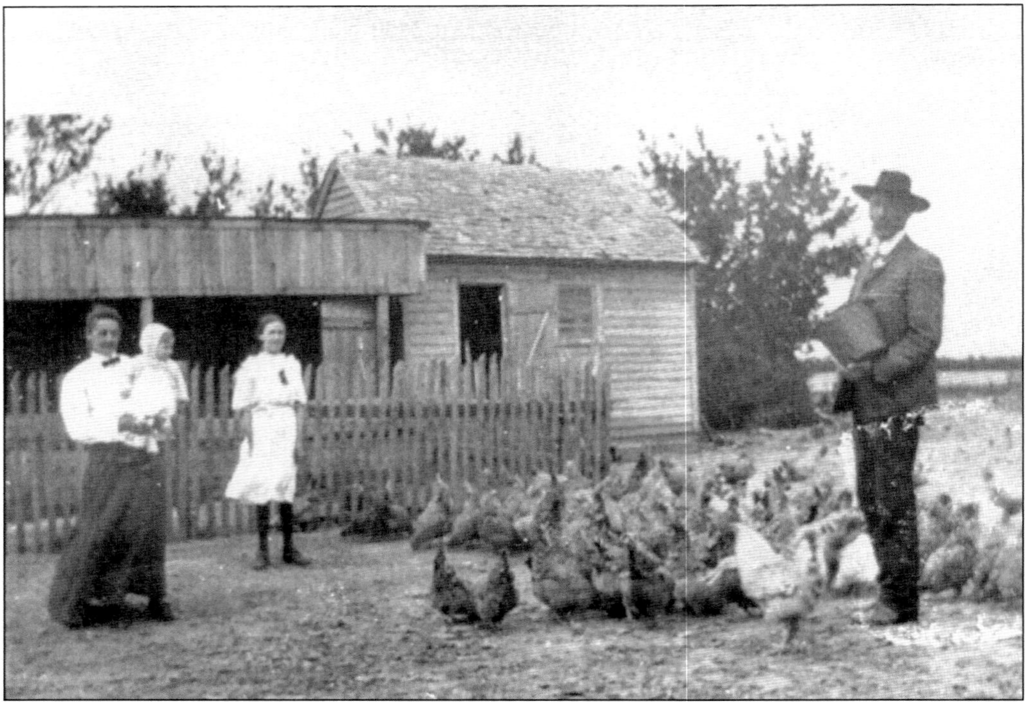

An unidentified family watches as the well-attired father attends to feeding the chickens on a 19th-century Cole Camp area farmstead.

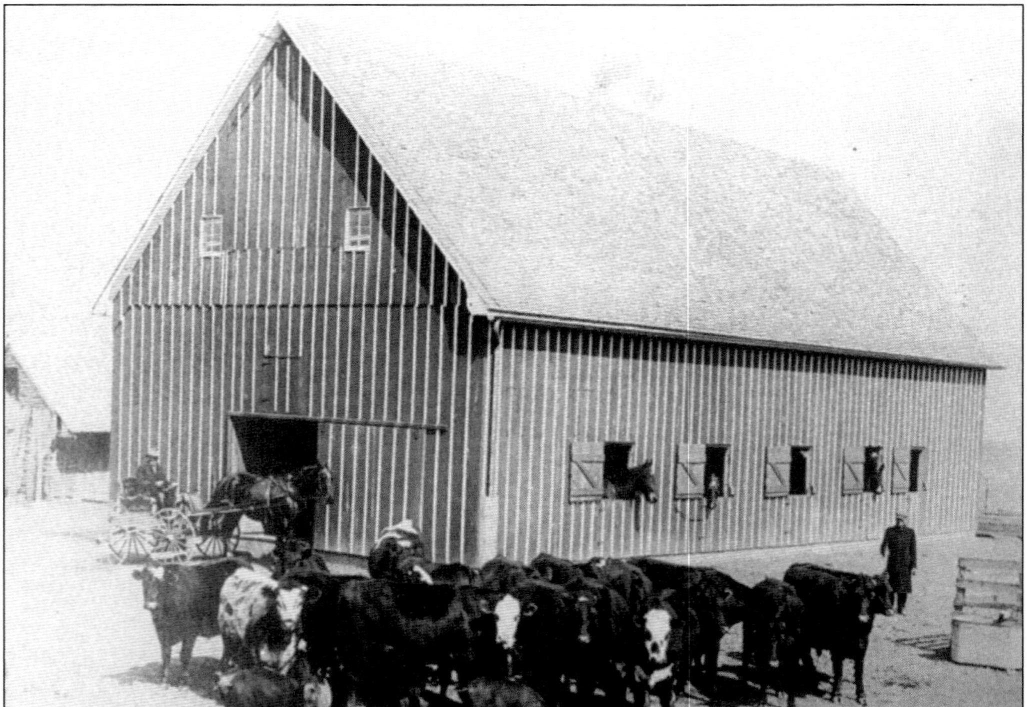

David T. Holtzen, in his buggy, is visiting the Herman Schnakenberg farm to buy cattle for his northern Benton County farm. The Holtzen family still farms the same ground.

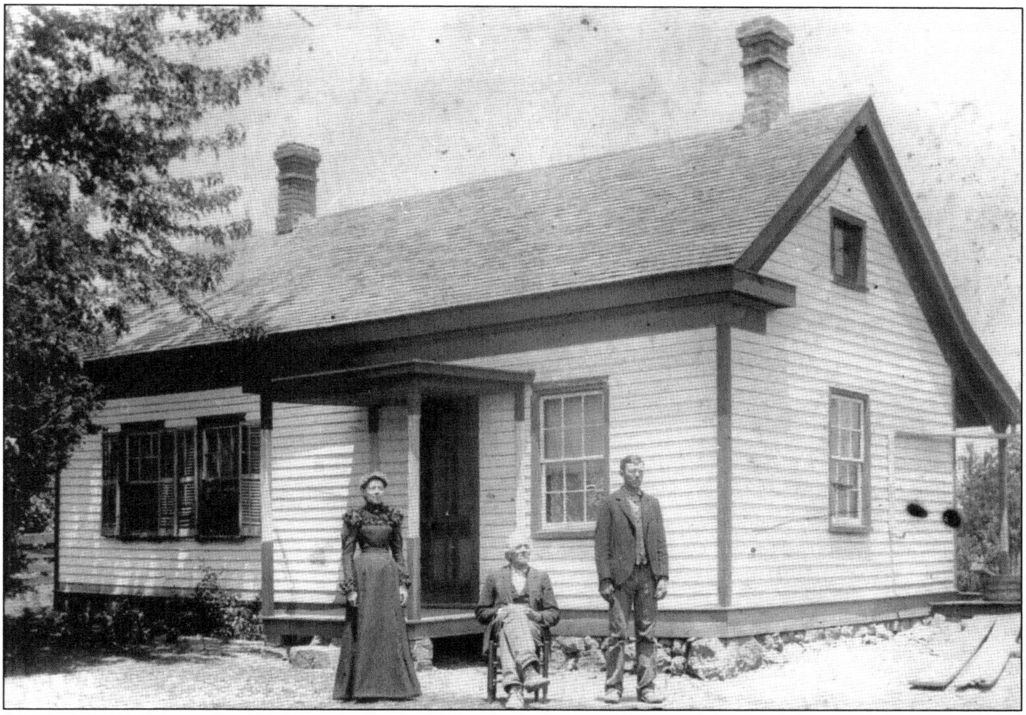

John C. Bockelman (center) emigrated from Germany and purchased 40 acres north of Cole Camp in 1859. He married Margaretta Bahrenberg, and they had seven sons and two daughters.

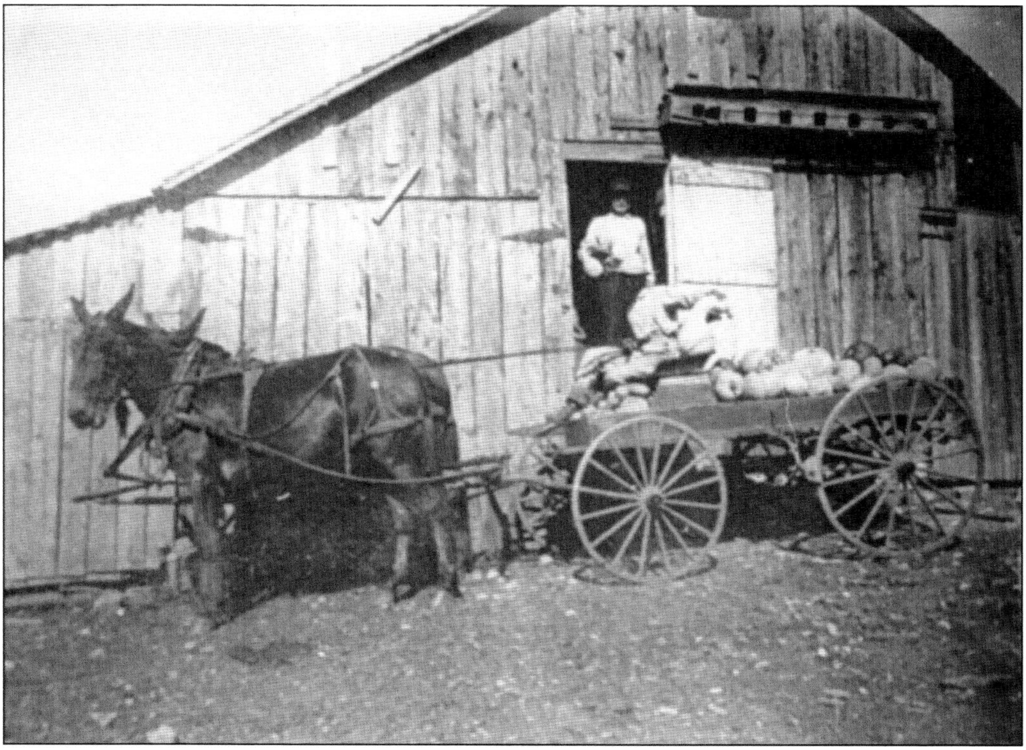

A wagon full of pumpkins is being stored for both food and feed in the Fowler farm barn in 1907.

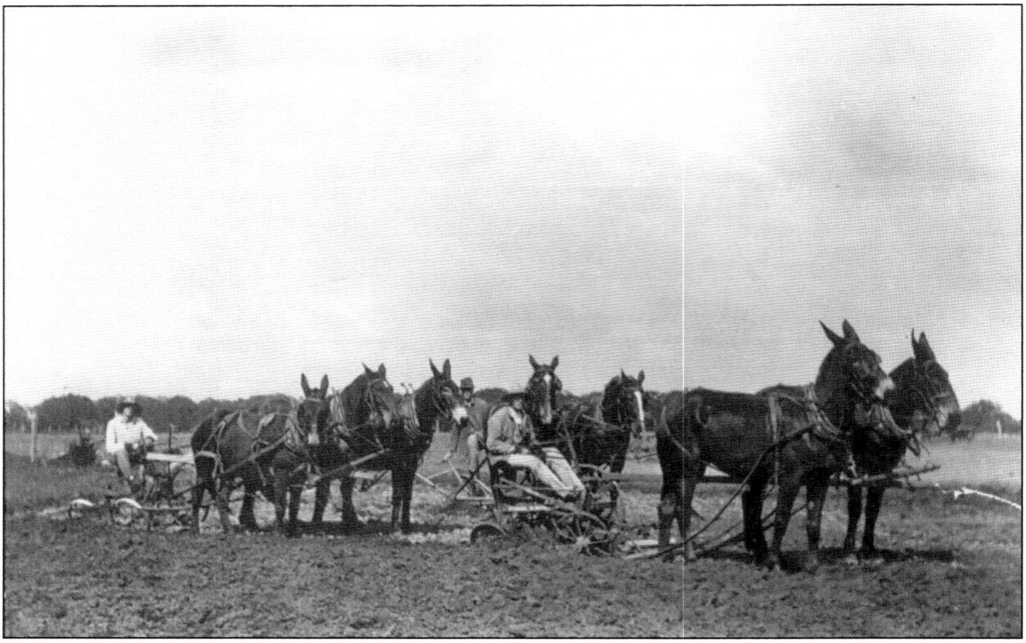

Spring plowing has two teams in tandem on the David Holtzen farm in the early days of the 20th century. David Holtzen has the rear team, while Paul Holtzen drives the first.

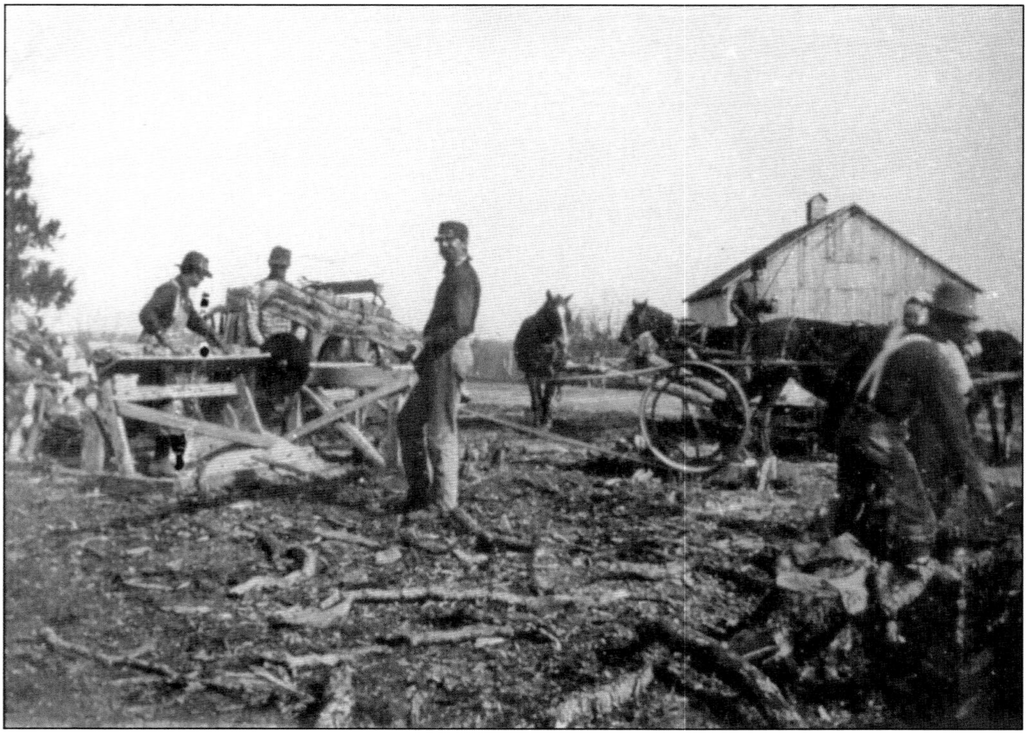

Four horses are being employed in operating this field sawmill on the Fowler farm. Fence posts and firewood are being produced.

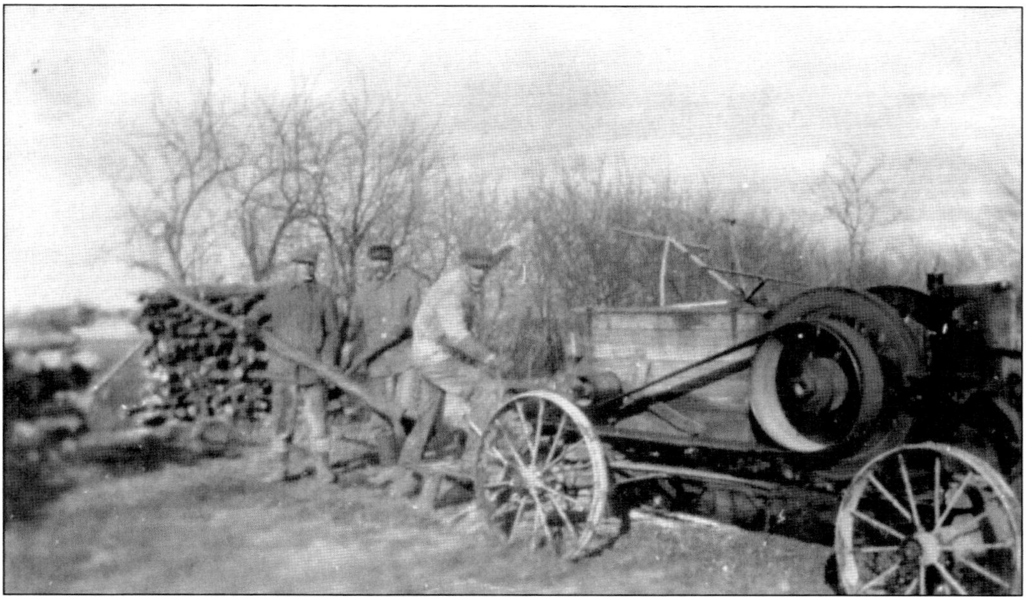

The introduction of the single-cylinder gasoline engine reduced the need for live horsepower. Here, a gasoline-powered rig is being used to sharpen fence posts.

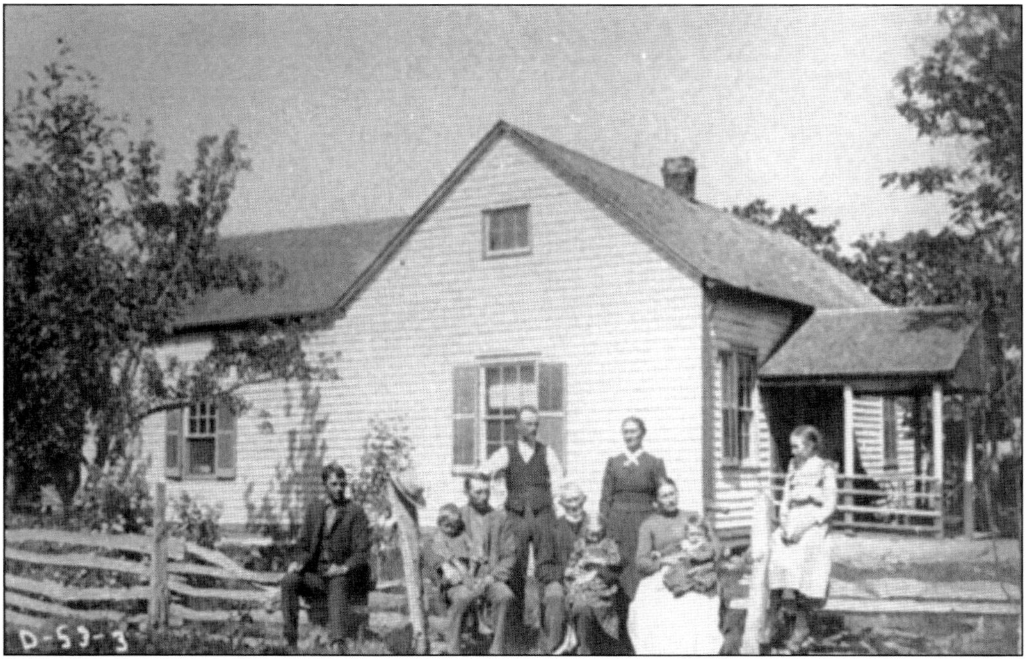

Members of the Herman Schnakenberg family pose outside of their 1870 farmhouse. In this image are, from left to right, (seated) Conrad, Herman (holding Ernest), Cord (holding Hulda), Catherine (holding Martha), and Minne; (standing) Henry and Margaret. They were typical of the German families that settled the Cole Camp area in the 1800s.

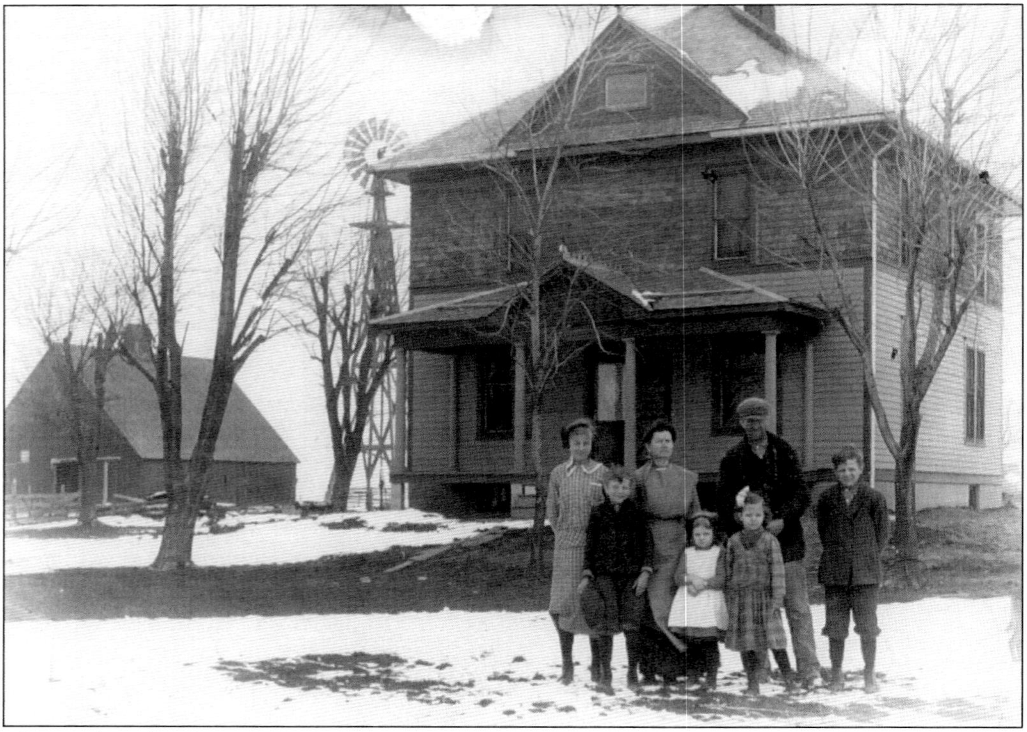

The Hoslten family is pictured on their farm in the winter of 1913. The ample front porch, large barn, and sturdy windmill proclaim the prosperity of this family.

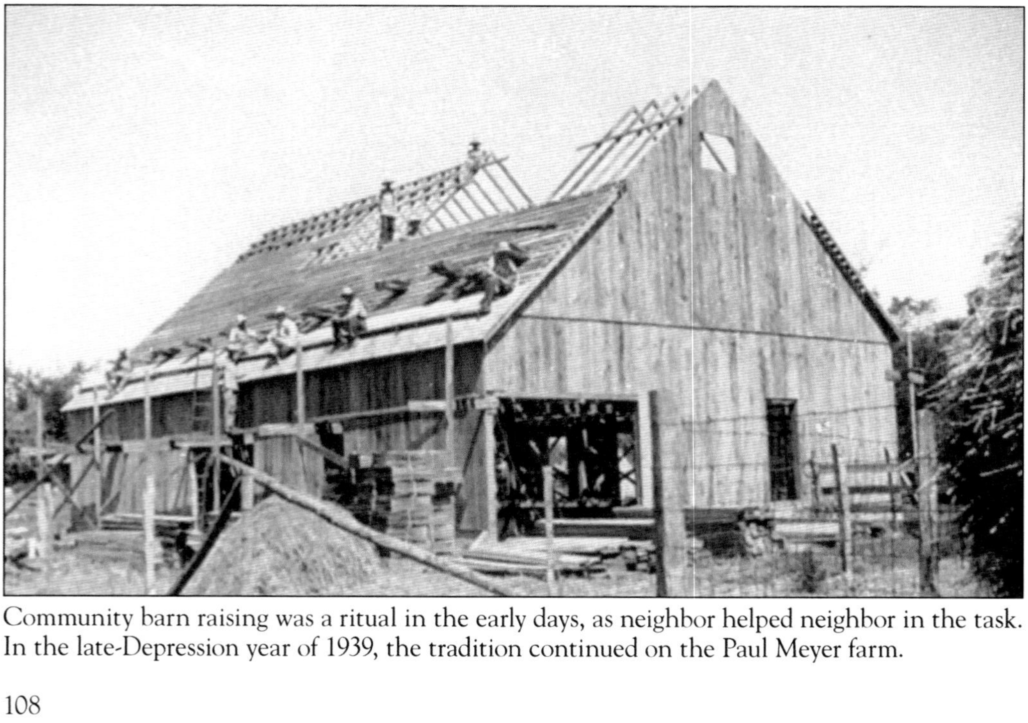

Community barn raising was a ritual in the early days, as neighbor helped neighbor in the task. In the late-Depression year of 1939, the tradition continued on the Paul Meyer farm.

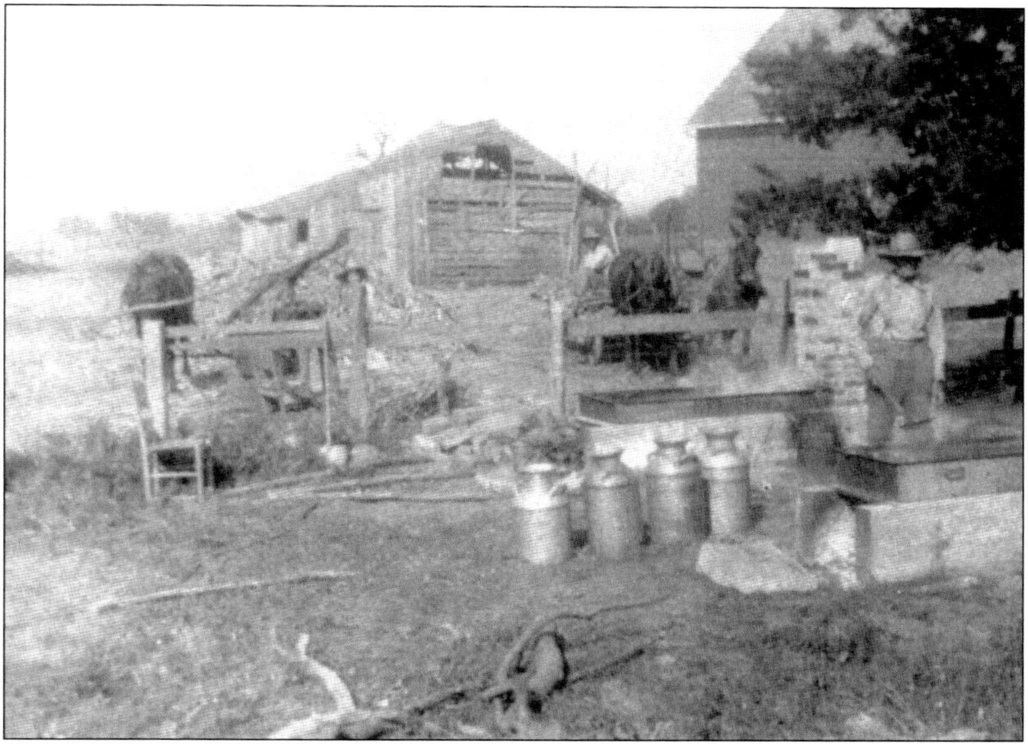

Herman Schnakenberg is making molasses, a valued product eaten by both animal and man alike. Poured on hot biscuits, molasses made a great breakfast treat.

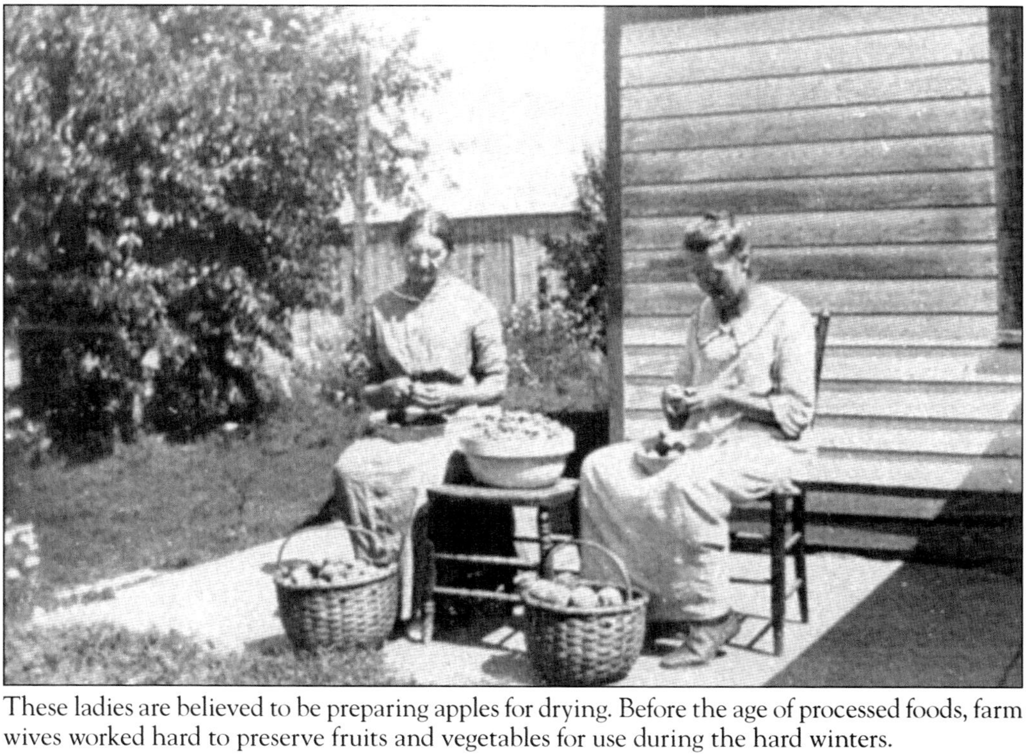

These ladies are believed to be preparing apples for drying. Before the age of processed foods, farm wives worked hard to preserve fruits and vegetables for use during the hard winters.

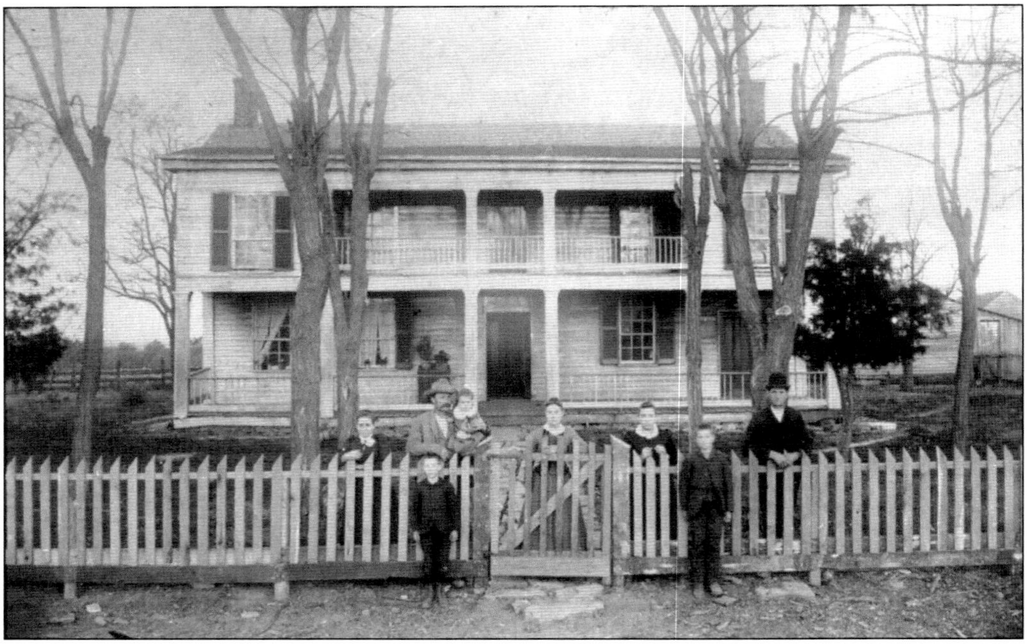

Built in the 1840s by Samuel Fowler, this farm home was located south on what is today Highway F, or Butterfield Road. The Henry C. Fowler family poses in front of their ancestral home.

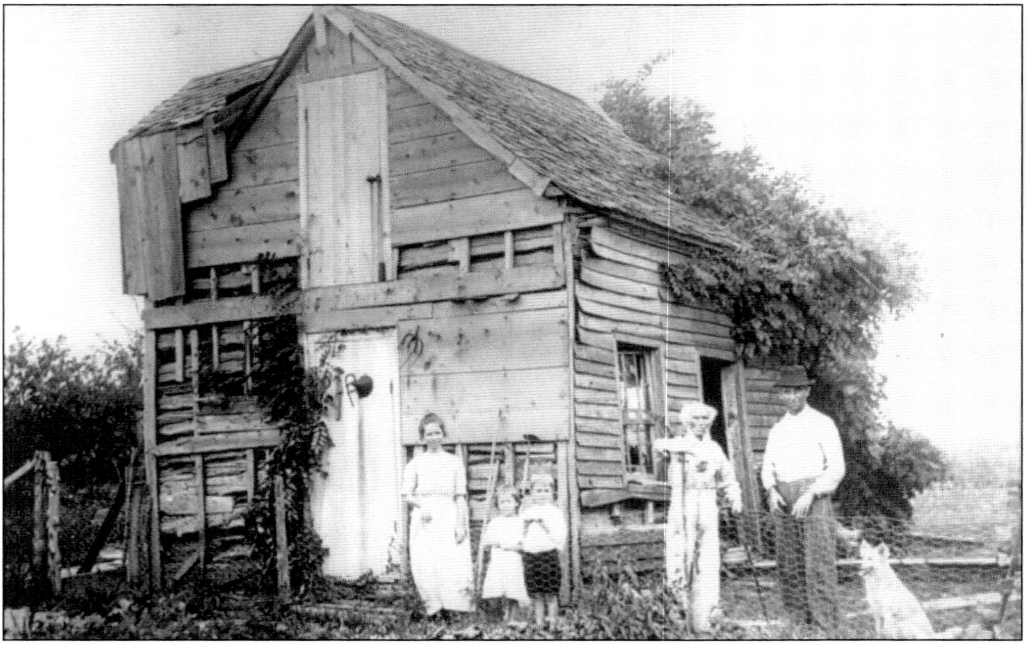

Those in this photograph are described only as the Anton Medek family near Cole Camp. Life was hard on the early farms, yet this family seems cheerful with their lot.

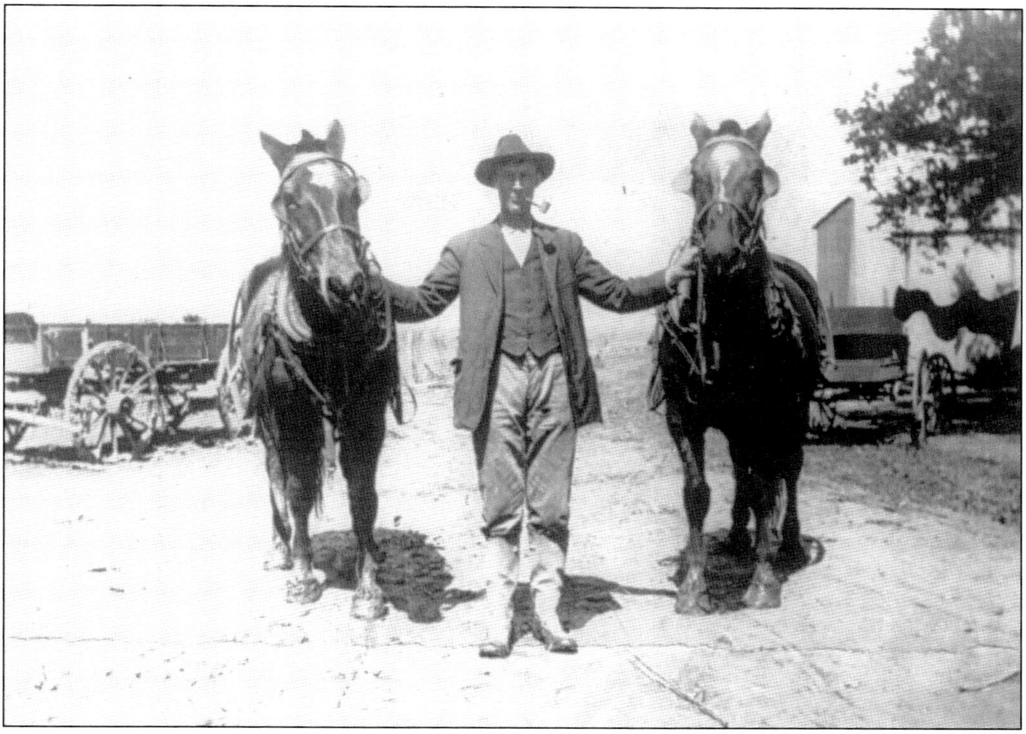

The horse was the most valued of livestock. Henry Stelling holds two of his prized steeds in this image.

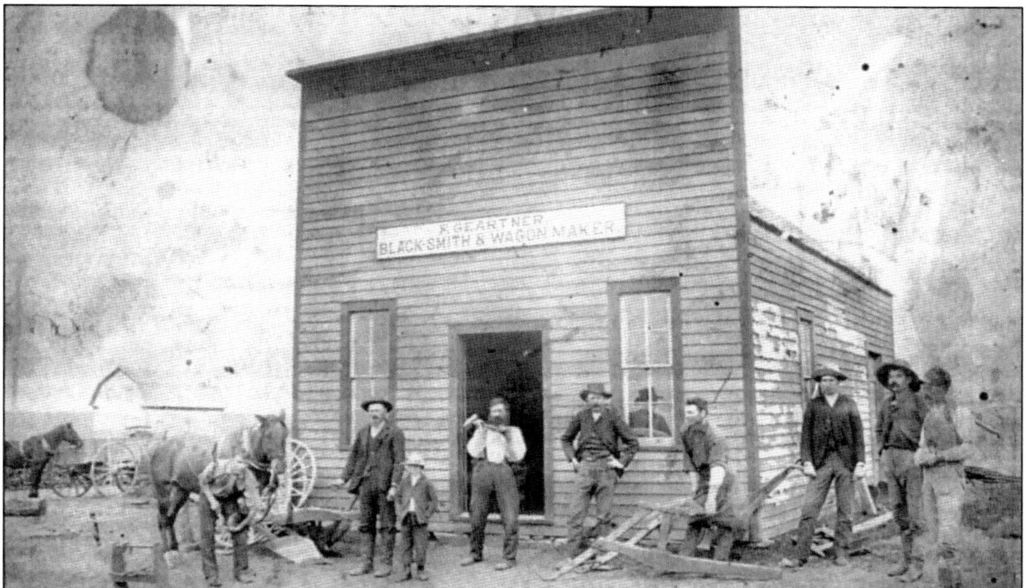

Horses need constant care to maintain their health and availability, and the rural blacksmith was a vital service to the community. Frank Geartner displays his hammer, while a worker shoes a horse and another repairs a plow in this 1902 image.

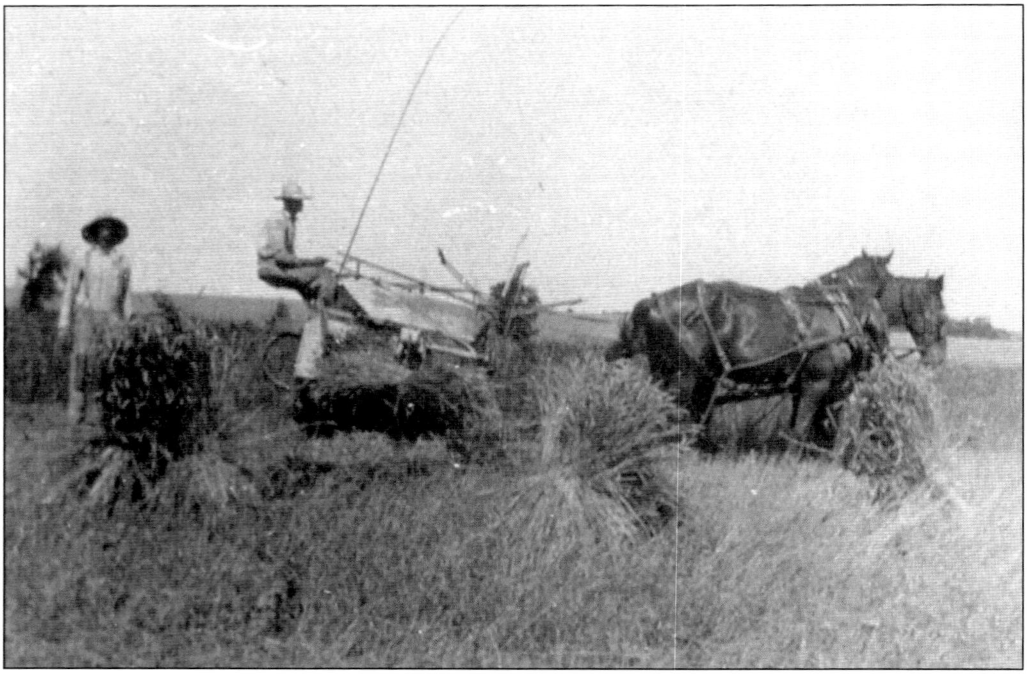

Wheat is cut on the Holtzen farm with a horse-drawn binder. Before the mechanization of farming, work was accomplished with animal and human power.

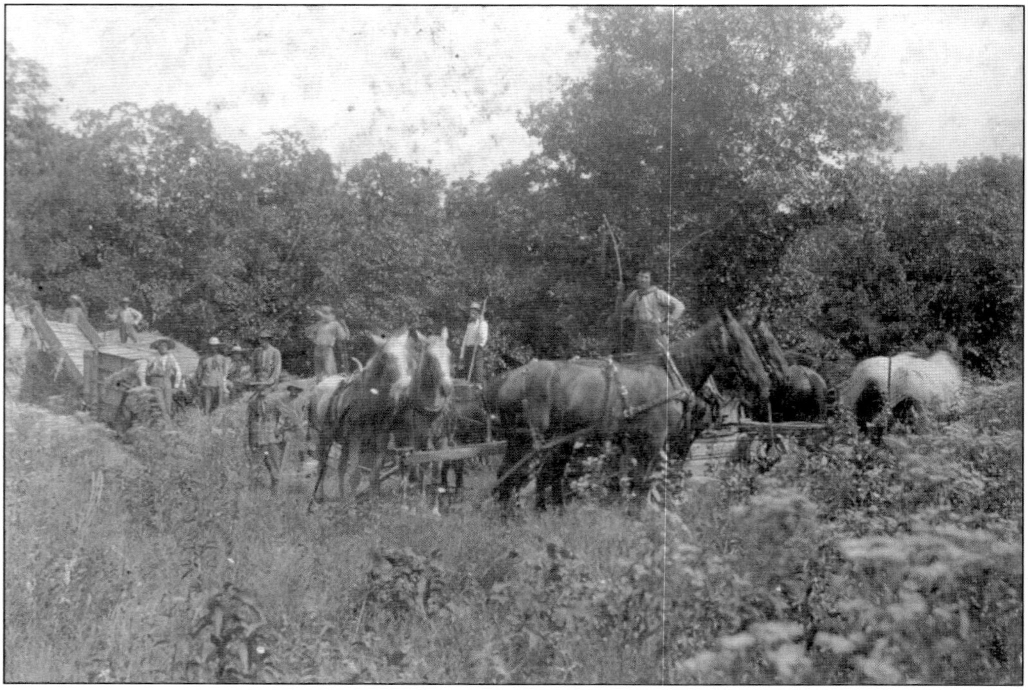

A horse-drawn thresher is pictured on the William Kreisler farm in 1910.

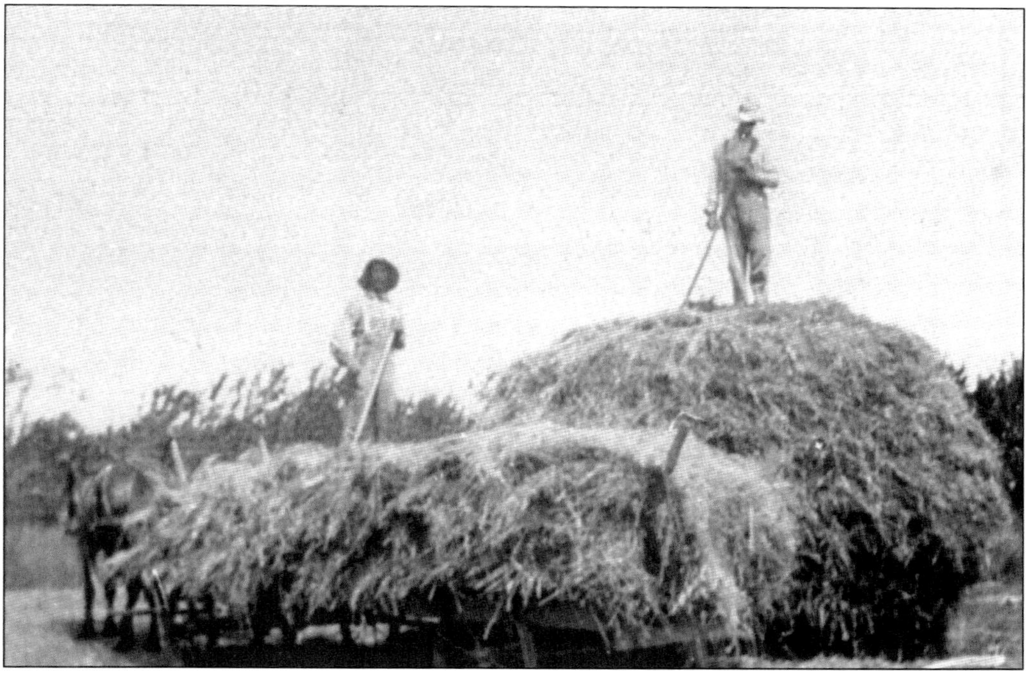
Cut bundles are being stacked for storage.

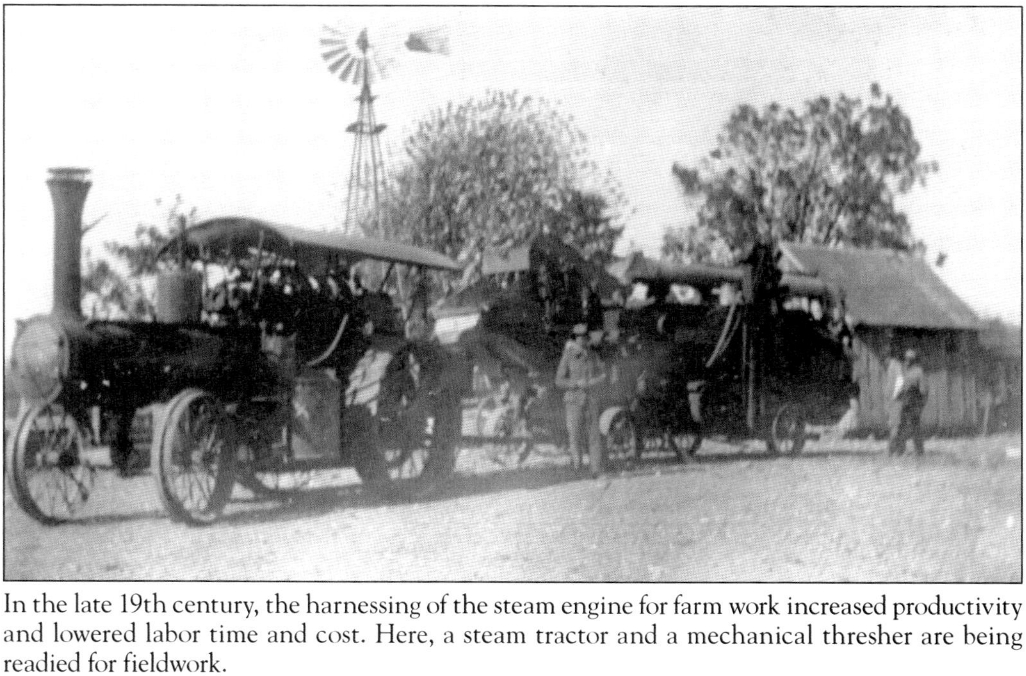
In the late 19th century, the harnessing of the steam engine for farm work increased productivity and lowered labor time and cost. Here, a steam tractor and a mechanical thresher are being readied for fieldwork.

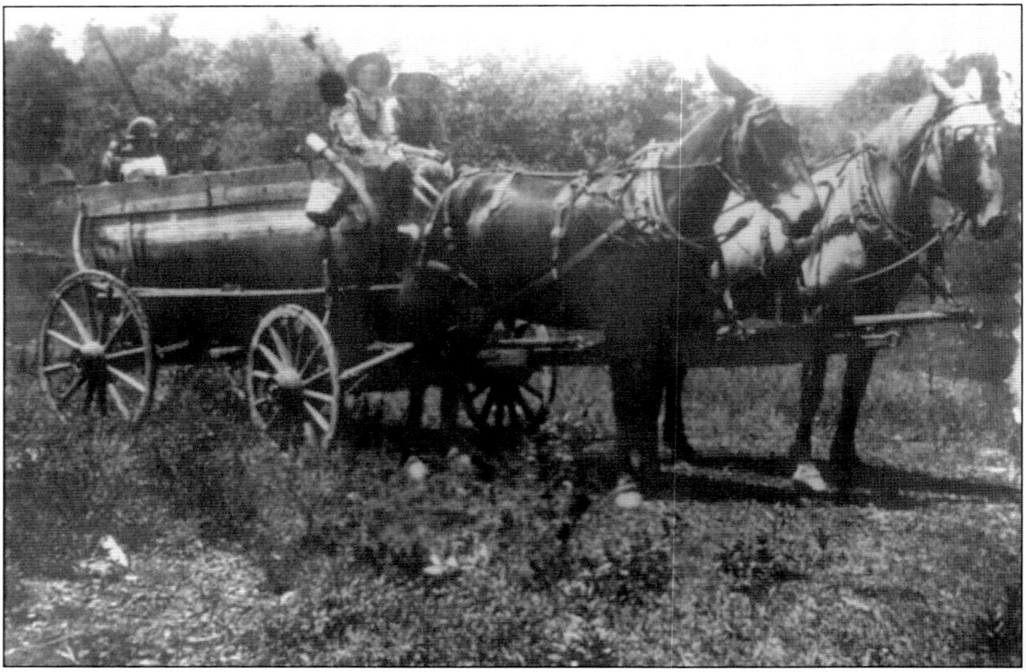

Like their railroad cousins, steam tractors needed a ready supply of water, and it was usually provided by a mule- or horse-drawn tanker, as pictured.

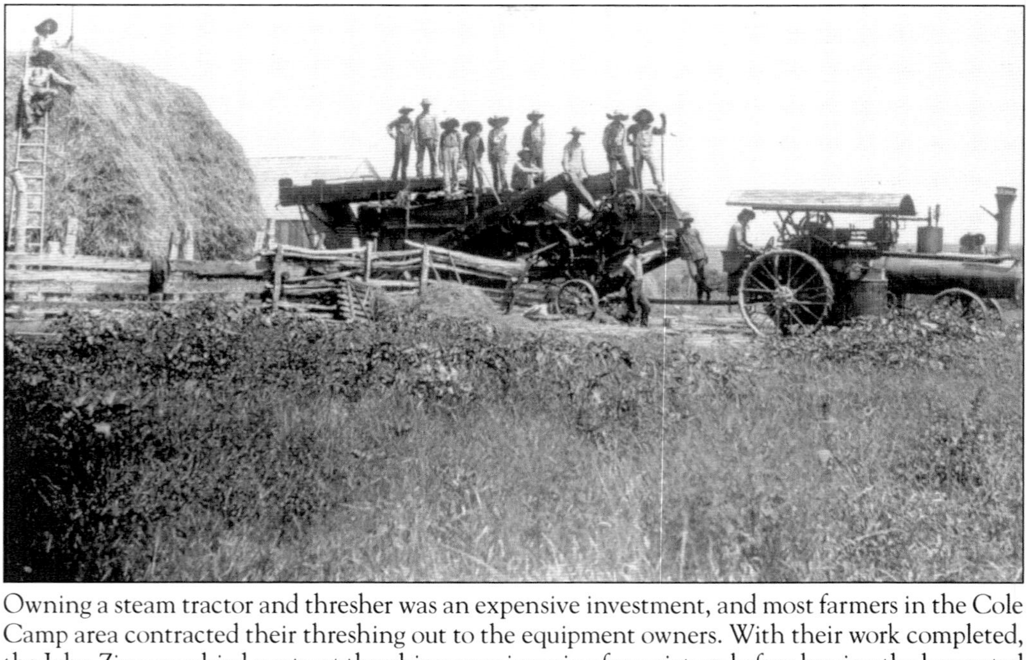

Owning a steam tractor and thresher was an expensive investment, and most farmers in the Cole Camp area contracted their threshing out to the equipment owners. With their work completed, the John Zimmerschied contract threshing crew is posing for a picture before leaving the harvested field for home.

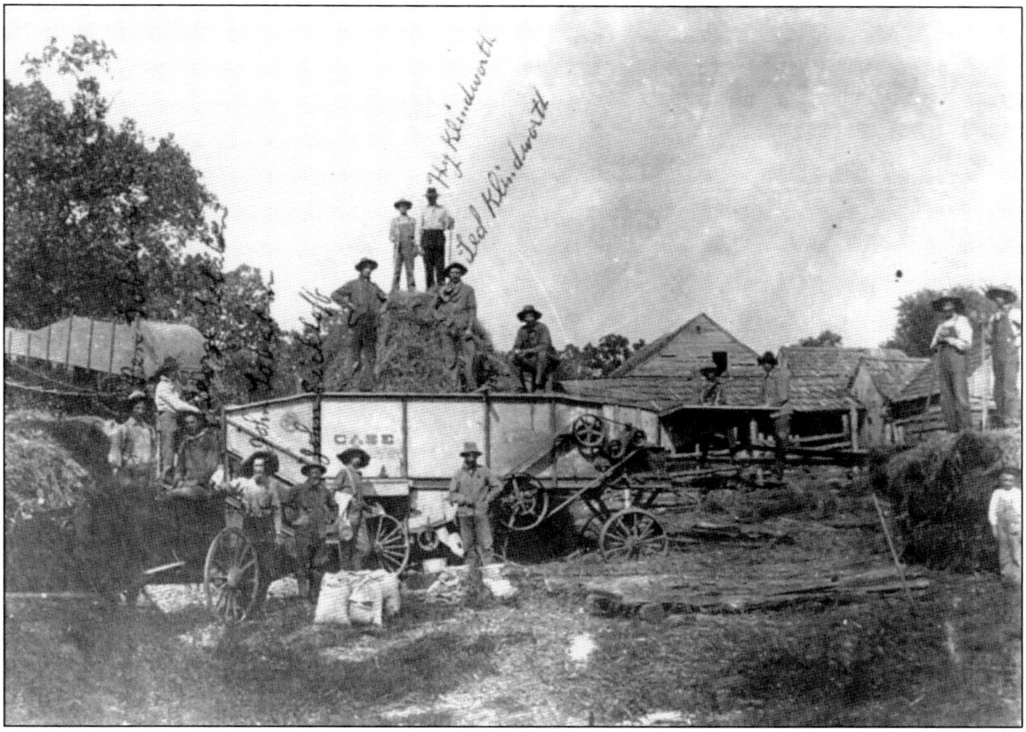

This threshing crew poses for the camera in 1910. From left to right are (standing in front) Ben Tobaben, unidentified, George Tobaben, John Tobaben, John Eickhoff, and two unidentified; (on the wagon) two unidentified, Henry Klindworth, Ted Klindworth, and unidentified; the others to the right are unidentified.

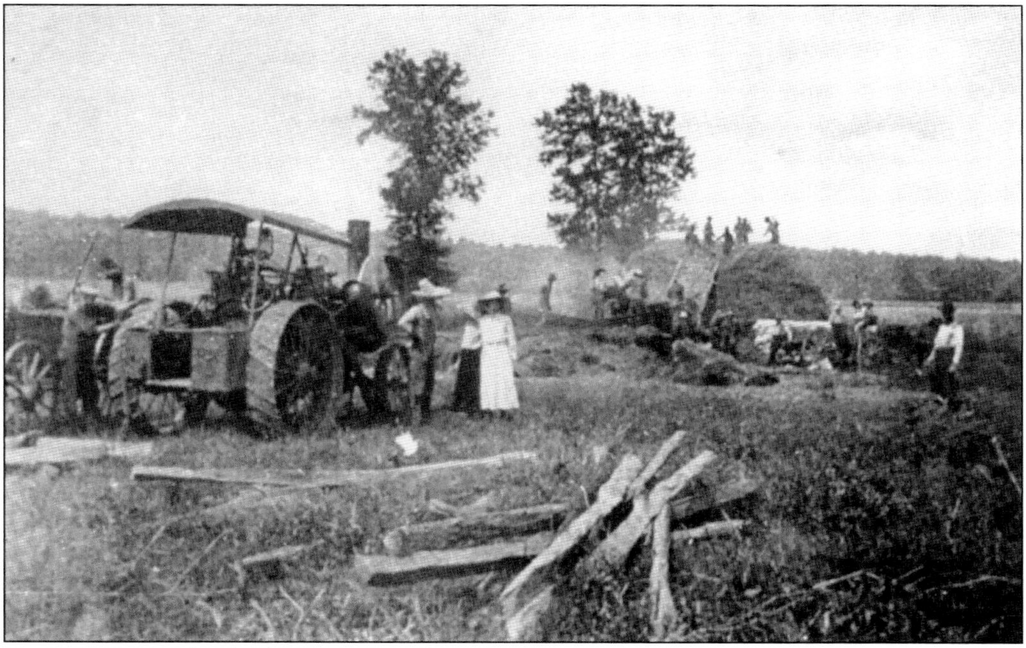

It was customary for the farm women to bring lunch to the field for the famished threshing crews. A lunch break is in process for the Kleinschmidt crew in this photograph.

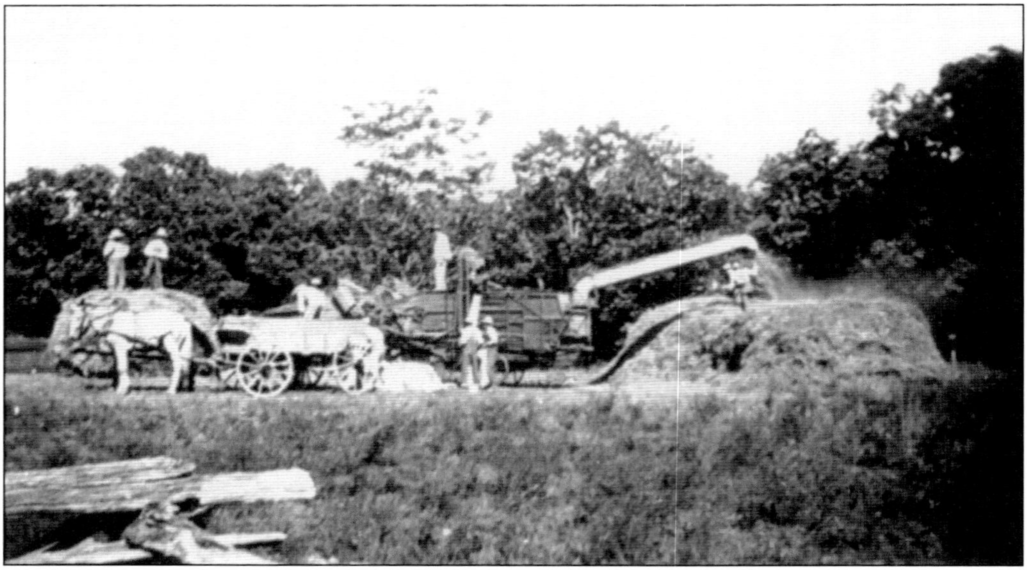
The Paul Meyer threshing crew is in the process of making a large stack of straw.

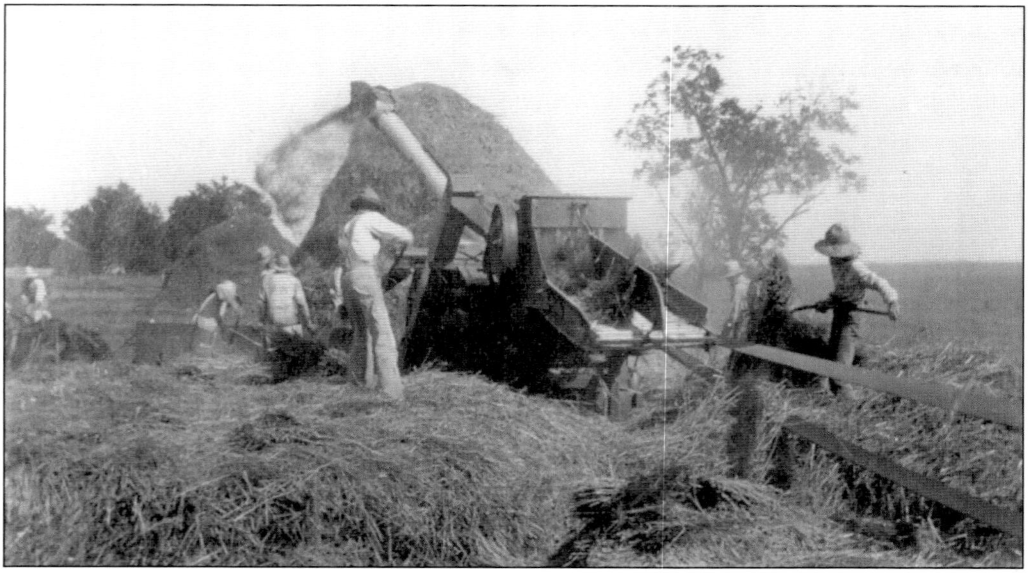
These men are feeding the wheat plants into the thresher. The stalk of the plant is blown out as straw, while the separated head of the plant becomes the wheat grain.

E.L. Eickhoff Sr. instructs three-year-old E.L. Eickhoff Jr. on the mysteries of the steam tractor. In 2010, Eickhoff Jr. is 93 and operating the 138-year-old Eickhoff Furniture Company on Main Street.

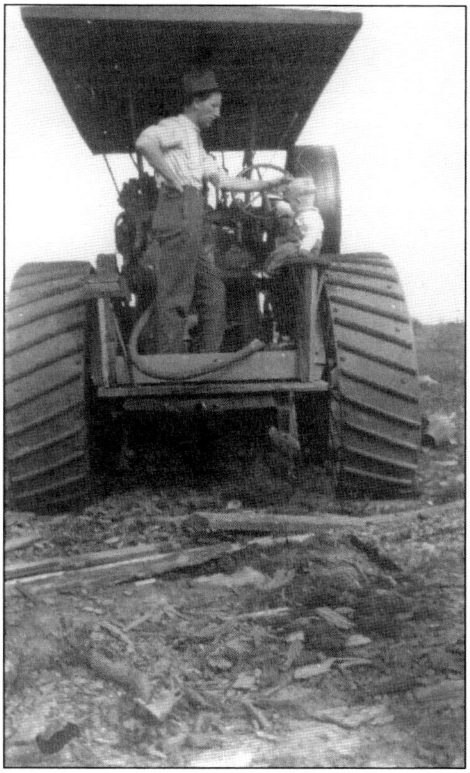

One of the early gasoline-powered tractors is in use by this crew on a farm in north Benton County in 1904.

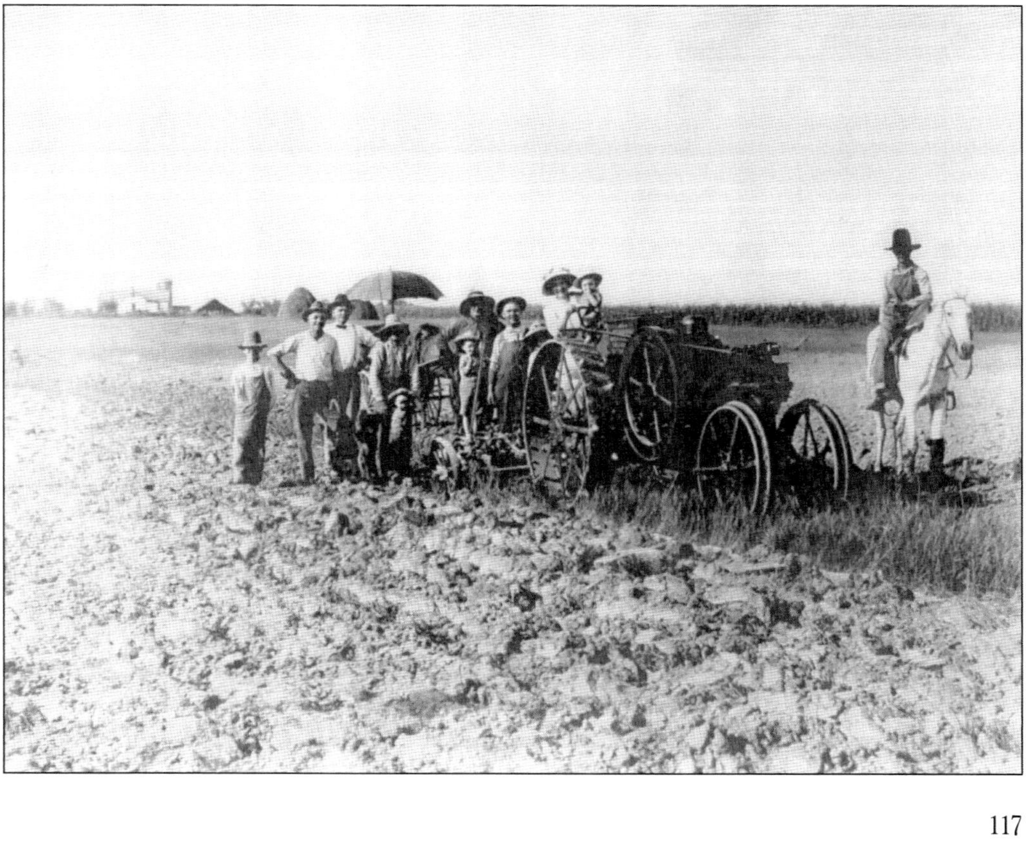

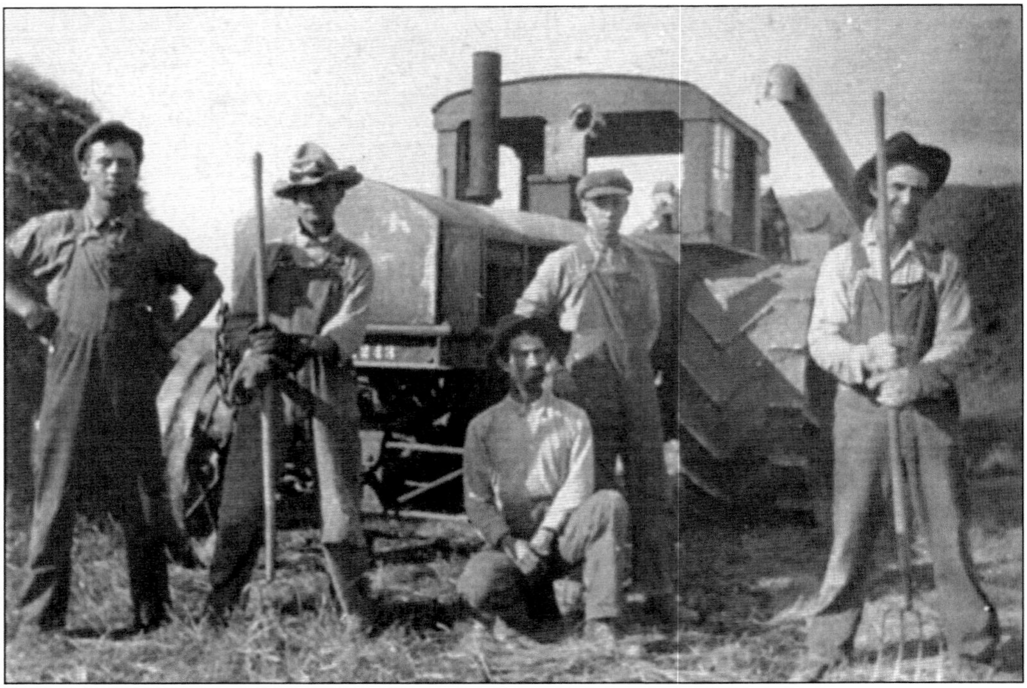

This crew, working on the farm of Theodore Howe in 1909, has a gasoline tractor to power the thresher.

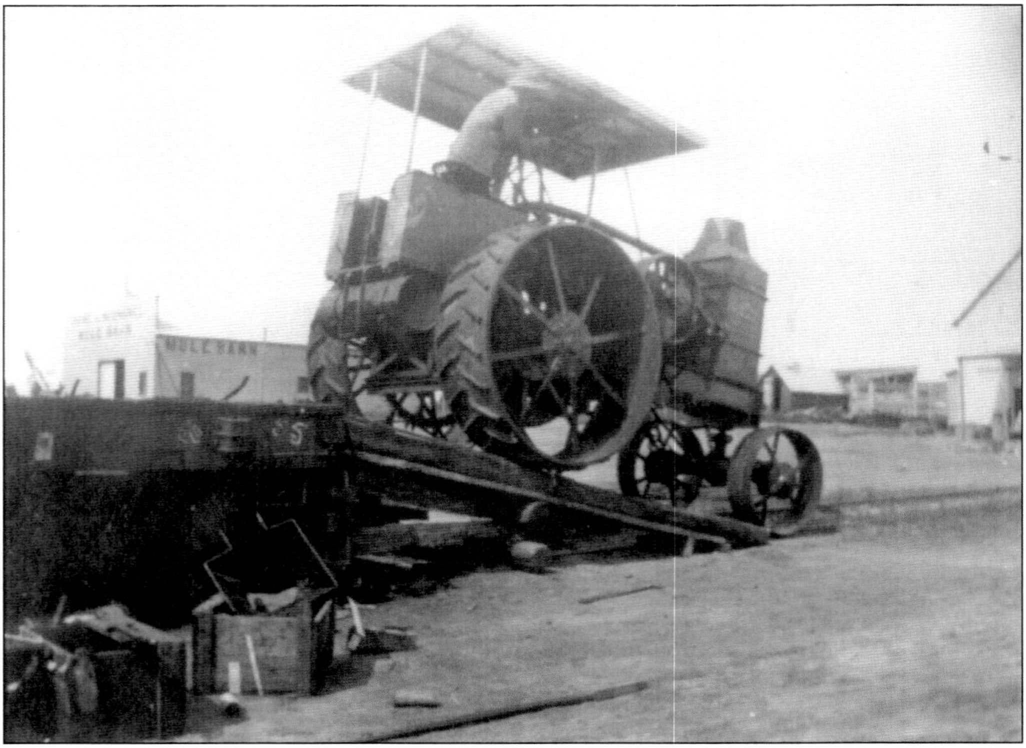

C.E. Muller unloads a new Rumely Oil Pull tractor off of a flatcar near the Cole Camp Rock Island Depot in 1917.

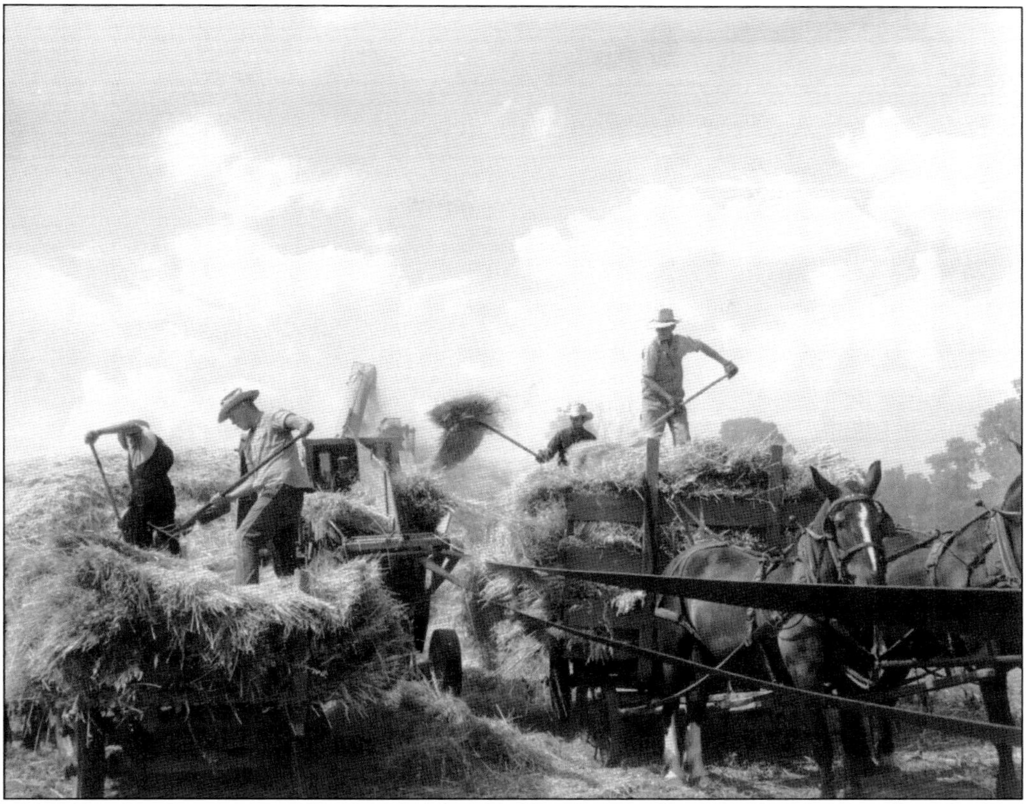

This photograph could have been taken in 1900, but it is 1953, and Henry Rotermund of Lincoln is seen using a steam tractor and horses to gather his crops. (Courtesy of the Flora Rotermund family.)

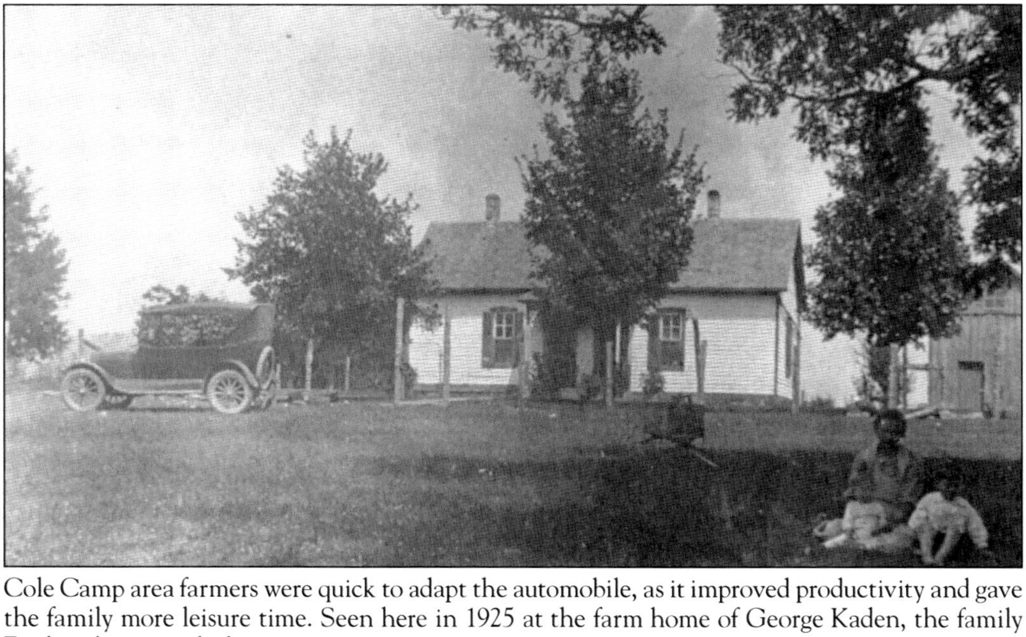

Cole Camp area farmers were quick to adapt the automobile, as it improved productivity and gave the family more leisure time. Seen here in 1925 at the farm home of George Kaden, the family Ford is always ready for a trip to town.

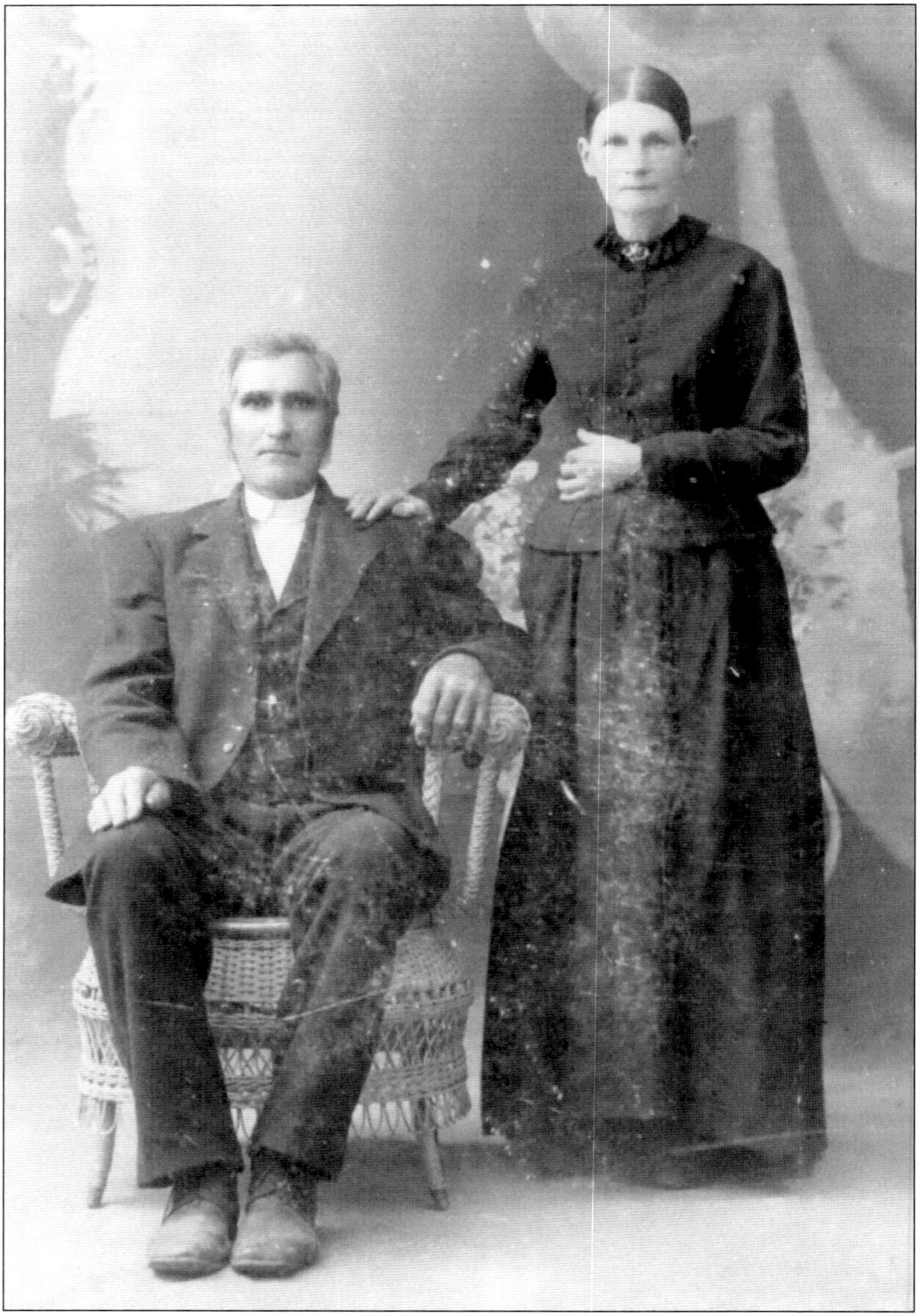

Henry Brauer and his wife, Margaretha, are examples of the early German pioneers to the Cole Camp area. Brauer arrived in 1844 from Hanover, Germany, and purchased 160 acres north of Cole Camp. Descendants of the Brauers still reside in the area.

Nine

People and Places

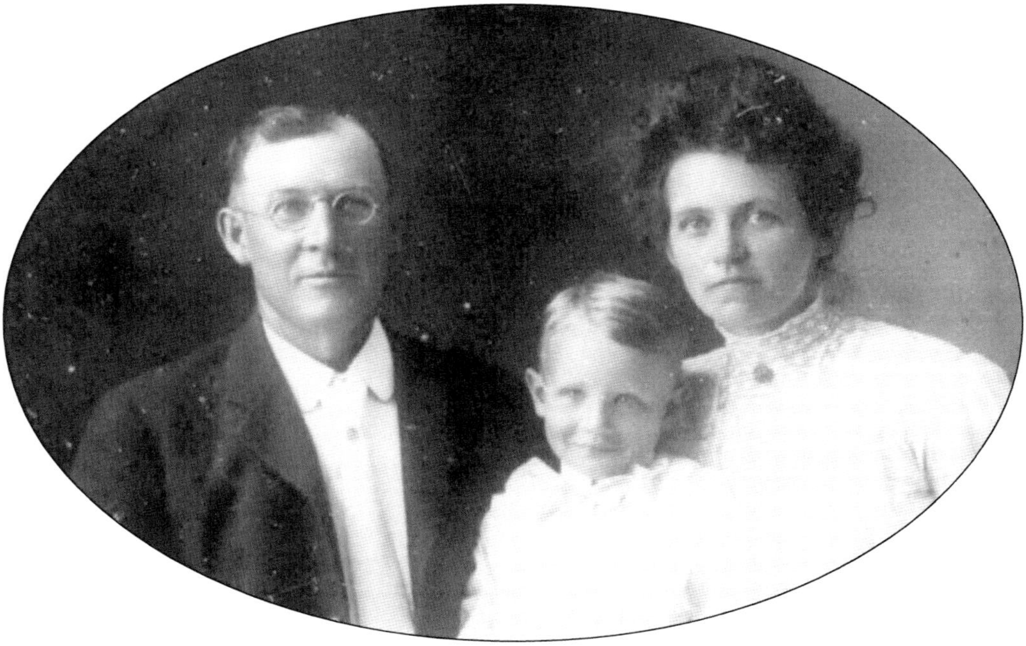

Space does not permit the mentioning of all the Cole Camp area families and places that played a part in its history, and only a few are included in the following pages. John M. Moss of Mora (1869–1926), his wife, Emma, and son Guido are pictured here. Moss was a Spanish-American War veteran, a farmer, school teacher, Benton County road engineer, Rock Island Railroad timekeeper, Missouri Pacific station agent, Mora Lumber Yard owner, and also the postmaster at Mora for 12 years.

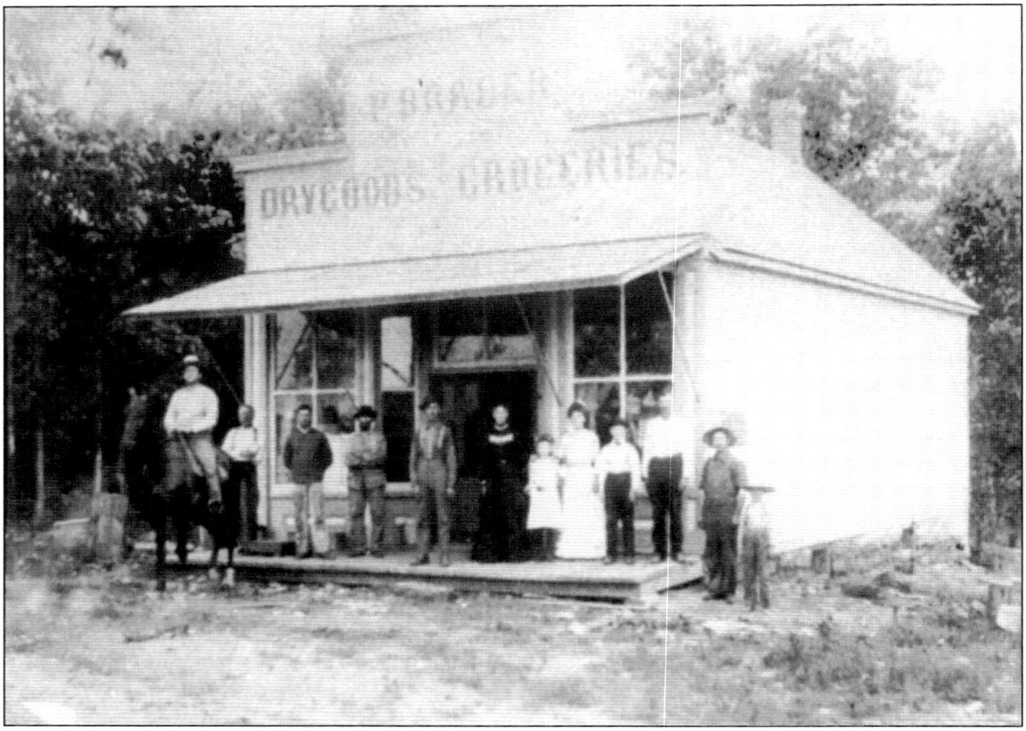

Crest was the highest point on the Rock Island Railroad and included the railroad station, a hotel, and this store owned by Peter Brauer, the great-grandson of Henry Brauer.

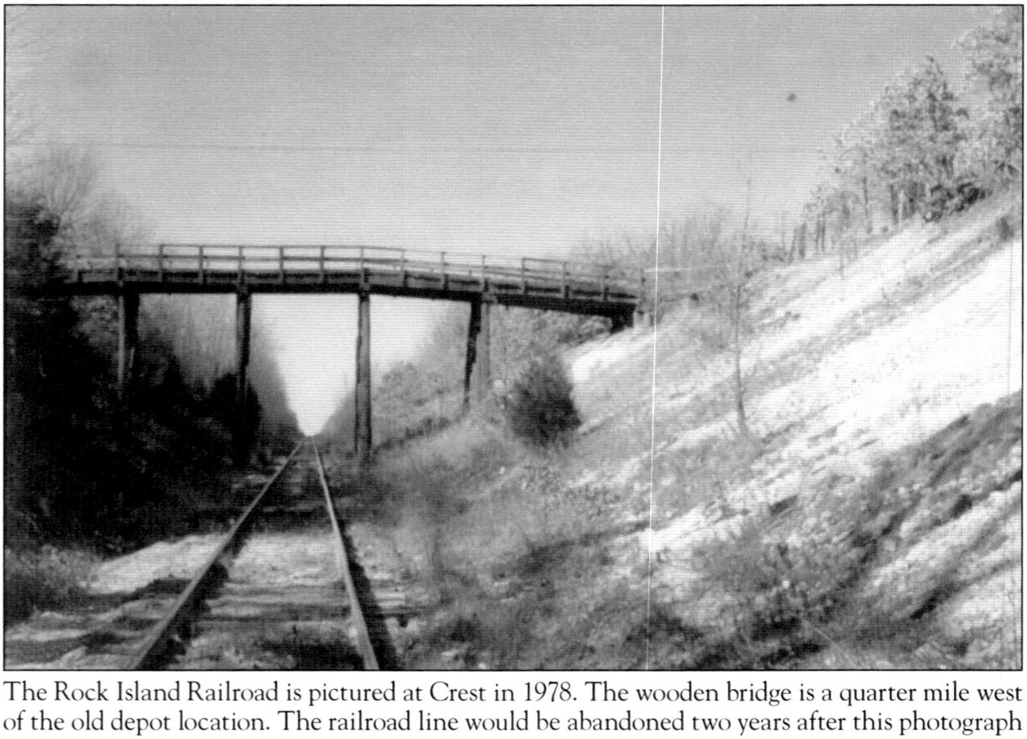

The Rock Island Railroad is pictured at Crest in 1978. The wooden bridge is a quarter mile west of the old depot location. The railroad line would be abandoned two years after this photograph was taken. (Courtesy of Forest Brockman.)

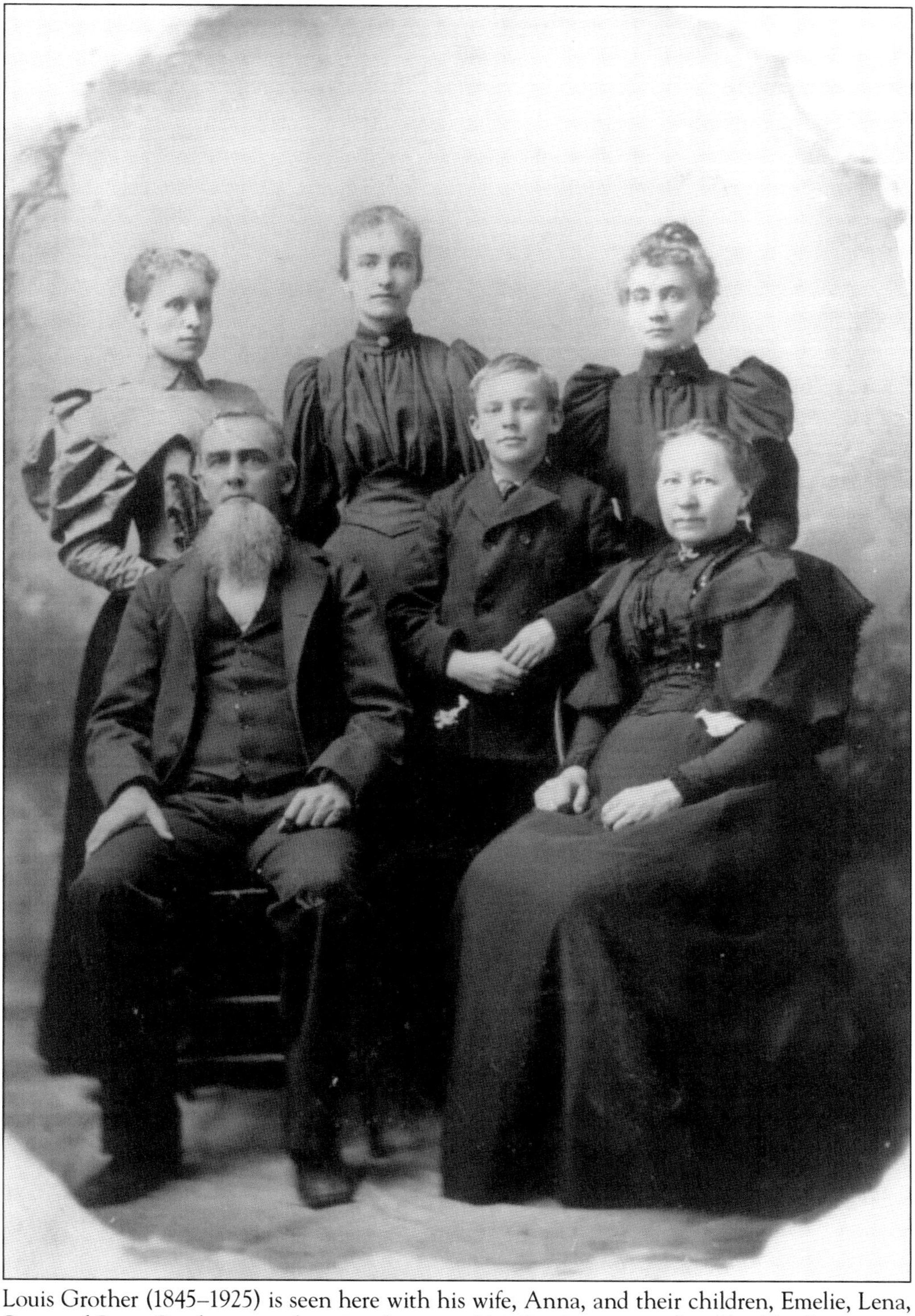

Louis Grother (1845–1925) is seen here with his wife, Anna, and their children, Emelie, Lena, Sam, and Sena. Grother was a druggist who opened his first business in the old public Square area in the 1880s (see page 18). He later moved the business to Maple Street. Grother was elected to the Missouri Senate in 1885 and later was the circuit clerk and recorder for Benton County.

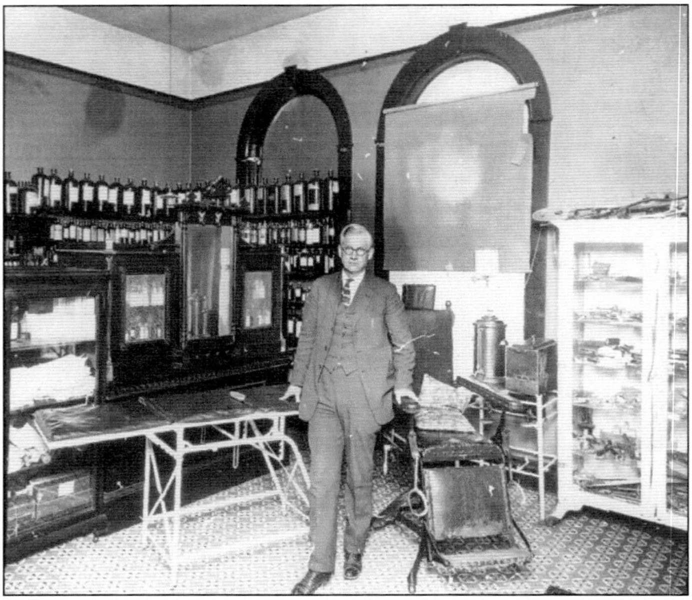

Dr. Harry Bay (1879–1938), pictured in his office in 1929, came to Cole Camp in 1909 and occupied rooms above Citizens Bank. He practiced until his tragic death on October 27, 1938. When on a sick call to the Martin Harms farm north of town, his 1938 Dodge was struck by an eastbound Rock Island freight train at a blind grade crossing. He was survived by his wife, Sophia, a son, Harry, and a daughter, Ruth Kersey, who at age 98 in 2010 still resides in her father's Short Street home.

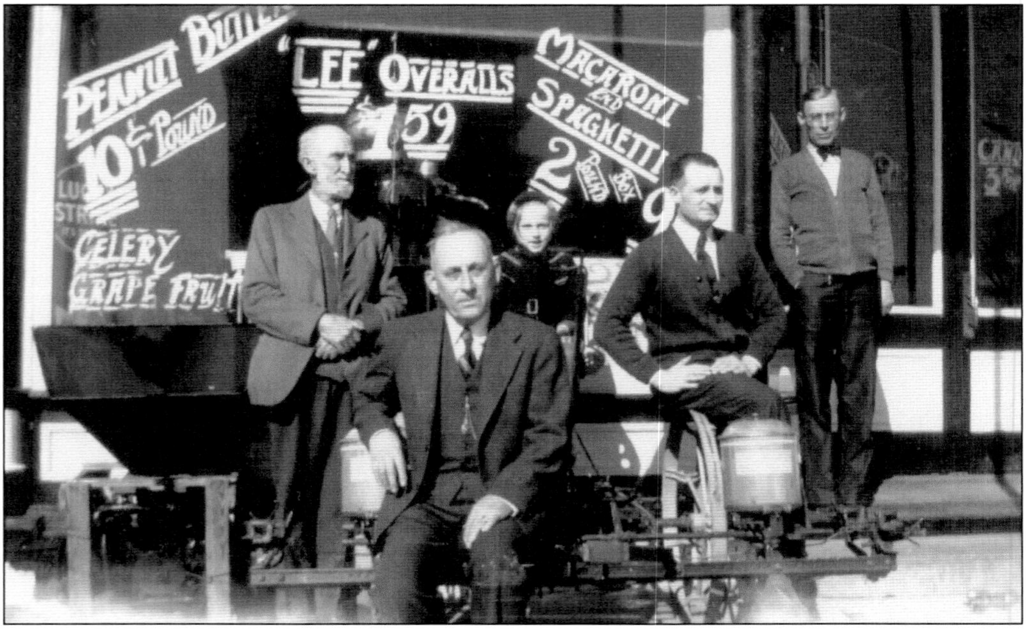

On February 8, 1939, C.D. Brill (1876–1952) poses on a corn planter in front of the Brill and Wisdom Store. The occasion was the 50th anniversary of the store's founding. Others in the photograph are, from left to right, W.W. Wisdom, Dorothy Ann Brill, J.L. Atwood, and H.F. Brill. The store changed hands over the years and finally closed in 1986. (Courtesy of Dorothy Brill Upton.)

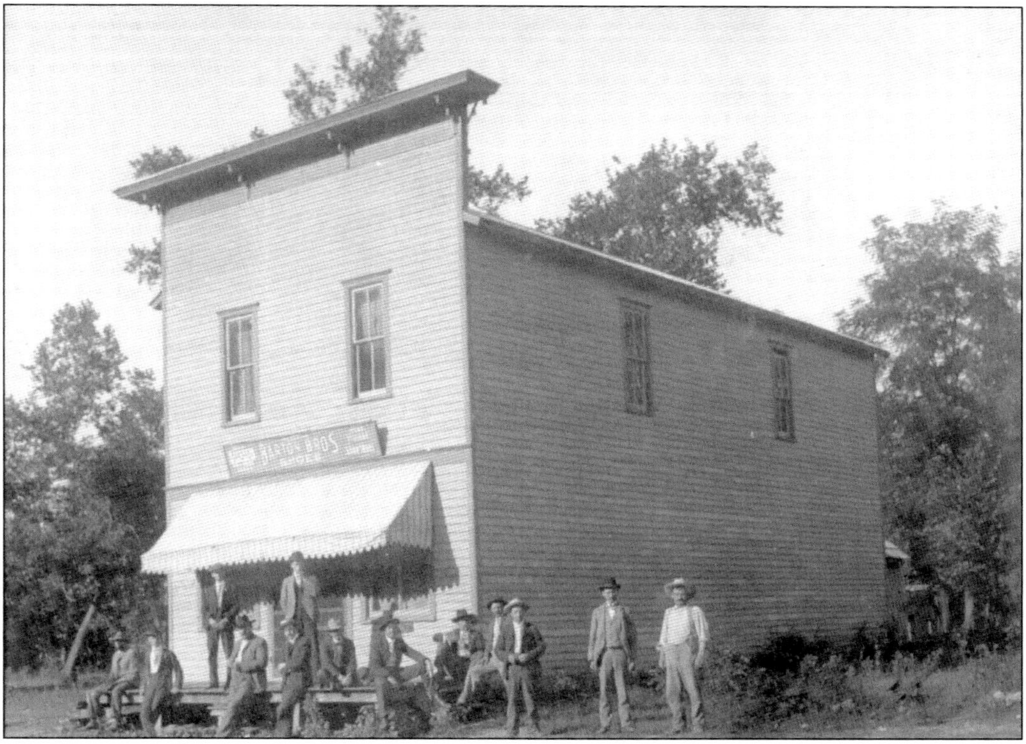

The Barton Brothers store was located at Boylers Mills, southeast of Cole Camp. It is typical of the country stores that served the farm dwellers in the area.

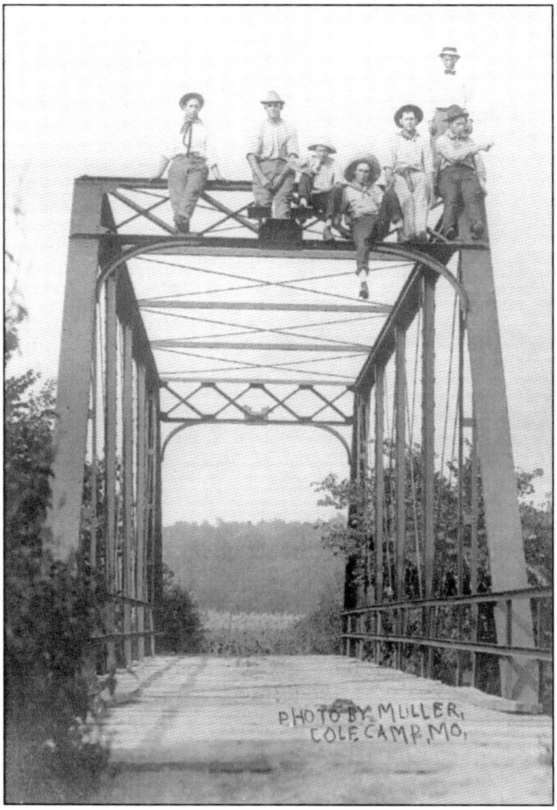

The c. 1880 Balltown Bridge carried the Butterfield Trail over Cole Camp Creek, six miles south of Cole Camp. When a new bridge was built in 1993, the old bridge was donated to the Cole Camp Historical Society by Benton County, and the bridge was moved in October of 1993 to the Ezekiel Williams Memorial Park in Cole Camp. Pictured on the bridge in 1915 are, from left to right, George Weymuth, Henry Fitschen, Bish Eickhoff, Theodore Fitschen, Walter McKinney (with gun), Ben Eickhoff, and Leo Eickhoff (with bow tie).

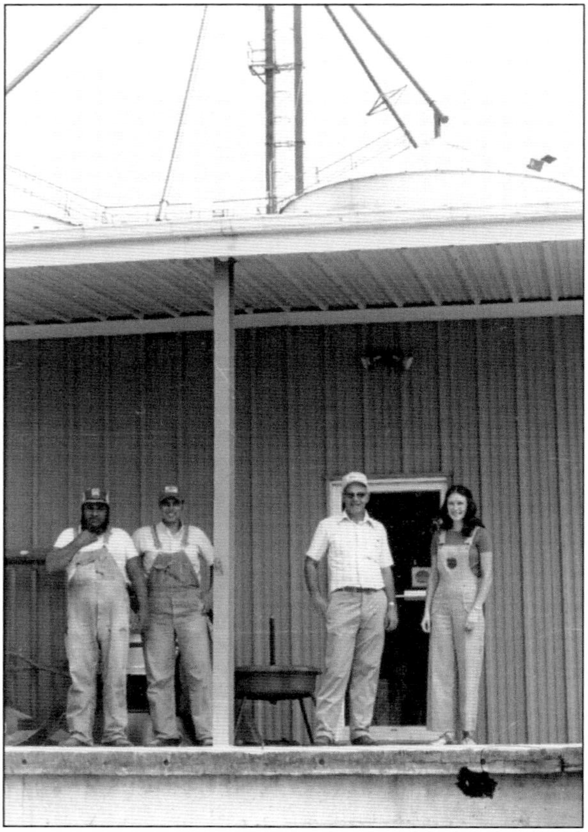

Harold Steffens is a descendant of Henry Steffens, who came to the Cole Camp Area from Hanover, Germany, in 1872. Harold started working at the Ionia Producers Exchange Mill in 1945, became the manager in 1958, and retired in 1991. He has also been the mayor and a councilman of Ionia, and in 2010 he still resides in the town with his wife, Mary Ann. This 1976 photograph includes, from left to right, Harold Schroeder, Harold Weinberg, Harold Steffens, and Elaine Friedly, all employees at the elevator.

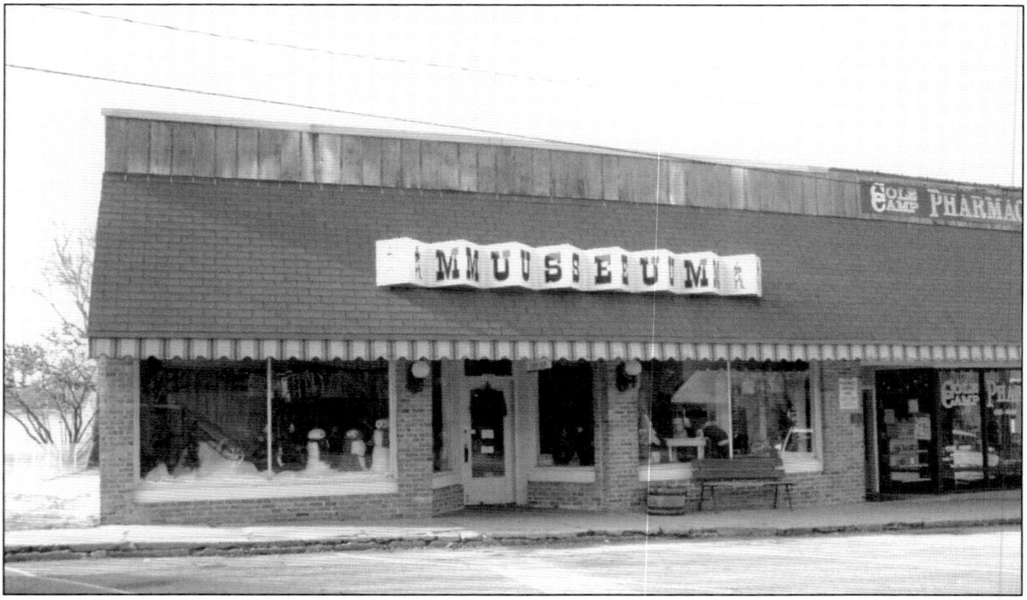

This book gives the reader just a glimpse of the rich history of the Cole Camp area. Those interested are encouraged to visit the Cole Camp Museum, established in August 1999 in the heart of historical district, for an in-depth presentation of area history with photographs and artifact displays.

BIBLIOGRAPHY

Bird, Kenneth L. *Rails to the Osage*. Lincoln, MO: Menwith Productions, 2009.

Cole Camp Area Historical Society. *Cole Camp Area History, 1839–1876*. Cole Camp, MO: Cole Camp, Missouri, Editing Committee, 1976.

Robert Owens. *Hier Snackt Wi Plattdutsch (Here We Speak Low German)*. Cole Camp, MO: City of Cole Camp, 1989.

White, Kathleen Kelly and Kathleen White Miles. *The History of Benton County Missouri*, three vols. Clinton MO: White & Miles, 1960–1971. (The three volumes were reissued on CD-ROM in 2007 by the Benton County Historical Society, Warsaw, MO.)